Germany
at the Crossroads

Published in cooperation with
The Robert Bosch Foundation, GmbH,
and
The Robert Bosch Foundation Alumni Association

Germany at the Crossroads

Foreign and Domestic Policy Issues

edited by Gale A. Mattox
and A. Bradley Shingleton

Westview Press
BOULDER • SAN FRANCISCO • OXFORD

All rights reserved. No part of this publication may be reproduced or transmitted in any form or by any means, electronic or mechanical, including photocopy, recording, or any information storage and retrieval system, without permission in writing from the publisher.

Copyright © 1992 by Westview Press, Inc.

Published in 1992 in the United States of America by Westview Press, Inc., 5500 Central Avenue, Boulder, Colorado 80301-2847, and in the United Kingdom by Westview Press, 36 Lonsdale Road, Summertown, Oxford OX2 7EW

Library of Congress Cataloging-in-Publication Data
Germany at the crossroads : foreign and domestic policy issues /
  edited by Gale A. Mattox and A. Bradley Shingleton.
    p. cm.
  Includes bibliographical references and index.
  ISBN 0-8133-1251-5
  1. Germany—History—Unification, 1990. I. Mattox, Gale A.
II. Shingleton, A. Bradley.
DD290.25.G48   1992
943.087'9—dc20   92-8202
                                                                                                  CIP

Printed and bound in the United States of America

⊚ The paper used in this publication meets the requirements of the American National Standard for Permanence of Paper for Printed Library Materials Z39.48-1984.

10   9   8   7   6   5   4   3   2   1

To the memory of Robert Bosch
(1861–1942)

"A New Beginning in Germany"*

The very name Robert Bosch suggests that this beginning has deep and reassuring roots. Bosch was born in 1861 near Ulm in a gemütlich, liberal part of southern Germany; he was a kind of practical polymath, a scientist-engineer. In his early twenties he studied in America, even with Thomas Edison. In 1886, together with two other men, he founded a workshop, destined to become a world-famous electrotechnical enterprise under his own leadership. In many ways he was an exemplar of the greatness of German science and technology, of the efficiency of the German economy. But he was also an exception among the powerful German industrialists. He was a liberal entrepreneur; he had advanced social and even political ideas. He came to be known as "the red Bosch," but that was only in comparison to his rather black or later brown contemporaries. No need to fear guilt by association; he was simply an enlightened industrialist who introduced the eight-hour day in 1906 and paid vacations thereafter. He was a liberal democrat who kept his distance from the Nazis. His biography was written by a fellow-Swabian, Theodor Heuss, whose moral authority as first president of the Federal Republic did so much to create a new political culture. If today we talk of a "new beginning" we should remember the deeper continuities as well. Historically, Robert Bosch was an ambiguous presence—precisely because politically he was an exception in the German entrepreneurial scene—but his American experience, his liberal outlook, and his commitment and adherence to excellence: these serve to strengthen my belief that a new beginning has roots in a difficult past. . . .

—*From a speech by Fritz Stern to the 1990 Annual Conference of the Robert Bosch Alumni Association, Washington, D.C., 6 October 1990

Contents

Foreword, *Rüdiger Stephan* — xi
Preface — xiii
Acknowledgments — xix
List of Acronyms — xxi

PART ONE: FOREIGN AND SECURITY POLICY ISSUES

1 A Unified Germany and European Security,
  Dana H. Allin and Daniel H. Mudd — 3

2 The Politics of Franco-German Arms Collaboration:
  Between Autonomy and Alliance, *Jonathan B. Tucker* — 17

3 German-American Relations After the Cold War,
  Dana H. Allin — 34

PART TWO: POLITICAL ISSUES

4 European Integration and the German *Länder:*
  Lost Competence or Found Opportunity?
  Jon M. Appleton — 51

5 Momper at Germany's Dawn, *John Meakem* — 67

PART THREE: ECONOMIC ISSUES

6 German Monetary Union: The Inevitable Experiment,
   Melinda Hargrave-Kanzow   83

7 German Trade and Joint Ventures with the East,
   Cole Thompson   94

8 East German Firms in the New Germany,
   J. Henrike Garkisch   111

PART FOUR: NEW TECHNOLOGIES AND PUBLIC POLICY ISSUES

9 Private Broadcasting in the Federal Republic
   of Germany, *Barbara Reilly*   123

10 Technology and the Competitive Advantage of Nations:
   The Case of Biotechnology, *Richard W. Morris*   135

11 Negotiation and Compromise in German Environmental
   Politics: Government, Industry, and the Public,
   Carol Deck   149

12 The Future of the German Electronics Industry,
   Lauren Kelley   162

Appendix One
   Martin Bangemann Speech: "The EC Internal Market:
     Internal Integration, External Trade Restrictions?"   174
   Rita Süssmuth Speech: "The German View of the World
     in the 1990s and Beyond"   181
   Carola Kaps Speech: "Germany in an Era of Change"   190

Appendix Two
   West German Federal Governments Since 1949   196
   Chronology of the Division and Unification of Germany   197

Articles of the German Basic Law with Respect to Unification	198
The New German States	199
About the Book and Editors	201
About the Contributors	203
Index	207

Foreword

It was not the trumpets of Jericho, nor the cannons and tanks that brought down the Berlin wall, but the desire of the people for freedom and democracy. In this way, "what belongs together could grow together" (*zusammenwachsen was zusammengehört*).

The problems of our time have national, transnational, and even global elements. We must therefore continue to recognize that these problems—between East and West, North and South—can be solved only through the lasting understanding that transcends daily politics. Although international understanding comes in many forms, it is impossible without an accurate knowledge of other countries. Such an understanding is based on the mutual knowledge of our various life-styles and visions for the future.

In addition to the fields of health care and social welfare, the objective of the Robert Bosch Foundation, a private philanthropic establishment, is to help secure the future for succeeding generations on the North American and European continents and in our two countries, the United States and the Federal Republic of Germany (FRG). The foundation considers its promotion of information, knowledge of foreign languages, and cultural comparisons to be its most important tasks, and it has focused its efforts on France, Poland, and the United States.

Every year since 1984 the Robert Bosch Foundation has invited fifteen young, highly qualified Americans for a nine-month stay in the FRG. The American Fellows of the Robert Bosch Foundation were able to experience how freedom and democracy tore down the iron curtain and created a new understanding between peoples. They were witnesses to the social processes that we hope will lead to a new European peace order. The foundation conceived the program and carries it out under its own auspices.

Participants are selected after a rigorous screening process. The applicants do not have to know German beforehand, but once chosen, they receive stipends to learn German or to improve their knowledge of it while still in the United States. For a successful stay in Germany, working and living in everyday German society, a good knowledge of the language is indispensable.

After arriving in Germany, the Bosch Fellows work at high levels in federal and regional establishments, businesses and banks, administrative bodies, television and radio stations, and on newspapers. They deal with current political, economic, and cultural problems—in Berlin with German unification and East-West relations, in Brussels and Strasbourg with the development of the European Community and the North Atlantic Treaty Organization, and in Paris with intra-European cooperation from the French perspective. The Fellows get to know Germany and Europe "from the inside." Based on these intensive experiences, they submit papers on topics of their choosing. The publication of many of these submissions, above all in professional journals, attests to the high quality of their efforts.

The rapid success of the program was manifested in the decision of the first group of Bosch Fellows to found an alumni association. The association has already been very active and organizes an ever-growing annual alumni conference, which has been held in Washington, D.C., New York, and Boston over the past six years.

Together with the Alumni Association, the Robert Bosch Foundation decided to establish a series of books in which the best papers submitted to the Foundation would be published. The authors themselves are responsible for the contents. The Robert Bosch Foundation wishes the series and its authors every success and hopes that this book and succeeding ones will contribute to German-American understanding.

Rüdiger Stephan
The Robert Bosch Foundation

Preface

The 1989 revolution in the German Democratic Republic (GDR) and the subsequent unification of Germany are among the most important political events of our time. At the same time, German unification took place within the context of profound regional developments: the emergence of Eastern Europe from Soviet domination and the economic integration of Western Europe. The geographical location of Germany—often cited as a primary influence in its history and development—has caused it to experience directly and, by necessity, to participate in these regional revolutions with substantial international repercussions.

The task of comprehending these dramatic developments in Germany and in Europe is immense. The pace of events and the complex interaction of a multitude of historical, economic, and political factors resist simplistic explanations. Their impact on international issues and the course of global events is almost impossible to judge.

The recent revolutions in Europe may be even more difficult for Americans to understand, given their geographical remove and the competing international concerns that occupy their attention. Nevertheless, the European revolutions affect the United States directly, and they should be studied on this side of the Atlantic as well. We hope that the essays in this volume will contribute to this task of understanding the new Germany—within a new Europe.

Today, Germany finds itself at a crossroads. Internally, it must redefine itself after the accession of territories whose population has not participated in a functioning democracy for more than fifty years. At the same time, it must help to shape a new political and economic structure for Europe, a continent that, like Germany itself, is unified by common cultural traditions and divided by vast economic and social disparities. In Germany, there is no sharp division between internal and external situations: the one conditions the other.

Above all, Germany is redefining itself. It must come to terms with the fact that it is no longer the same state or society that it was before 3 October 1990. The incorporation of the German Democratic Republic into the Federal Republic ignited excitement over the prospect of bringing democratic reform and better living conditions to the East but also gave rise to concern over united Germany's ability to do so while maintaining its own economic vitality. While supporting unification overwhelmingly by any measurement, the East and West German publics are also confronting the realities of the difficult tasks before them to secure an equality of opportunity in both halves of the country.

These changes are symbolized by the relocation of the capital and seat of government from Bonn to Berlin. Chancellor Konrad Adenauer promoted Bonn, the "federal village," as a provisional capital in 1949, in large part to anchor the Federal Republic in the West. Berlin, at that time an island in the Soviet occupation zone, had ceased to be a viable choice for a capital, and instead became a symbol of the endurance of the German question. With Berlin's return as the capital of a united Germany, a chapter has closed on the evolution of postwar Germany, and a new epoch has begun. The immense challenges of reconstruction described in several of the following essays are truly formidable. In addressing these challenges, Germany is coming up against the realities of its past, while confronting the immediate, pressing demands of the present.

This great process of national reconstruction is occurring while deep changes sweep across Europe. The European Community (EC), well on the way to the creation of a unified internal market, confronts the economic challenges of developing a common currency and a common financial institution. At the same time, Europe is groping for a structure for political and, eventually perhaps, military cooperation. Postwar German foreign policy has long emphasized active commitment to the European Community. This will continue, but under more challenging and ambitious circumstances than the EC has ever experienced.

Europe also will face the task of redefinition as it confronts the dual challenges of integration within its current borders and pressures from outside its borders to expand. Not only has a NATO country, Turkey, applied for membership, but neutral countries such as Austria are also lining up for membership. In addition, many former Eastern bloc countries have expressed interest in joining the EC. Germany will play a major role in future decisions on the myriad issues which will confront the EC, including membership.

The role of Germany in the international arena also may be expected to undergo substantial transformation in the longer term as it puts the postwar period and cold war behind it. In part this larger role will be within and through the European Community, but Germany will inevitably assume an increasingly larger independent role as it overcomes and absorbs the problems of incorporating the eastern half of the country.

* * *

The chapters selected for inclusion in this volume represent the broad range of issue areas in which the Bosch Fellows were involved. They also reflect the varied viewpoints and interests of the Fellows—a strength of the program. The chapters were selected as contributions to the literature in each particular field. Although there was no attempt to cover all of the Fellows' fields of endeavor, the chapters reflect the diverse interests of the participants in the program. The nearly one hundred Fellows who have traveled and lived in the Federal Republic of Germany during the first seven years of the program represent a broad spectrum of interests and career paths, including law, business, government, academia, international banking and economics, chemistry, and journalism. These essays are drawn from the Fellows who were in Germany over a period of four years, from 1987 to 1991. Not only were the participants able to bring their wide-ranging experience and background to their German colleagues, but each participant also contributed to the general knowledge of their U.S. colleagues.

The essays in this book are divided into four parts: foreign and security policy, politics, economics, and new technologies and public policy issues. These four categories are not as distinct as they may appear; some of the chapters on new technologies necessarily address foreign policy and security issues, and several of the chapters deal with both economic and political themes. This overlap also applies to foreign and domestic policy issues. In contemporary Europe, the national and supranational realms cannot be separated, as several of the chapters concretely demonstrate.

The chapters in Part One address some of the momentous events and resultant political and security questions confronting the new Germany. Dana Allin assesses the impact of unification on the German-American relationship, and, in a jointly authored essay, Allin and Daniel Mudd analyze the impact of German unification on NATO and European security. In his chapter on the security relationship between Germany and France, Jonathan Tucker discusses the politics of arms collaboration and suggests that the relationship has been complicated by a variety of political and economic, as well as strategic, factors. Part Two groups two essays dealing with political issues. In a chapter on a topic not often addressed outside of specialist circles, Jon Appleton discusses the relationship between the federal states in Germany and the European Community. John Meakem provides a vivid chronicle of the early stages of German unification through the example of Berlin and its mayor, Walter Momper. Part Three surveys economic topics. Melinda Hargrave-Kanzow analyzes the evolution of the monetary union created in July 1990 between the Federal Republic of Germany and the German Democratic Republic. Cole Thompson discusses the historical trade relationships between Germany and Eastern Europe and the Soviet Union and the prospects for those relationships in a time of upheaval. He offers insights into the rapidly evolving endeavor of joint ventures. Finally, the troubled situation of many eastern German business firms in unified Germany is discussed in the essay by Henrike Garkisch.

The fourth part of the book is devoted to issues of public policy generated by new technological developments in communications, biotechnology, electronics, and environmental protection. In a chapter that addresses the advent of privately controlled entities in a field that has been publicly controlled, Barbara Reilly discusses the evolution of private broadcasting in Germany. Lauren Kelley describes the economic impact of international competition on the German electronics industry. The chapters by Richard Morris and Carol Deck treat topics on which relatively little has been written in English, particularly from a comparative perspective. Morris discusses the organizational and economic structure of biotechnology research in Germany, and Deck compares German and American regulatory approaches to environmental protection.

Appendix One contains addresses by European Commissioner Martin Bangemann, *Bundestagspräsidentin* Rita Süssmuth, and Carola Kaps of the *Frankfurter Allgemeine Zeitung* to the annual conferences of the Robert Bosch Foundation Alumni Association. The Bangemann speech, delivered in October 1988 in New York, addresses foreign—especially American—concerns about the 1992 Internal Market program of the European Community. Rita Süssmuth's address, delivered in October 1989 at Harvard University, focuses on important factors in the history of German-American relations and vital mutual goals for the future. Carola Kaps addressed the alumni in 1990 at the conference in Washington, D.C. She focused on the importance of the human dimension of relations among different countries, especially relations between the United States and Germany. In dedicating this volume to the memory of Robert Bosch, we excerpted remarks made by Fritz Stern in an address to the Fellows in 1990.

The Robert Bosch Foundation selects fifteen Fellows each year on the basis of expertise in a particular field. We believe this is a strength of the Fellowship program and of the book. With few exceptions, the authors pursue careers in the United States in the same general field as the work performed at their guest institutions in the Federal Republic. The Fellows brought to their German colleagues several years of experience, and the benefit typically proved mutual. The publication of *Germany at the Crossroads* is intended to apply the varied experiences and backgrounds of the Fellows to a wide range of contemporary German issues.

Taken together, we hope that the essays in this book will provide a sense of the tremendous changes—political, social, and technological—that Germany has recently confronted. It has been our intention that these

Preface   xvii

essays contribute in a modest way to a better understanding of the enormous challenges these changes have produced.

* * *

The objective of the Alumni Association in publishing this volume is to reinforce and further the purposes outlined in the association by-laws, which include:

- To provide a continuing education for former Bosch Fellows on current German and European social, political, and cultural issues
- To provide a forum for maintaining personal and professional contacts with German counterparts
- To create and foster contact and communication among successive groups of Bosch Fellows
- To encourage and foster any other such activity that has the purpose of promoting the long-term improvement of German-U.S. relations

The process of intensifying knowledge of Germany as well as exposure to the interests of U.S. colleagues continues today in the Alumni Association. The establishment of the Alumni Association has served the purpose of maintaining the high level of interest in Germany that the Fellows brought back to the United States. Many former Fellows participate in the regional alumni organizations that have been formed throughout the United States. Others participate in the various committees aimed at strengthening German-U.S. relations. The Association has made particular efforts most recently to broaden its activities with Germans from the five new states of the Federal Republic. Finally, each year there is an annual conference to bring the alumni together for discussions and debate with one another and with guest speakers. These conferences enable the alumni of the region in which they are held to identify the community interested in German affairs and to give impetus to continued involvement by alumni in German-American affairs.

Gale A. Mattox
A. Bradley Shingleton

Acknowledgments

The authors owe a debt of gratitude to a number of people for their assistance in the publication of this volume. The Alumni Association and the authors have benefited foremost from the financial support and encouragement of the Robert Bosch Foundation, its executive directors Ulrich Bopp and Hans Glücker, and the Robert Bosch Foundation Board of Trustees. The authors submitted their chapters as papers to the Foundation from 1988 to 1991, and their contributions reflect their professional experiences as Bosch Fellows in the Federal Republic of Germany. The Bosch Foundation's deputy director, Rüdiger Stephan, and other staff members, in addition to CDS International, Inc., deserve special thanks as well for their assistance. Peter Payer, now retired, has also been a source of continuing support for the publication.

A board of outside experts including Lily Gardner Feldman, Werner Hein, Stephen Szabo, and Peter Pfund, reviewed the chapters. We would like to thank them for their time and efforts.

Many individual alumni were supportive in a number of ways in our efforts to publish the book. We particularly thank the past two presidents of the Alumni Association, Nancy Walker and Kathryn Mack, and their executive boards.

Of course, the authors themselves deserve the most credit for their hard work and persistence in updating and revising their papers—often under considerable time pressure and from a transatlantic distance. Their good nature was unfailing, and their responsiveness truly appreciated.

The views expressed in the volume are those of the authors and do not represent the views of the institutions with which they are affiliated, the Robert Bosch Foundation, or the Robert Bosch Foundation Alumni Association.

G.A.M.
A.B.S.

Acronyms

AG	Aktien Gesellschaft (Stock Corporation)
AL	Alternative List
BHE	Block party of Refugees and Disenfranchised
CAP	Common Agricultural Policy for the European Community
CDU	Christian Democratic Union
COMECON	Council of Mutual Economic Assistance
CSCE	Conference on Security and Cooperation in Europe
CSU	Christian Social Union
DASA	Deutsche Aerospace
DM	deutsche mark
DP	German party
EC	European Community
EFA	European Fighter Aircraft
EMS	European Monetary System
FAR	Rapid Action Force
FDP	Free Democratic party
FRG	Federal Republic of Germany
GDR	German Democratic Republic
GG	Basic Law/constitution
INF	intermediate-range nuclear forces
MBB	Messerschmitt-Bölkow-Blohm aerospace firm
NATO	North Atlantic Treaty Organization
R&D	research and development
SEA	Single European Act
SED	Socialist Unity party
SPD	Social Democratic party

PART ONE

Foreign and Security Policy Issues

1

A Unified Germany and European Security

Dana H. Allin and Daniel H. Mudd

"Drained of Meaning"

Not long ago, when pessimists brooded about the specter of Soviet hegemony over Western Europe, they imagined a catastrophe that would occur even while the Atlantic Alliance remained formally intact. The West Europeans would continue to pay lip service to their Atlantic commitments while in reality competing for Moscow's favor. West Germany would lead the bidding. In the face of overwhelming Soviet military power and political ruthlessness, the alliance would be progressively "drained of meaning," as Henry Kissinger put it.[1]

During the cold war, Soviet hegemony provided a wonderful focus for the Western mind. For forty-five years there was a clearly defined, objectively proveable foe with both the capability and, arguably, the intention of exercising influence over all of Europe. If nothing else could bring Western heads of state to a conference table, then 4 million Red Army troops, 25,000 Soviet warheads, and Kremlin foreign policy doctrine could. These things gave meaning to the North Atlantic Treaty Organization (NATO).

Today it is not Soviet power but Soviet decrepitude that haunts the Western imagination. The authoritarian reaction against the disintegration not only of Communist party control but also of the country itself confirms the Soviet Union's growing weakness. The problem of Soviet disintegration is coupled with the emergence of German strength at the center of Europe.

This combination will create two sorts of pressure: on the one hand, to give NATO a new, political, mission in the world, and on the other, to provide perfect security for both Western and Eastern Europe against the continued uncertainty in the Soviet Union. These pressures should be resisted. NATO had a specific culture developed for a specific task—a task it performed well. Enlarging its mission to regions and missions outside of pure European defense risks overburdening an organization that is likely to become more rather than less prone to divisions in coming years. Moreover, efforts to construct a perfect military mechanism against every conceivable danger run the risk of actually provoking conflicts. Far better to treat the organization to a kind of managed, benign neglect. Preserve NATO, but let its profile recede in proportion to the threat it was founded to deter. Because that threat is not likely to go away completely, neither should NATO.

Of course, NATO will endure, at least formally, for the foreseeable future. No one is about to disband it. The decisive moment in favor of NATO's survival came July 1990, with the Bonn government's insistence on, and Soviet president Mikhail Gorbachev's assent to, a unified Germany within NATO. This triumph also brought ambiguous implications for the future of the Western alliance. The new German-Soviet partnership was codified by a formal treaty that reflects the deep commitment of German elites to helping Gorbachev succeed, i.e., to preserve enough central Soviet power to ensure that any devolution of authority occurs peacefully and slowly.[2]

German-Soviet Bedfellows

The summer of 1990 took the German-Soviet relationship to a new, higher realm, comparable not so much to the 1922 Rapallo Treaty as to the Russo-German relationship of the nineteenth century before the Franco-Russian alliance. In the summer of 1990 the relationship was at once hopeful (who else but Germany could help to modernize the Soviet Union and thereby stabilize the East?) and also, for many obvious reasons, disturbing. The two great troublemakers of the twentieth century had become bedfellows. And they were doing so when everyone was starting to realize that the post–cold war era was full of perils, one of which was the unprecedented possibility that a nuclear superpower might collapse into civil war.

In the following months, danger signals became even more acute, including the Eduard Shevardnadze resignation, Gorbachev's alliance with conservative figures against separatist movements, a curiously ineffective repression in the Baltics, and a divisive result on the referendum for unity. The future of German-Soviet relations became correspondingly more problematic for the Germans, the Soviets, and everyone else.[3]

Compounding these untoward events is the controversial and theoretical assertion that a bipolar system, such as has existed since 1945, is inherently more stable than a multipolar system—such as prevailed throughout most of modern European history.

The Balance of Power Returns

"The root causes of war and peace," argues John Mearsheimer, lie in "the distribution and character of military power." Noting that anarchy characterizes an international system, Mearsheimer observes that states "seek to survive . . . by maximizing their power relative to other states, in order to maintain the means for self-defense."[4] If the system is multipolar, a state can best maximize its power by seeking alliances with other powers. But this alliance building tends to be both competitive and confusing: Opposing states will also seek power-maximizing alliances, the new alliances will threaten any state that is left out, and the whole edifice will be prone to uncertainty and miscalculation. With four or five "poles" of power, it will be very difficult to determine where the real balance of power lies, i.e., to distinguish between military and economic power. Moreover, given numerous poles in the system, there will be a correspondingly greater number of potential conflicts.

According to the theory, bipolarity is simpler and therefore more stable. Two opposing powers have no important allies to seek and can therefore increase their relative power only through internal efforts (e.g., rearmament). Power balances are easier to calculate and thus more likely to be achieved. The two opposing powers understand the "rules of the road" for avoiding conflict; they can recognize and avoid encroaching on interests that the opponent might deem worth going to war over. With only two major poles, there is only one potential major conflict. And that conflict is so potentially cataclysmic that "sophisticated" powers can avoid it.

Around 1963, after a series of crises in the early cold war era, the two superpowers succeeded in establishing a stable bipolar modus vivendi—a mutual recognition of the "rules of the road," as Mearsheimer put it.[5] Since then, Europe has lived without any grave disturbance to its peace. But the predictability that has prevailed since 1963 is no longer guaranteed. If a new multipolar system is coming, and it appears to be, then new rules will have to be established.

The Elements of a "New Peace Order"

What will a successful multipolar system require? The question is impossible to answer in any conclusive or schematic way. Peace, like war, tends to be an organic, unpredictable affair, the causes of which are difficult to identify in retrospect. But Europe's history and present circumstances suggest at least four general considerations.

First, a new peace order should contain some structure or structures that preserve as many of the virtues of bipolarity as possible. Specifically, the system must be highly predictable. Multilateral relations should not be superseded by unpredictable, suspicion-arousing bilateral relations.

Second, it should manage to "integrate" all the European powers—a vague and abstract notion that may be slightly easier to understand in the negative. The structure should somehow avoid imposing on the Soviet Union, or any other power, that beleaguered isolation that produces a virulent revanchism—the road from Weimar to the Third Reich.

Third, these structures should have the gravity and influence (money and political power) to bring order to an environment where the old structures—Council for Mutual Economic Assistance (COMECON), the Warsaw Pact, the Union of Soviet Socialist Republics, the Yugoslavian central government—are being demolished, and in lieu of replacement structures, entire politico-economic orders are imploding.

Fourth, the new order should provide a military balance which is stable enough to withstand the shocks accompanying the decline of bipolarity.

Alternatives to NATO

If NATO were to wither away entirely, what other organizations and arrangements could satisfy these requirements? Three existing institutions seem to be the most likely candidates: a European Community (EC) that develops a political and military dimension; the Western European Union (WEU) or a European defense community that remains essentially independent of the EC; and the Conference on Security and Cooperation in Europe (CSCE). A brief consideration of these three organizations reveals why NATO still has a role to play.

The European Community

The EC plays a critical role in preserving Europe's peace. The democratic market economies of Europe have developed over a period of four decades into a zone of stability and unprecedented prosperity. This zone exerted a magnetic pull on the Communist societies of the East (along with Madonna, Levis, and Marlboro)—ultimately bringing about their peaceful collapse. Western Europe was aided in this achievement by the Treaty of Rome (1958), which established an organization that set aside old enmities and opened up new trade and other forms of economic cooperation. Since the 1986 Single European Act, the EC has gained in real and perceived importance as a motor of European economic development and economic integration.

The European Community can serve many of the integrative and multilateral requirements of the new order. The dissolution of borders within the EC and the computerized march of the modern corporation have already brought a degree of integration that offers some hope for the wane of European separatism.

Though the EC is taking shape, the achievement of a bona fide European union is not yet within the grasp of its twelve members. While the first phase of the EC's agenda (reducing internal trade barriers) is under way, it is far from complete. The second and third parts of the community agenda—currency and political union—are barely on the drawing table. There is significant dissent over the structure of the monetary regime, the role of the European Parliament, the distribution of regional development funds, not to mention the establishment of a common foreign policy or a European defense force. And now the once-powerful Eastern bloc nations, cast adrift from the Warsaw Pact, are threatening to pull the EC under before it can set a course.

When these new democracies of Eastern Europe talk about rejoining Europe, it is membership in the European Community to which they most aspire. Their aspirations present the European Community with a historic opportunity as well as a number of dilemmas. The opportunity is to use these desires for membership as a lever for encouraging further democratic and economic progress. By offering the East Europeans a reasonable expectation and a realistic (if necessarily loose) timetable for membership, the EC can continue to provide powerful incentives for the peaceful consolidation of the 1989 revolutions.

The dilemmas number at least three. First, it is practically impossible to construct a timetable for membership because it is impossible to say when the eastern economies might be strong enough to survive integration with their robust capitalist neighbors.

Second, it is not at all clear that EC membership for the new democracies in Eastern Europe would be compatible with some of the more grandiose plans for European political union now circulating. If a truly federal Europe, akin to the United States of America, is envisioned, then there comes a point where the structure is too large and the population too diverse to be governed effectively. These first two dilemmas concern economic and political questions, including a long-standing debate about European federalism, that are beyond the scope of this chapter.

But there is a third, related, dilemma that goes to the heart of the current topic. Discussion of a European political union inevitably includes talk of a common defense policy, even a European army.[6] But this would be a dubious contribution to peace if East European nations were admitted into a European Community that included a strong military dimension. Such a development would amount to a serious geostrategic defeat and humiliation for the Soviet Union, and would quite possibly trigger the dangerous revanchism warned about earlier. These worries and a sensible reluctance to push the historic Western victory to the point of Soviet humiliation are already being voiced at the highest levels of NATO.

With regard to the EC as a military force, as the *Economist* noted, "Europe's capacity to speak and act as one is still almost entirely theoretical."[7] The Gulf war did little to advance the realization of united EC military action. The questions and conundrums arising from the concept could be so serious as to jeopardize the community's essential economic programs. For example, would military action be taken on the basis of a majority or a unanimous vote? Could dissenting nations pursue independent military action or refuse to participate? How would French and British nuclear weapons be factored into the equation? How about Ireland, an EC member that is militarily neutral? Or Germany, where non-NATO operations in Europe, or non-United Nations operations outside Europe are unconstitutional? These and other questions, all involving the lives and deaths of young citizens of sovereign nations, will prove immensely more difficult to resolve than economic issues.

The Western European Union

One way out of this dilemma, it is suggested, would be to establish a European defense community independent from the European Community. Currently a formal and rather meaningless construction, the WEU has been suggested as a possible vehicle for this development. Separate economic and defense communities (essentially the situation that exists today) would allow Eastern Europe to join the former without being implicated in the latter. This arrangement might nonetheless offer some small measure of security to the East Europeans, since the essential congruence between the two communities might give pause to a potential aggressor. A West European defense community along these lines seems to make sense, though the idea does suffer from a certain sophistry (East Europeans are neutral but enjoy implicit WEU protection all the same). There would also be a further advantage to maintaining a formal separation between European defense and economic communities: a defense community would be capable of greater decisiveness if it consisted of fewer countries grouped around French, German, and British leadership.

But ultimately, the WEU cannot replace NATO, even if, in the area of European defense, it rivals NATO in importance. It cannot replace NATO because only NATO establishes the American military presence in Europe. That military presence, however much reduced in size, serves as a reassurance, a symbolic link to the past bipolar stability at a time when power relations are increasingly multipolar. To the extent that the WEU can perform functions that are not excessively duplicative of NATO missions, and do not detract from the effectiveness and readiness of NATO forces, it could be a welcome integrative structure.[8]

The Conference on Security and Cooperation in Europe

If the EC is having difficulty reaching a consensus on assisting Eastern Europe, the notion of integrating the Soviet Union into the EC is inconceivable. The organization's political balance and direction would be hopelessly upset. This fact underscores the real importance of the CSCE. The Soviets have always looked at the conference as a forum for legitimizing their status as a European power. Of course, they wanted to do so in a way that would ratify their World War II victory and hence their brutal East European hegemony. One of the delightful ironies of history is that the dramatic December 1990 CSCE meeting in Paris did just the opposite: it ratified the end of Soviet hegemony.

But the Soviets still appear to place significant hopes in the organization as the foundation for a Common European House to which they have a key. It seems reasonable to encourage these hopes. The house would remain largely symbolic, but not unimportant. The CSCE "process" would carry moral authority that might help to settle disputes in the Balkans or even between Moscow and the Baltic republics. Recent history tells us that this moral authority should not be underestimated, for it was real force on the side of such people as Vaclav Havel, the current President of the Czech and Slovak Federal Republic.

By the same token, moral force should not be overestimated. Any structure intended to integrate the Soviet Union into a community of Western values functions tautologically, that is, it would keep the peace to the extent that its members are peacefully inclined. Here again, the function should not be dismissed: aspirations to live in the European House can encourage cooperative and peaceful forces in the Soviet Union. Thus, like the EC and WEU, the CSCE would best serve the cause of peace in Europe by focusing on what it does best. In the case of the CSCE, this means resolving crises before they become conflicts. But when the task is not to integrate the Russians, but to hold them at arm's length, or to fight a war if that fails, there remains but one obvious organization.

The North Atlantic Treaty Organization

NATO was created to meet a real need and to accomplish something that no nation could accomplish alone. It thrived in direct correlation to the gravity of the Soviet threat to the sovereignty of the nations of Europe. Although it is inevitable that the community and various economic relations will tend to eclipse NATO as the focal North Atlantic organization, there is no reason, *prima facie*, to rue the replacement of a military organization with commercial ones. Nor is there a need for concern over various suggestions, be they from Jacques Delors, Manfred Wörner, or others, that the Western European Union, or some other exclusively European body, stand as the community leg of NATO. There is concern, however, if these concepts walk hand in hand with the idea that the American military presence in Europe should vanish.

The Theory Behind NATO

In many ways, NATO has worked as an intricate mousetrap. It was designed to make the members do things automatically that they would not do reflectively: thus would the trap slam shut if the Soviets nibbled the cheese. Specifically, this means that the British, the Americans, and (presumably) the French would come to the aid of the Germans, and if the Soviets advanced too far, all three would launch nuclear warheads into the twilight of humanity. Europe's acceptance of the mousetrap was driven by the immediacy of the threat. Today, the mousetrap remains important, because the Soviet Union retains the world's largest arsenal of nuclear weapons, and only the American arsenal can counterweigh it; the link to the American arsenal, in the minds of Europeans and the hearts of Americans, is the presence of the U.S. Army. Without the American presence, Europe faces the choice of building large nuclear forces or living helplessly between Washington and Moscow. The key is to keep the mousetrap intact while reducing the economic costs of maintaining it.

Lord Hastings Ismay, the first NATO secretary-general, once summarized the purpose of the alliance as "to keep the Russians out, the Americans in, and the Germans down." While the goals remain valid, subject to subtle modification, the question is how to best accomplish them.

"Keep the Soviets Out." It may well be that in the near future the Western democracies will be required to mount a common deterrent against a renewed Soviet threat—a threat that does not exist today in the direct form it took for four decades. Nevertheless, the danger of war has not disappeared from Europe. Quite the contrary. Soviet troops have not disappeared from eastern Germany and central Europe. They remain under arms at a time when elements of the Red Army along with the KGB and Communist apparatchiks are fighting the consequences of Gorbachev's reforms and may hold Gorbachev himself as a kind of political hostage. Should the USSR split into an array of independent republics, the Russian Republic alone would still be the most powerful military force in Europe.

However, the Soviet Union has survived so far and has committed itself in a series of treaties to removing all of its troops from central Europe and to cutting its offensive weaponry west of the Urals. While it is possible that the Soviets will renege on this commitment, it is more likely that they will honor it. If that happens, the Soviet threat will no longer exist in the essential form we have known for almost half a century: the Red Army, offensively armed, just days away from Paris and Bonn. For now, however, the Soviets are out and only the Germans can let them in.

"Keep the Americans In." The United States now returns home from the gulf the undisputed end-of-century superpower, but one with a mixed record of following through on the results of its military handiwork. The stark realities of the deficit, growing social-services expenditures, and a reluctance to raise taxes exert mounting pressure on the federal budget. There is a clear tendency to bring the boys home and bar the door. NATO needs the United States as the arbitrator, and the force that divides German-French domination of the continent's western defense, to the detriment of the noncentral nations (Britain, Spain, Italy, Belgium, Denmark, Norway, Turkey).

The United States needs Europe, a peaceful and secure Europe, not simply as its $1 trillion trading partner but more importantly because Europe is home to shared values and traditions. Without Europe, America would be lonelier in the world. NATO will no longer provide the central focus for U.S. involvement in Europe, but a benign neglect of NATO will, for Lord Ismay's purposes, keep the Americans in Europe in the event of a military crisis.

"Keep the Germans Down." The assumptions of Konrad Adenauer and Dean Acheson formed the basis for the postwar transatlantic community. Those assumptions included a rearmed (West) Germany, tightly imbedded in NATO and the EC; and a major U.S. military presence and leadership in Europe/Germany. They also included, consciously in Acheson's mind, a Pax Americana: the United States as the preeminent source of finance capital, and the dollar as the reserve currency anchor of a fixed exchange international monetary system.

Westerners quite rightly granted the Federal Republic of Germany sovereign status, but never considered the possibility of a German-Soviet rapprochement counter to their perceived interests. The *Ostpolitik* of Brandt and his successors unsheathed the double-edged sword of Germany's role as a senior player in the postwar world, and as recently as July 1990, Helmut Kohl's direct negotiation with Gorbachev was a cause for concern. As Roger Morgan noted, Western fears more often reflect feelings than rational responses:

> There is no use facing the 21st Century with the fears of the 19th: the prospect of any future German government resorting to armed force to

recover lost territory is remote in the extreme, and so is the risk of German economic power being used to exercise political hegemony in order to exact support for German policies or interests. Rather, there is simply a feeling among Germany's neighbors—diffuse but still real—that the might of a united Germany will be so great that it needs to be contained firmly in a sound framework for the good of the Germans themselves as well as everyone else.[9]

The West cannot overlook the fact that Soviet policymakers vest great hopes in their German ties. Therefore, the German role in the new order will clearly involve a tricky balancing act: serving as the conduit for Soviet relations with Europe while remaining outwardly committed to Western economic and military structures.

Foreign policy tension is exacerbated by the internal pressures facing the Germans. Following the heady euphoria of the unification, Germans have been progressively turning inward. They neglected the Persian Gulf partly because the political leadership was consumed with unification. After desultory debates and pro forma peace demonstrations, the government called for a $50 billion tax hike to pay for $6.6 billion in aid. Despite statements to the contrary, the tax increase was a fait accompli as far back as the currency union in 1990, which converted the East German mark into the deutsche mark at a rate seven times the market. Thus the "taxes for the Gulf" sleight of hand will actually be used to pay the costs of unification (which include $9 billion to house redeployed Soviet troops). The government will also draw down the several billion dollars left in the German part of the Marshall Fund and borrow heavily. All of these funds will go to the bailout of eastern Germany, but it will not be enough.

Unemployment in the eastern part of Germany has topped the cataclysmic levels of the Weimar era; immigration from the flanks of the community and Turkey exacerbates the problem; the tax bite (already over 50 percent), climbing interest rates, and the resurgence of the dollar combine to block up goods within Germany and stall business growth. The inability of investors to purchase unencumbered assets or properties in the new *Bundesländer* has killed new business growth in the eastern half.

Worst of all, most who could leave the East have left. This means that the skilled workers, young families, and students are gone. A recent poll indicated that less than half of those between the ages of eighteen and twenty-four thought they would "probably stay" in the eastern half.[10] The remaining generation, now middle aged, will not outlive the problems begotten during the Communist era. The odds are strong that a still prosperous and democratic Germany will eventually emerge—but it will not be the same country as the beholden and divided land that once lay on the edge of the Western world. Instead, the Soviet Union, borders again laid bare, will demarcate the edge of the West.

A Prescription for NATO

The alliance must continue to operate at a level in proportion to the threat to peace in Europe. It cannot be constructed or configured for any other mission. The ideas currently in vogue—"out of area operations" and "crisis management"—are unnecessary baggage that will sap NATO's strength and guarantee its irrelevance. NATO and most of the member's armed forces were built to fight the hot war that could have been the nightmarish progeny of the cold war. The planning systems, the procurement policies, the training exercises, the stationing of troops and finally the philosophical bridge to nuclear war—all of these things evolved for the single purpose of halting a Soviet invasion of Western Europe. Momentum exists in every organization, and this is especially true in one as large and successful as NATO. To suddenly reorient the system to some new (and possibly contrived) goal is to beg disaster and failure.

NATO should continue to exist in order to "promote stability and well-being in the North Atlantic area" and to "unite [members] in their efforts for common defense and for the preservation of peace and security."[11] This mandates four essential characteristics for the future structure of NATO forces: the capability to mobilize against a renewed threat to the center; the ability to react to threats around the periphery on shorter notice; the retention of a range of weapons that can deter nuclear aggression; and continued centralized planning, coordination and training of NATO forces. These characteristics are nothing new, and they were virtually adopted in the London Declaration of the NATO ministers of July 1990.

As with the EC, the success of NATO in fulfilling its role will hinge on integrative structures. NATO forces should, insofar as possible, be highly specialized within the alliance; there is no real reason for all the members to maintain fully capable general purpose forces. This is true not only for reasons of military effectiveness but also because Europe's political landscape makes some missions impossible for certain nations and relatively simple for others. Support functions such as transport, mess, field wiring, and engineers could easily be assigned to specific countries.

Attention should be given to improving the effectiveness of multinational fighting units, such as the German-French Brigade and the Jutland Division. Critics and commanders contend that these organizations are highly desirable from every standpoint, except that they are not always as effective as single-language, similarly equipped units. NATO needs to find the optimal level of integration (i.e., division or corps) that maximizes both integration and effectiveness. These units should be the sort of integrative structures that encourage cooperation and provide a bellwether for the broader health of inter-European relations.

The tactics and strategy of the cold war, principally "flexible response" and "follow-on forces attack," are no longer valid and are currently under review in Brussels. The battlefield for World War III is now a fragile field of nascent democracies. Attacking targets in these countries is a perverse if not incredible exercise. Instead, while retaining focus on the Atlantic bridge, NATO needs to develop a conventional counterpunch strategy that goes deeper than follow-on forces and strikes at war-making machinery and the politically vulnerable heartland. Such a force, constituted for a counterattack, would serve as a truly credible conventional deterrent. At the nuclear level, the progress of arms control and pressure for European denuclearization means a renewed reliance on strategic systems. Given the environment of instability that is likely to attend the coming period of realignment, it is a reliance that should be avoided.

In particular, intermittent calls for a German nuclear capability should be resisted.[12] The provision of nuclear protection for NATO countries is the ultimate guarantee of a relevant American military voice in Europe. For a host of other reasons, including proliferation, specialization, domestic tranquility, and constitutionality, Germany should stay out of the nuclear club. Furthermore, the configuration of that club, the United States, the USSR, China, France, and Britain (at the strategic level), is one of the few stable power balances in the new order. The addition of new poles or control-sharing arrangements would serve only to increase uncertainty and bilateral suspicion.

The European defense industry is already highly integrated. Messerschmitt-Bölkow-Blohm (MBB), the German contractor, can no longer manufacture its fighter planes or space technology alone because of the massive capital requirements and development risks. In addition, the cancelation of a major contract can devastate a single concern. As a result, MBB and firms like it are integrated on a project basis across Europe. The further interdependence of the Western arms industry should be encouraged, if not directly supported, by the United States.

With regard to Eastern Europe, the path to the West, meaning membership in the EC and NATO, should be clarified. These countries suffer from the aftermath of communism in a structural sense, for as George Kennan has noted, one of the worst ravages of Soviet rule was that it left client states unable to replace it with anything better. Both NATO and the EC should play a role in developing replacement international structures. For now, it is clear that Eastern European economies are too weak, their forces too incompatible, and their dreams too threatening to the Soviets for them to join NATO or the EC. But then again, as Czech foreign minister Jiri Dienstbier pointed out, they would hope to be treated at least as well as Kuwait if they were threatened.

Russian disintegration, German unification, and American overstretch[13] have severed the ties that made balance-of-power politics a game of the past in Europe. NATO, the focus of U.S.-European relations for forty years, can no longer serve all three goals envisioned for it: NATO can keep Russian divisions on the far side of the Elbe (not the Oder), but it cannot keep a swarm of immigrants there; it can keep an American nuclear tripwire stretched across Western Europe, but it cannot maintain transatlantic commercial ties; it can protect Germany from others, but it cannot protect Germany from itself. Therefore, if NATO is to wane in the coming of the New World Order, it must do so only when something else fills the roles articulated by Lord Ismay.

Keeping the Soviets out means helping the new democracies in Eastern Europe while somehow stabilizing the Soviet Union itself. Keeping the Americans in requires a workable Atlantic trading regime to replace a declining military presence. Keeping Germany down really means integrating Germany into (not against) the new arrangements. NATO alone cannot accomplish these goals. But it can, and should continue to do its part: to provide the bulwark of defense for Europe. It will do so if neglected, benignly.

Notes

1. Henry Kissinger, *Years of Upheaval* (Boston: Little, Brown, 1982), p. 147.
2. A more general reflection of the German commitment is the remarkable response to the appeals for food aid to help the Soviet Union through the winter of 1990–91. Germany has provided 80 percent of such aid. In his final Bundestag speech, Egon Bahr, the SPD veteran, compared the effort to the 1948 Luftbrücke— the American airlift to relieve Stalin's blockade. There are emotional sources at work here that are more or less impervious to cool observations that the actual Soviet situation was far from catastrophic, or that there was far more pressing hunger in other parts of the world.
3. Until November 1989, serious voices were still warning that the whole recent astonishing turn of events might be a Soviet trick. It is impossible to make this claim any more, the Gorbachev leadership having given up its entire claim on Eastern Europe and struggling now to hold together its remaining union. But things are starting to look like a trick of history—this "peace" may be more dangerous than the cold war.
4. John Mearsheimer, "Back to the Future," *International Security* 15, no. 1 (Summer 1990): 6.
5. Ibid., pp. 26–27.
6. In October 1990 Roland Dumas proposed a unanimous decision from the heads of the 12 EC governments, indicating that a "European response" was

needed. The Council of Ministers would then shape the policy. In December, the EC then agreed to use the WEU in this respect.

7. *Economist*, 23 March 1991, p. 24.

8. See Hans Binnendijk. "How NATO + EC + WEU Can Equal Security for Europeans," *International Herald Tribune*, 2 April 1991.

9. Roger Morgan. "Germany in Europe," *Washington Quarterly* 13 (Autumn 1990): 153.

10. *Wall Street Journal* (Europe), 20 March 1991, p. 1.

11. North Atlantic Treaty, 4 April 1949, Preamble, from *The North Atlantic Treaty Organization. Facts and Figures* (Brussels, 1989), p. 1.

12. See, for example, David Garnham, "Extending Deterrence with German Nuclear Weapons," *International Security* 10 (Summer 1985). He argued that in the face of the declining credibility of the American deterrent, a German deterrent should be installed to guarantee a strong link between the weapon and the defender.

13. Paul Kennedy, *The Rise and Fall of Great Powers: Economic Change and Military Conflict from 1500 to 2000* (New York: Random House, 1987).

2

The Politics of Franco-German Arms Collaboration: Between Autonomy and Alliance

Jonathan B. Tucker

In February 1991 the first prototype of the Franco-German *Tiger* antitank helicopter was unveiled at the German aerospace firm Messerschmitt-Bölkow-Blohm (MBB) near Munich and transferred to southern France for flight testing. It was the most recent example of Franco-German arms collaboration, which began in the mid 1950s with the licensed construction of French military transports in West Germany and later expanded to include the joint development and production of missiles and combat aircraft. The transformation of France and Germany from "hereditary enemies" (*Erzfeinde*) that fought three wars between 1870 and 1945 into close allies engaged in arms collaboration is one of the most remarkable developments of postwar European history. How did this entente develop, and how have its dynamics changed over the past three decades as the balance of technological and economic strength between the two countries has shifted in Germany's favor?

The initial impetus for Franco-German arms collaboration came from the economics of defense procurement, in particular the rapidly increasing cost of research and development (R&D) for advanced weapon systems. In the late 1950s Britain, France, and West Germany recognized that if their national aerospace industries were to survive in the face of intense U.S. competition, they had no choice but to collaborate. Joint development, while more expensive overall than purchasing U.S. aircraft "off the shelf," enabled the participating countries to save money by sharing R&D costs and pooling national markets to achieve economies of scale in production. Each country thus retained a national aerospace industry for reasons of security, prestige, skilled employment, and technological spinoffs.

France, in particular, viewed arms collaboration with allies as a means of maintaining a national defense industrial base capable of producing the full range of major weapon systems. As former French defense minister Charles Hernu once wrote,

> Although it seems paradoxical, our main objective in cooperation is to have control over our arms policy and thus an autonomous defense policy. . . . Without this cooperation, our arms industry would have to abandon the presence it has today in all key spheres; it would have to specialize, which would inevitably lead to a loss of independence in the abandoned sectors.[1]

Arms collaboration is much more than a business transaction between governments; it is also a matter of high politics, all the more sensitive and critical because it impinges directly on core security issues that have traditionally been of supreme value to the nation-state. From the beginning, Paris and Bonn used military-aerospace collaboration to further their respective foreign policy goals. Joint weapons-development projects provided a tangible symbol of reconciliation between the two former adversaries and created new channels of communication between their military establishments. Nevertheless, the politicization of arms collaboration has tended to diminish its economic benefits. According to RAND analyst Mark A. Lorell, joint military aircraft projects in Western Europe "have been dominated by national industrial and political priorities to such an extent that military requirements and cost and schedule objectives were seriously compromised."[2]

At the same time, Franco-German arms collaboration has been constrained by two essential tensions: on the one hand, French ambivalence between the quest for national autonomy in defense production and the desire to strengthen political and economic ties with its neighbor across the Rhine, and on the other, German ambivalence between its European and transatlantic security relationships. These tensions have caused arms collaboration to proceed on an ad hoc, project-by-project basis, driven more by political opportunism and industrial interests than the desire for economic efficiency or military standardization. Finding an optimal balance between autonomy and alliance will be increasingly important if the Franco-German security relationship is to provide the nucleus of a West European defense identity—a task that will become more important as the United States reduces its military presence in Europe.

Sources of Franco-German Arms Collaboration

In the aftermath of World War II, the victorious Allies dismantled Germany's military-industrial infrastructure. But the emergence of the cold war and the 1950 invasion of South Korea by the Communist North convinced the United States of the need to rearm West Germany as a bulwark against Soviet aggression. The 1954 Paris Agreements ended the Allied occupation, made the Federal Republic a full member of the North Atlantic Treaty Organization (NATO), and allowed it to establish a Federal Defense Force (*Bundeswehr*) of a half-million men. These new forces had to be equipped and trained, yet there was no West German defense industry. As a stopgap measure, Washington and Bonn signed the Mutual Defense Assistance Agreement of June 1955, which pledged the United States to provide the first generation of arms and equipment for the *Bundeswehr* free of charge. This gift was not entirely altruistic because it created a vast new market for the U.S. defense industry.

Although France had long opposed West German rearmament, the government under President Charles de Gaulle reacted pragmatically with a fundamental shift in policy toward its former enemy. If direct containment of Germany was no longer possible, then it was imperative to control and integrate the rearmament process through arms sales and collaborative procurement efforts, thereby harnessing the growing German wealth and military power to benefit French interests. France's other objective was to create a continental European bloc centered on Franco-German cooperation (with Germany in a subordinate position) as a political counterweight to U.S. hegemony in Europe. This latter ambition was strengthened by de Gaulle's anger over the U.S. refusal to support the Franco-British military intervention in Egypt during the 1956 Suez crisis.

Chancellor Konrad Adenauer sought to rebuild West Germany's defense and aeronautics industries as an instrument of national political rehabilitation. Although the burdens of the Nazi past precluded the Federal Republic from engaging in power politics or pursuing national autarky in arms production, Bonn could enhance its political and military weight by becoming a valued partner in collaborative arms projects with France, Britain, and the United States. In this way, the Federal Republic would achieve a "capability for partnership" (*Partnerschaftsfähigkeit*) that would further its goal of political equality and strengthen its influence on NATO policies affecting its security.[3] Defense minister Franz-Josef Strauss was also convinced of the economic importance of the military-aerospace sector, with its new technologies of benefit to civilian industry.

At the end of World War II German engineers had been at the cutting edge of aerospace technology with the invention of the jet fighter and the V-2 ballistic missile. But the decade-long ban on the industry meant that by 1955 they had missed an entire generation of aircraft development. Although renowned aeronautics firms such as Messerschmitt, Heinkel, Focke-Wulf, and Dornier had reestablished themselves in West Germany, they required a major infusion of foreign know-how to recoup their technological lag. Because the U.S. aircraft industry refused to engage in joint development efforts, the German firms turned to the French industry as the best possible alternative. Furthermore, if Bonn was to overcome its pariah status and become an influential player in Europe, it had to allay the fears of its suspicious neighbors about resurgent German militarism by integrating itself fully into the community of Western nations. Close cooperation with France, Germany's traditional rival, was the keystone of this strategy.

In January 1957 the two governments formed a joint military committee to explore possibilities for the codevelopment of aircraft, missiles, and tanks. It was agreed that France would supply most of the technical expertise and the Federal Republic much of the financing. The colonial war in Algeria had depleted the French defense budget, forcing Paris to slash research and development funds and to cancel several ongoing projects. Since the West German "economic miracle" was in full swing, France turned to its prosperous neighbor for the resources that would enable it to maintain a broad-based defense industry, narrowing the gap between its modest economic base and great-power ambitions. French defense minister Jacques Chaban-Delmas even met with Strauss to discuss the possibility of West German funding for the development of French nuclear weapons, although these negotiations were aborted in 1958 when de Gaulle returned to power and asserted the independence of the French nuclear deterrent.[4]

The first Franco-German arms project involved the licensed production in West Germany of two French aircraft: the *Noratlas*, a military transport, and the *Fouga Magister*, a jet trainer. But the nascent defense-industrial partnership suffered a major setback in October 1958 when the German Defense Ministry selected the Lockheed F-104 *Starfighter* over the Dassault *Mirage II* as the primary fighter for the new German Luftwaffe. The American aircraft prevailed less on technical grounds than because of the need to reinforce transatlantic political ties and to satisfy Washington's demands for arms purchases to offset the costs of stationing U.S. troops on West German soil. Another key factor was Bonn's desire to participate in the NATO "nuclear sharing" program, in which Luftwaffe fighter-bombers would be armed with U.S. nuclear gravity bombs. Washington made clear that the condition of German participation in the program was the purchase of an American aircraft.

Losing the fighter contract to the United States only strengthened French determination to capture a major share of the West German arms market. As the U.S.-French rivalry intensified, arms procurement became a key element in the struggle between Paris and Washington for political influence with Bonn. But Franco-German arms collaboration was limited by countervailing interests on both sides. Paris vacillated between the pursuit of national independence and the economic benefits of joint weapons development, while Bonn was torn between its competing alliances with France and the United States. Although Strauss considered strong ties with both countries vital to West German security, it was clear that the United States had priority because France was neither able nor willing to replace the U.S. nuclear guarantee or troops deployed along the inner-German border. For this reason, Bonn was careful to balance Franco-German arms projects with off-the-shelf purchases of U.S. weapons.

The Transall *Program*

The first Franco-German joint development effort was the C-160 *Transall* military transport, which was launched in 1958 as compensation for Bonn's choice of the *Starfighter* over the *Mirage*. At the outset, the airlift requirements of the two air forces were diametrically opposed: the French needed a long-range transport optimized for use in the North African desert and for export sales on the global market, while the Luftwaffe wanted a short-range transport optimized for weather conditions in central Europe. The Germans made most of the concessions and thus ended up with an aircraft that did not meet their military needs. In addition, the participating firms, two German and one French, carried out the development jointly but produced the transport on three separate assembly lines. This arrangement, driven by industrial-policy objectives, limited economies of scale and greatly increased the unit cost of the aircraft.

Nevertheless, the *Transall* program was mutually beneficial from a political and industrial standpoint, establishing what William Wallace has termed a pattern of "complementary advantage" between French design leadership and German cost and production sharing.[5] For the Federal Republic, the project helped to rebuild the national aircraft industry within a politically acceptable framework by providing access to French technology and design know-how. For France, collaboration with West Germany permitted a major aircraft development project that would not have been affordable with national means alone. The joint project also furthered France's ambition of creating a European aerospace capability under its leadership that could compete with the dominant U.S. industry. In this sense, the *Transall* program was the technical and political forerunner of the Airbus commercial aircraft consortium, founded in 1967.

The Elysée Treaty

A second phase of Franco-German armaments collaboration began on 22 January 1963, when Chancellor Adenauer and President de Gaulle signed the Treaty on Franco-German Cooperation at the Elysée Palace in Paris. One provision of the accord called for extensive defense cooperation between the two countries, including collaboration in weapons development and production "from the stage of developing suitable armaments projects to the preparation of finance plans."[6] In this way, the treaty codified the joint programs that had emerged on an ad hoc basis during the mid-1950s.

The Elysée treaty was motivated by de Gaulle's desire to create a "Paris-Bonn axis" as the nucleus of a more independent Europe under French political and technological leadership, thereby balancing the strong ties between Bonn and Washington. But the treaty's implicit anti-American slant did not sit well with the Atlanticist majority in the West German parliament, or Bundestag. During the ratification debate in May 1963, a majority of the Bundestag repudiated de Gaulle's vision by voting to add a preamble to the treaty reaffirming the priority of the German commitment to NATO.

Although the preamble was a bitter political setback for de Gaulle, the Elysée treaty gave new impetus to Franco-German arms collaboration. On the day the treaty was signed, representatives of the French firm of Nord-Aviation (later Aérospatiale) and the German firm of Bölkow (later Messerschmidt-Bölkow-Blohm, or MBB) met in Paris to plan the joint development of a family of tactical missiles. This partnership led to agreements to codevelop the *Milan* and *Hot* antitank missiles and the *Roland* antiaircraft missile. Here again, the partners had complementary interests. Whereas the French aerospace industry needed German capital, the West German industry benefited from transfers of French technology and—given Bonn's restrictive export-control policies—was happy to let the French take the lead in overseas sales of the jointly produced weapons. After 1964, however, the German ability to launch new projects with Paris was constrained by the need for offset purchases of American arms.

French Isolationism

The late 1960s were a period of turmoil in Franco-German security relations. France deployed an independent nuclear deterrent (*force de frappe*) and in 1966 withdrew its forces from NATO's integrated military structure. Although France remained a member of the alliance and did not rule out participation in a joint defense against Soviet aggression, Paris reserved for itself the decision to go to war. This shift in policy came as a severe blow to the Federal Republic, which lost not only the automatic French commitment to the conventional defense of the central front but also the geographic depth, supply lines, and reinforcements that France had provided.

Even during the most isolationist period of Gaullist defense policy, however, Bonn was able to preserve some elements of French military support through bilateral defense arrangements. France kept troops deployed in the Federal Republic to maintain a symbolic influence over German defense policy and ensure its continuing status as one of the four guarantee powers in Berlin. Moreover, although Paris closed all NATO facilities on French territory, the *Bundeswehr* was allowed to keep important supply bases. Bonn also sought to strengthen the bilateral defense relationship with Paris in the hope of ultimately drawing France back into the NATO alliance. To achieve this long-term objective, the Federal Republic was prepared to make major concessions in joint arms projects.

The next opportunity was a multilateral European project to develop a multirole combat aircraft, later named the *Tornado*. Yet France refused to participate in this program, both because it was unable to reconcile its military requirements with those of the other partners (West Germany, Britain, and Italy) and because it wished to retain an autonomous capability to develop and manufacture high-performance military aircraft. As an alternative, Paris invited the West German industry to collaborate in developing a modified version of the *Mirage III* fighter, but Bonn was already committed to the *Tornado* consortium.

Changes of government in both Paris and Bonn soon created strong political incentives for a new collaborative arms project. In 1969 de Gaulle resigned the French presidency and was replaced by Georges Pompidou. Relations between the new French president and German chancellor Willy Brandt were strained, most notably by the deployment of French *Pluton* tactical nuclear missiles. Designed for use against Warsaw Pact forces in the event that they broke through NATO's defensive positions, the French missiles had such a short range that they could hit targets only on West German soil. This shortcoming provoked concern in Bonn and motivated German defense officials to seek some influence over French nuclear planning. Pompidou viewed Brandt's new *Ostpolitik* with considerable mistrust, fearing that the rapprochement between the two German states would lead sooner or later to a resurgence of German nationalism.[7] Paris was therefore interested in new initiatives that would bind the Federal Republic more tightly to France and thus to the West.

The Alpha Jet *Program*

An opportunity for Franco-German arms collaboration soon presented itself. Although the Luftwaffe trained most of its pilots in the United States, the high costs led the air staff to consider transferring its program back to Europe. Discussions between the French and German air forces raised the possibility of establishing a joint pilot-training center in southern France. This objective would be facilitated by the codevelopment of a jet trainer to replace the *Fouga Magister*, which had been developed in France and built under license in West Germany during the mid 1950s.

Although the idea of a Franco-German flight school was still embryonic, the joint-trainer proposal was catapulted to the level of high politics. Shortly after Bonn declined the French offer to coproduce the *Mirage III*, West German defense minister Gerhard Schröder made the opportunistic decision to "compensate" the French by offering to codevelop the jet trainer. Because a trainer was not a critical weapon system like a fighter, the French had no reservations about collaboration. In 1969 Paris and Bonn announced their intention to purchase 200 aircraft each, and launched a design competition with participation limited to Franco-German industrial teams. The West German firm of Dornier and its French partner Dassault won the contract with a design called the "Alpha Jet."

Midway through the definition phase, however, Washington informed Bonn that the Luftwaffe was obligated by contract to continue pilot training in the United States with U.S.-built aircraft. Since West Germany no longer had a requirement for a new trainer, the *Alpha Jet* had lost its rationale, yet the political imperative of collaborating with Paris made it necessary to salvage the program. At this point, the German Defense Ministry recalled that it needed a light fighter-bomber for close air support of ground forces and that with a few design modifications the *Alpha Jet* might be adapted to this role. Luftwaffe pilots protested that the trainer-turned-fighter would not have the thrust, maneuverability, and weapons payload required for combat and called instead for purchasing a heavier aircraft with more powerful engines. But political pressures to preserve the collaboration, combined with concerted lobbying of both governments by Dornier and Dassault, prevailed over the Luftwaffe's objections. According to one account, Luftwaffe inspector Günther Rall "ordered" the pilots to cease their criticism of the program immediately.[8]

After feasibility studies by industry, Paris and Bonn agreed to produce two different versions of the *Alpha Jet:* a trainer version for France and a fighter-bomber version for the Luftwaffe. The two versions would use the same fuselage, engines, and basic equipment, differing only in such secondary features as avionics, pylons, brakes, armament, and ejection seats. Nevertheless, the Luftwaffe insisted on increasing the thrust of the French-designed jet engines to meet combat requirements. (The Germans favored using a more powerful engine already available from General Electric, but the French rejected this idea out of hand.) Unfortunately, the development of higher-power French engines led to technical problems that substantially increased the cost of the aircraft.

The hybrid trainer-fighter that emerged from the collaboration was an awkward compromise that failed to satisfy the needs of either air force. Although the French acquired a high-quality trainer, the more powerful engines necessitated by the German combat version made the aircraft considerably more expensive than Paris had planned. As a result, the

Alpha Jet sold poorly on export markets, particularly in competition with simpler, cheaper trainers such as the British *Hawk*. The Luftwaffe, for its part, found the subsonic *Alpha Jet* too light and slow to perform its assigned combat missions against increasingly lethal Soviet air defenses. Thus, in 1987 the German Defense Ministry, after investing billions of marks to procure and upgrade the *Alpha Jet*, decided to abandon the aircraft's combat role and use it primarily as a trainer—an ironic outcome given its original mission.

From a political standpoint, codevelopment of the *Alpha Jet* symbolized the continued interest of Paris and Bonn in security cooperation despite France's isolationist defense policy. The program was also a pragmatic response to the French need for German financial aid to fund new conventional weapons systems, particularly now that a third of the French defense budget was devoted to the nuclear strike force. Yet the *Alpha Jet* itself proved to be an unwanted child that satisfied the desires of neither parent—a clear example of the negative consequences of using arms collaboration to achieve political objectives. Beyond its symbolism, the codevelopment effort had no discernible effect on French defense policy. After the plan for a joint Franco-German flight school was abandoned, the *Alpha Jet* program did not compel Paris to modify its independent defense posture or to make a tangible commitment to West German security. Because the two sides ended up procuring different versions of the aircraft, it contributed little to the military standardization of the two air forces.

The program also undermined Bonn's principled policy on arms exports outside the NATO region. In 1971 the Brandt government issued strict policy guidelines designed, in principle, to ban all transfers of German-made weapons to Third World "areas of tension" (*Spannungsgebiete*), as defined by the Foreign Office. At the same time, however, the Pompidou government began to promote arms sales to the Third World as a means of financing the national defense industry. As a condition of French participation in the *Alpha Jet* program, Paris insisted on the right to export all codeveloped military equipment without restrictions, creating a direct conflict with the Brandt policy.

After much internal debate, the West German government signed a secret agreement in 1972 creating a major loophole in its restrictive arms-export laws. The German defense industry would be allowed to participate in export sales of codeveloped weapons systems to conflict areas such as the Middle East as long as the German-made components were first exported to France for assembly. Although Bonn could decline to produce its share of a jointly developed weapon system for export if it judged the sale would harm its vital interests, the German share of production would have to be transferred to the French industry. In practice, however, this option was rarely used. When the terms of the secret Franco-German arms agreement were leaked to *Der Spiegel*, Bonn's moral standing was tarnished at home and abroad. Franco-German arms collaboration had been preserved, but at the expense of Bonn's relations with the rest of the world.

Revived Defense Cooperation

The coming to power in 1974 of Helmut Schmidt in Bonn and Valéry Giscard d'Estaing in Paris led to a new mutual commitment in defense cooperation. France's chief motivation for this shift away from isolationism was its anxiety over *les incertitudes allemandes*, or the unpredictability of West Germany's relations with the Eastern bloc. In particular, the French were concerned about the emergence of neutralist elements in the West German political debate, including the Greens, the left wing of the Social Democratic Party (SPD), and the peace movement, which won a large popular following after the announced deployment in 1979 of new U.S. intermediate-range nuclear (INF) missiles on West German soil.

The worst-case scenario for French defense planners was that the Federal Republic would leave NATO in exchange for the Soviet promise of a reunified, neutralized Germany. That eventuality would eliminate the shield of West German and U.S. forces defending France's vulnerable eastern border and also result in the withdrawal of the U.S. nuclear umbrella, exposing France directly to the full weight of Soviet military power. Thus, in a great historical irony, French preoccupation with the "German problem" shifted 180 degrees from fears of German militarism to apprehensions about German pacifism.

In fact, French concerns were greatly exaggerated: The Schmidt government was in the mainstream of Western defense policy and supported the deployment of the American INF missiles. Bonn sought to gain a stronger French commitment to the conventional defense of West Germany, to establish a framework for Franco-German consultations on the employment of French tactical nuclear weapons, and to reopen discussions on the use of French territory and supply lines by NATO forces.

An important step in closer defense cooperation was the establishment of an institutionalized dialogue on security issues. At the biannual Franco-German summit in February 1982, Chancellor Schmidt and French president François Mitterrand agreed to create a joint steering committee for this purpose, with three subsidiary working groups focusing on arms collaboration, military cooperation, and political-strategic affairs. Nevertheless, a renewed attempt at bilateral arms collaboration stalled when a French proposal to develop a Franco-German main battle tank was opposed by the West German defense industry, which feared that the

French partner firms would appropriate Germany's superior armor and diesel-engine technology to increase French tank exports. The Defense Committee of the Bundestag finally canceled the project in May 1982. A more positive development came in late 1983, when the French government deployed the Rapid Action Force (FAR), a new military organization designed both for overseas intervention and conventional conflict in Europe. In Bonn's view, the FAR was the first tangible evidence of a new French commitment to the conventional defense of West German territory.

Parallel to the expanded Franco-German security dialogue, the Federal Republic sought to involve France in an ambitious project to develop a new European fighter for the 1990s. In December 1983 the air force chiefs of staff of West Germany, Great Britain, France, Italy, and Spain signed an agreement specifying a joint military requirement for the European Fighter Aircraft (EFA), the first time all five major European countries had agreed to develop a common weapon system.[9] Although the participating countries managed to harmonize their military requirements, the French decided in July 1985 to withdraw from the EFA consortium and develop a competing fighter, the *Rafale*, on a national basis.

The primary reason for this decision was the uncompromising attitude of the French defense industry, in particular Dassault and SNECMA (National Company for the Design and Construction of Aircraft Engines), which demanded the leadership of both the EFA airframe and engine development programs despite the insistence of the British and West German industries on an equitable division of benefits and responsibilities. The French government was also split between Europeanists, who favored greater defense cooperation, and Gaullists, who wanted to retain a domestic capability to develop major weapons systems as a guarantee of national independence. In the Gaullists' view, participation in the EFA program would have led France down a slippery slope toward reintegration with NATO.[10] The decision to leave the EFA consortium was thus a major setback to Bonn's attempt to draw France back into the military structures of the alliance.

The *Tiger* Helicopter

After the French withdrawal from the EFA consortium and the failure of other efforts at bilateral arms collaboration, both governments came under intense pressure to succeed with the one remaining joint program: the Franco-German antitank helicopter, later named the *Tiger*. The project had been launched officially in October 1976, when the two defense ministries signed a memorandum of understanding to begin conceptual studies of a military helicopter. While the German Army had a near-term requirement for an antitank helicopter capable of night-combat operations, the French Army needed an escort and fire-support helicopter to protect its existing *Gazelle* antitank helicopters, which would not have to be replaced until after the year 2000. The joint program foresaw the development of a basic helicopter from which would be derived three national versions: a German antitank version and separate French escort and antitank versions.[11] Because the two sides were unable to reach a compromise between their divergent military requirements, the program was put on hold in the late 1970s.

In May 1982, however, the Bundestag's cancelation of the Franco-German tank project changed the political context and created strong pressures for a new joint arms initiative. In November Bonn tried to soothe the bad feelings in Paris by proposing to revive the quiescent helicopter project. The new government under Chancellor Helmut Kohl was anxious to have at least one major Franco-German arms project under way as a tangible demonstration that the partnership was moving forward. A breakdown in collaboration would send the wrong signals to Paris and Moscow, while allowing the joint structures built up over the 1960s and 1970s to erode. Thus, ironically enough, the antitank helicopter replaced the joint tank as the major collaborative venture of the 1980s. According to a German defense official, "It's traditional that there be at least one major Franco-German program. Had the joint tank project gone ahead, there would have been no political need for the anti-tank helicopter."[12]

In May 1984, after arduous negotiations, the two governments signed an agreement authorizing the codevelopment of three versions of the *Tiger* by the helicopter divisions of Aérospatiale and Messerschmitt-Bölkow-Blohm (MBB). Meanwhile, political pressures to move forward with the joint helicopter program were strengthened by two other failed attempts at collaboration: the French withdrawal from the EFA consortium in July 1985 and Bonn's decision a few months later to turn down a French offer to codevelop a military reconnaissance satellite called *Helios*. Paris had offered to share the project leadership as an indication of its desire to deepen defense cooperation. But German participation was blocked by financial constraints and the clear separation in the West German bureaucracy between civilian and military space research. (France later codeveloped the *Helios* with Italy and Spain.)

West German efforts to deepen defense cooperation with France were also driven by what Bonn perceived as a weakening of the U.S. nuclear commitment to its security. The Reagan administration launched its Strategic Defense Initiative (SDI) in 1983. Combined with negotiations on reducing intermediate-range nuclear forces in Europe, SDI appeared to signal a U.S. shift away from an emphasis on nuclear deterrence. Although the French nuclear strike force was much smaller than the U.S. arsenal, it offered the advantages of being based and controlled from Europe and less susceptible to arms-control reductions. Bonn therefore sought closer coordination with Paris on the targeting and use of French tactical nuclear weapons.

Yet while the *Tiger* program had strong political incentives to succeed, it was plagued by spiraling costs and delays, leading the French Army in early 1986 to consider abandoning the program in favor of a national development. President Mitterrand and Chancellor Kohl urged both sides to compromise on a configuration and night-vision equipment that would be mutually acceptable, but the revised cost estimates provided by industry were so high that in September 1986 the two sides agreed to halt the development program pending a review of the military requirements and system specifications. The military staffs reworked the definition of the basic helicopter, reducing the number of versions from three to two. In March 1987 the French and German defense ministers approved the common antitank configuration and launched the full-scale engineering development.[13] Flight testing of the first prototype began in the spring of 1991.

The *Tiger* helicopter is a clear example of a collaborative armaments program created almost entirely for political and industrial reasons, with little if any military or cost-saving rationale. According to an estimate by the Social Democratic fraction in the Bundestag, the program will cost about DM 2 billion more and take several years longer than the purchase or licensed-production of a comparable U.S. helicopter, the AH-64 *Apache*.[14] Moreover, the two armies have different tactical conceptions for the use of the *Tiger* helicopter and have not engaged in joint planning for future military operations.

By the late 1980s Franco-German defense collaboration appeared to have reached an impasse. Paris agreed in February 1986 to consult with Bonn in some circumstances prior to the use of its "prestrategic" (short range) nuclear weapons on German soil, and in 1987 their armies carried out a large joint exercise called "Bold Sparrow" and agreed to create a joint army brigade under alternating French and German command—a step with greater political than military significance. In January 1988 the two governments established a Franco-German Defense and Security Council, made up of the heads of state and the foreign and defense ministers, to underline the continued solidarity between them. Nevertheless, more far-reaching forms of collaboration were blocked by the two countries' incompatible military doctrines. Paris was unwilling to revise the basic tenets of Gaullist defense policy by rejoining the NATO wartime command structure or by "sharing" its nuclear deterrent, while Bonn refused to enter into bilateral relationships that would weaken the NATO alliance, despite Germany's growing disillusionment with U.S. policy.

Another reason for the difficulty of Franco-German arms collaboration was Bonn's demand for equal status, based on its increasing political self-confidence and the financial and technological strength of its aerospace industry. Beginning in the mid-1980s, the Federal Republic was determined to pursue its own interests within collaborative projects and to prevent its domination by partners.[15] During the *Tiger* program, Bonn made clear that it was no longer willing to sacrifice its military requirements for the sake of collaboration. As a result of this new assertiveness, the negotiations with France lasted more than twelve years before the development phase began, and a compromise was reached only after intense pressure from the highest political levels.

The Impact of Germany's Increased Power

With the opening of the Berlin wall in November 1989 and the prospect of rapid German unification, Franco-German relations suddenly experienced new tensions. Chancellor Kohl's initial hesitation to recognize the Oder-Neisse line as the definitive border between Germany and Poland, and President Mitterrand's outspoken support of Poland even after the Bundestag passed a resolution affirming the existing border, reawakened long-buried resentments. Fortunately, the French government recognized that there was no holding back the German people's irresistible drive for unity and that seeking to slow the process would merely poison future Franco-German relations.

French elites remain concerned that a united Germany with 80 million inhabitants will create a new imbalance between the two countries. Unification has transformed the Federal Republic into the largest non-Russian continental state, fundamentally changing the political and economic balance of power within both the European Community and Europe as a whole. Although France strengthened its political standing in Europe by participating in Operation Desert Storm while Germany remained on the sidelines, the end of the cold war has diminished the importance of France's special status as a nuclear power and its military contribution to the conventional defense of Germany.

Meanwhile, France is increasingly overshadowed by its neighbor's growing economic power. According to *Business Week,* "Germany's $1.8 trillion economy is suddenly 40 percent bigger than France's. A year ago, it was just 25 percent bigger. The gap will only widen as eastern Germany rebuilds."[16] The Federal Republic already leads France in automobiles, machinery, electronics, and chemicals, and it may soon move ahead in aerospace. In 1989 the German aerospace industry was consolidated into a giant Daimler-Benz subsidiary known as Deutsche Aerospace (DASA). With annual sales of about $7.5 billion, DASA is larger than the French firm Aérospatiale and roughly the same size as British Aerospace, greatly enhancing Germany's ability to compete at the European level.[17]

According to Thomas-Durell Young, from the perspective of French policy, unification has "killed once and for all the perception (greatly encouraged by Paris and tacitly accepted by Bonn) that France was the senior partner in the bilateral relationship. . . . Just as Bonn must come to terms with the fact that it has all but become an incomplete superpower, so must Paris accept its new status in Europe and refocus its political aspirations."[18] As a check on Germany's growing financial power, France is seeking to accelerate the EC's economic and political integration, including the development of common monetary, foreign, and security policies. But while both Chancellor Kohl and President Mitterrand have endorsed the concept of political union, there is far from a consensus within the EC on the ultimate goals of the integration process.

The Future of Collaboration

Over the past thirty-five years France has used arms collaboration with Germany as a means of maintaining an independent defense posture in the face of limited financial resources by sharing the development costs of specific weapons programs and military technologies. At the same time, Germany has sought to use high-profile collaborative arms projects as a political instrument for extracting tangible French security commitments. While Franco-German defense cooperation remains politically important as a driver of European political integration, the bilateral relationship will play a useful role in the future only if it complements multilateral defense cooperation efforts within NATO and the European Community.

As long as France strives to preserve a large degree of autonomy in matters of defense, arms collaboration will remain a marriage of convenience in which the partners merely aggregate their national interests instead of pursuing a broader European common interest. Paris still procures nearly all of its weapons from domestic sources, including nuclear missiles, the *Leclerc* tank, and the *Rafale* fighter. Yet because the French defense industry can no longer count on arms exports to finance the spiraling costs of defense research and development, French firms have begun to enter into strategic alliances with other West European contractors, most notably the 1990 merger of the helicopter divisions of Aérospatiale and MBB to form a joint-venture company called Eurocopter. The growing French emphasis on collaboration was reinforced by the Persian Gulf war, which revealed the operational and logistical importance of standardized weapons in coalition warfare.

Given the French interest in ensuring that a united Germany remains enmeshed in Western security structures, Paris has also supported the first tentative steps by the EC toward the development of a common defense policy, with the long-term objective of establishing a cohesive West European defense identity. At a meeting in Rome of the European Council in December 1990, the member-states agreed to consider the gradual expansion of EC responsibilities in the security area, including "economic and technological cooperation in the armaments field, coordination of arms-export policy, and non-proliferation."[19] In March 1991 former French president Giscard d'Estaing made a more ambitious proposal for the creation of a European armaments agency that would manage programs for equipping the forces of the EC member-states, pool defense research and development efforts, and establish a common set of rules for limiting arms exports.[20]

Implementing this proposal, however, would require a fundamental shift in French defense policy. Although there are indications that French policymakers recognize that the Gaullist tenets of national autarky in defense and arms procurement are no longer realistic, domestic political constraints may prevent Paris from abandoning its traditional defense posture until political conditions become more clear. Because German defense policy is also in flux in the wake of the Gulf war, a restructuring of the Paris-Bonn axis will have to await the definition of French and German national goals within the new European security architecture.

Notes

1. Charles Hernu, cited in Edward A. Kolodziej, *Making and Marketing Arms: The French Experience and Its Implications for the International System* (Princeton, N.J.: Princeton University Press, 1987), p. 166.

2. Mark A. Lorell, *Multinational Development of Large Aircraft: The European Experience* (Santa Monica, Calif.: RAND, July 1980), p. 73.

3. Regina H. E. Cowen, *Defense Procurement in the Federal Republic of Germany: Politics and Organization* (Boulder: Westview, 1986), p. 219.

4. Francois Puaux, "La France, l'Allemagne et l'atome: Discorde improbable, accord impossible," *Défense Nationale* 41 (December 1985): 9–18.

5. William Wallace, "The Defence of Sovereignty, or the Defence of Germany?" in *Partners and Rivals in Western Europe: Britain, France and Germany*, ed. Roger Morgan and Caroline Bray (Hants, England: Gower, 1986), p. 231.

6. "Vertrag zwischen der Bundesrepublik Deutschland und der Französischen Republik über die deutsch-französische Zusammenarbeit," *Parlament*, No. 6–7, 7–14 February 1987, p. 2.

7. Hans-Peter Schwarz, "Die Entente: Perspektiven der deutsch-französischen Zusammenarbeit," *Politische Meinung* 32, no. 236 (January-February 1988): 11.

8. Alfred Mechtersheimer, *MRCA Tornado: Rüstung und Politik in der Bundesrepublik* (Bad Honnef: Osang, 1977), p. 132.

9. Erhard Heckmann, "Das europäische Jagdflugzeug: Vision, Alptraum oder Hoffnung?" *Wehrtechnik* (June 1985), p. 41.

10. "Militärluftfahrt: Alleingang oder europäische Gemeinschaft?" *Interavia* (May 1985), pp. 474-75.

11. François Heisbourg, "Für Einen Neuen Anfang," in *Deutsch-Französische Sicherheitspolitik*, ed. Karl Kaiser and Pierre Lellouche (Bonn: Europa Union, 1986), p. 131.

12. Ulrich Bewerunge, director Air Armaments Division, Ministry of Defense, Bonn, 1988.

13. "Die Entwicklung des gemeinsamen Hubschraubers gegen Panzer," *Wehrdienst*, no. 1107, 30 November 1987, p. 2.

14. SPD-Fraktion im Deutschen Bundestag, Arbeitsgruppe Sicherheitsfragen, "Positionspapier zur Streitkräfte-, Personal-, Rüstungs- und Finanzplanung der Bundeswehr" (mimeo), 28 April 1988.

15. Trevor Taylor, "European Armaments Cooperation: Competition for Resources," in *Brassey's Defence Yearbook 1987* (London: Brassey's, 1987), p. 158.

16. Stewart Toy, "La Republique Isn't Feeling So Grand Anymore," *Business Week*, 11 March 1991, p. 45.

17. "Daimler-Benz: On the Runway," *Economist* 311, no. 7597, 8 April 1989, p. 72.

18. Thomas-Durell Young, *The Franco-German Relationship in the Transatlantic Security Framework* (Carlisle Barracks, Penn.: Strategic Studies Institute, U.S. Army War College, July 1991), p. 3.

19. European Council, "Presidency Conclusions, Part I," Rome, 14-15 December 1990, Document No. 424/1/90 (OR.f) REV I, p. 6.

20. "Giscard Presents European Defense Proposals," Paris Antenne-2 Television Network, 20 March 1991 (translated in FBIS-WEU-91-056, 22 March 1991, p. 12).

3

German-American Relations After the Cold War

Dana H. Allin

What effect did the extraordinary events of 1989 and 1990 have on German-U.S. relations?

In attempting to answer this question, one should avoid the mood of the moment. Moods change quickly. Nor should one be too distracted by current tensions or preoccupations—whether it be disputes over trade, interest-rate coordination, or contributions to the Gulf war. Clearly, the historic events in Europe—reforms in the Soviet Union, revolutions in Eastern Europe, German unification—changed a great deal in the world. But did they change the fundamental nature of German-U.S. ties?

The answer is yes and no. The relationship looks set to endure. But with the passing of the cold war, there is a subtle but important change in the *basis* of that relationship. Whereas the German-U.S. alliance was once a strategic necessity, it has now become a political choice. It will consequently require greater cultivation and care.

Obviously this statement oversimplifies a more complicated reality. From the very beginning of the cold war, the alliance had been the result of conscious choices by such men as Konrad Adenauer and Dean Acheson. And there is no denying that many objective circumstances even today dictate a continued close German-U.S. partnership.

However, the demise of the cold war has removed the most dramatic of those circumstances: the fact that the inner-German border was literally the front line in a global confrontation between the United States and USSR, between East and West. What remains of the Soviet threat will no longer be the focus of U.S.-German ties.

An earlier version of this chapter was prepared as part of a Deutsche Bank Economics Department study.

Germany and America During the Cold War

Why should special German-American ties remain so important? Why, after the end of the cold war that made this relationship so critical, should there not be a return to normality? Germany and America would always have much in common: two of the most powerful world economies, sharing democratic values, a common European heritage, an important trade relationship, and so forth. Should it be any more than that? The answer is not altogether obvious. But one answer, often implicitly understood rather than explicitly stated, is that there was something inherent in the German-American relationship during the cold war that was important in its own right, and should survive the East-West confrontation. In rough terms, there was a feeling that Germany must somehow be anchored to the West, and that the United States should remain anchored to Europe.

To understand this feeling, one must understand its history. The German state created at the center of Europe by Bismarck was too big, powerful, populous, and dynamic to be integrated peacefully into the existing European order. It naturally excited the envy and fears of its neighbors, spurring military competition and a destabilizing competition for allies. Bismarck himself was skilled enough to maintain an acceptably stable balance of power. His successors were less skilled. The effect was two catastrophic world wars.[1]

After the second of these wars and defeats, leaders of the prostrated Germany argued about the kind of diplomatic orientation and political economy that might allow the Germans to escape a third disaster. In the western Trizonia, this debate pitted Christian Democratic Konrad Adenauer against the Socialist Democrat Kurt Schumacher. Schumacher conceived of a reunited, pacified Germany, neutral in the emerging Soviet-American conflict, enjoying a humane and democratic socialism distinct from both American-style "monopoly capitalism" and Stalinist communism. Adenauer imagined a westward-looking Federal Republic, embedded in the nascent (West) European Community and in a Western military alliance. The country would combine free-market capitalism with social welfare that was an integral tenet of the new Christian Democratic ideology. It would enjoy special ties with America and France.[2]

Adenauer's view, of course, carried the day. (He was helped immensely by Stalin's blockade of Berlin, and the resulting Allied Airlift, which overnight transformed the image of Americans from conquerors to saviors.) The "Adenauer Germany" turned out to be a historically unprecedented success economically, socially, and diplomatically. The price of this success was forty years of division—a price paid mainly by East Germans.

On the American side, there was an equally heated (though perhaps more complicated) debate about America's future ties to Europe in general and to Germany in particular. By logical extension, this debate also concerned the future shape and diplomatic orientation of Germany. There was a strong current of old-style isolationism, with its traditional anti-European ideology represented by right-wing congressional Republicans and General Douglas MacArthur, who saw the real American future in the Pacific. But not all of the American opposition to a permanent, massive U.S. presence in Germany can be dismissed as provincial isolationism.

By far the most interesting opponent of a permanent U.S. military presence in Germany was George F. Kennan. By no means anti-European or anti-German, Kennan, on the contrary, favored the rapid restoration and rehabilitation of German power and economic vitality as a bulwark against Soviet expansionism. German nationalism could be constructively channeled into a confederal European Community. Kennan believed a settlement was both possible and desirable, viewing it as a deal under which the Soviets would accept reunification and real German independence in exchange for a vow of neutrality. With its economic health restored, a neutral Germany would be able to resist Soviet pressures and blackmail. In a sense, Kennan believed it was possible to recreate a Bismarckian balance of power in Europe while avoiding the fatal errors of Bismarck's successors. Above all, Kennan feared a long-term American military hegemony in Europe as something that would damage both American and European societies. (He later admitted that he had been overly pessimistic in this regard.)[3]

In his espousal of most of these views, Kennan was very much a lone voice. The man who was much more influential in shaping the German-American relationship was Dean Acheson. In part this was because he so faithfully represented what the Europeans themselves (and especially the Germans under Adenauer) wanted. This Adenauer-Acheson interpretation formed the basis for the postwar transatlantic community. It included a rearmed (West) Germany tightly embedded in NATO and the EC and a major U.S. military presence and leadership in Europe/Germany. It adamantly rejected any deal with the Soviets that would attenuate Germany's economic and military ties to the West. And it also included, consciously in Acheson's mind, an American recreation of the financial aspects of the former Pax Britannica: an open trading system with America as the preeminent source of finance capital and the dollar as the reserve-currency anchor of a fixed-exchange international monetary system.[4]

It bears repeating that this Atlanticist creation—a Federal Republic "anchored" to the West and a United States anchored to Europe—has proved remarkably successful. European peace and stability were preserved. American troops in Germany arguably reassured Germany's neighbors and therefore made possible the historic Franco-German reconciliation. Above all, the whole construction undergirded a postwar

European prosperity that ultimately had a magnetic pull on the Communist societies of the East.

Despite all successes, there were of course tensions in the German-American relationship. For simplicity's sake, these tensions might be seen in two phases. The first phase, covering approximately fifteen years from the founding of the Federal Republic until Adenauer's retirement in 1963, was a period marked by the immediate threat that armed confrontation on the inner-German border would lead to real war.

The focus of this threat was Berlin, and the series of Berlin crises fed by the tensions of four-power jurisdiction over a city deep inside the Soviet-occupied zone of Germany. The crises carried the superpowers to the brink of the nuclear abyss. They also started, slowly at first, to pull the veil away from a recurring conflict between the Americans and their West German allies—over the proper balance between willingness to negotiate and readiness to go to war. This is not to say that repeated expressions of German-American solidarity were insincere. Quite the contrary. But there was a natural conflict of interests between the two allies. The Bonn government under Adenauer (which refused to recognize not only the GDR but also any other government that recognized the GDR) was troubled by the suspicion that America would ultimately sacrifice German interests at the negotiating table. The Americans, on the other hand, especially the incoming Kennedy administration, could not help but fret over their commitment to a city that they knew they could not defend without resorting to nuclear war.[5]

In August 1961 the Soviets constructed a virtual prison wall through the center of Berlin. With this act, some of the worst fears in both Bonn and Washington were realized. The United States looked on helplessly as the Soviets and their East German clients flagrantly violated the four-power agreement. The slow death, near Checkpoint Charlie, within view of American soldiers and West Berliners, of construction worker Peter Fecter, who was shot by East German guards while trying to scale the wall, became a wrenching symbol of the limits to American power. The hard-line Adenauer strategy for negotiating German reunification only from a position of overwhelming Western strength was revealed, at least for the moment, as a failure.[6]

And yet, despite all the horrors of the Soviet-imposed regime in the East, the 1960s ushered in a long period of peace—both in the cold war confrontation and in German-American ties. The Americans, although at a loss to preserve their rights in the Soviet zone, made it clear that they would go to war to defend the western half of the city. President Kennedy's rapturous welcome by Berliners during his June 1963 visit underscored that West Germans were supportive of the United States. Correspondingly, fundamental German allegiance to the Western alliance was, and remained, unquestioned.

A second phase in relations, from 1963 until the 1989 collapse of the Berlin wall, was a time of clarity as well as stability. Despite occasional bouts of fashionable pessimism, the German-American alliance was never in doubt. In fact, those problems that did arise between Washington and Bonn might best be understood as products of the stability. The respective German-American roles in the alliance, and their expectations of each other, changed only very slowly, even though their relative economic weight in the international system changed very quickly. From this somewhat anomalous situation, there arose a series of disputes over military strategy, eastern diplomacy, and the structure of economic relations (including the distribution of defense burdens).

Military Strategy

The German-American security debate has always been a rather confusing drama in which roles changed frequently: The Germans sometimes worried about U.S. reluctance to defend Europe and at other times about its overeagerness to challenge the Soviets. Americans habitually performed a similar switch, worrying one day about how their German commitments would drag the United States into a nuclear war, and concerned the next about a rise of German pacifism.

Simple geography explains much of this confusion. The West German state was a narrow band on the map, one border of which teemed with Soviet troops. If those troops had ever broken through NATO lines, they were expected to overrun the country very quickly. West German elites were committed to a concept of "forward defense"—repelling the invader along the border rather than falling back for a strategically more feasible "defense in depth." But without a massive increase in NATO conventional forces, this forward defense most likely could only be accomplished by an early resort to nuclear war. In fact, this explicit strategy of nuclear "first use" did not trouble German leaders greatly, since they believed that any European war would be catastrophic and probably lead to nuclear war in any case. The best way to prevent war altogether was to make clear that any battle in Europe would quickly turn nuclear.

American leaders could not help but have a different perspective. They imagined a European conflict drawing them into global nuclear war. It seemed more sensible to prepare for conventional war, and it should have been possible to mount an adequate conventional defense—a "firebreak" between the nonnuclear and the nuclear—if the Europeans were willing to raise sufficient forces.

The result of these conflicting perspectives was the strategy of "flexible response." Flexible response was very much a compromise. The original American proposal, forwarded by Defense Secretary Robert McNamara in the Kennedy administration, put much greater emphasis on conventional forces, but European governments would accept the strategy only if it contained an explicit threat to use nuclear weapons relatively early in a conflict.

Flexible response was officially adopted as NATO strategy in 1967. On the level of German-American political relations, the strategy experienced its crisis, so to speak, ten years later. With concern that the Soviet Union was achieving a superiority of nuclear firepower in the European theater, West German chancellor Helmut Schmidt issued a somewhat ambiguous call for an American response.[7] The Carter administration decided, rather reluctantly by most accounts, to deploy a new generation of European-based nuclear missiles: the Pershing IIs and ground-launched cruise missiles. But a wave of antinuclear sentiment in Germany took both governments by surprise. When the Reagan administration came into office, bringing with it a strident anti-Soviet rhetoric, it became popular to assume that the United States was forcing these weapons on the Germans. In fact, the Americans, although originally skeptical about the military rationale for the new missiles, feared that backing down now would hand the Soviets a diplomatic victory, with dire consequences for the cohesion of NATO, and they began to deploy the missiles in 1983 as scheduled.[8]

In 1985, the new Soviet leadership under Mikhail Gorbachev showed remarkable willingness to negotiate seriously about this and every other outstanding East-West conflict. During President Ronald Reagan's second term, a treaty was negotiated to remove the so-called Euromissiles from the Soviet and American arsenals. During these negotiations, when word leaked out that Reagan, at the Reykjavík summit meeting, had considered agreeing to the abolition of *all* nuclear weapons, German leaders once more worried that the United States might abandon nuclear deterrence.[9]

There was hardly a consistent pattern to this confusion of roles, but there was a consistent problem. In the area of military security, a combination of German dependence on the Americans plus the highly emotional dependence on nuclear weapons posed political difficulties—difficulties that German and American governments certainly were able to manage without the basic partnership ever being endangered. But these difficulties, precisely because they did involve emotional issues of life and death, tended to poison the overall relationship—producing, for example, a significant (though not to be exaggerated) current of anti-Americanism in the FRG. If such nuclear strategic questions are becoming less important for the future, that could be a good sign for transatlantic ties.

Ostpolitik

A similar confusion of roles characterized attitudes about diplomacy with Moscow. Sometimes Washington took the lead in negotiating a relaxation of tensions, and sometimes Bonn was out ahead. Consistently, however, whenever one partner was cultivating friendlier relations with the Soviets, the other partner tended to worry.

It was at the end of the 1960s, under the Socialist-Liberal coalition government of Chancellor Willy Brandt, that West German policy turned decisively toward negotiations with both Moscow and East Berlin. Brandt decided, and explained his decision explicitly, that it was necessary to recognize Germany's division in order to have any hope, in the long run, of overcoming that division. This *Ostpolitik* developed into a policy of small, practical steps—easing travel between the two Germanies, buying with deutsche marks the right of East Germans to move West, among others. But in order to achieve these small openings in the Berlin wall, Brandt's government first had to establish friendlier relations with Moscow.

The Americans reacted ambiguously. Watching Brandt's diplomacy from the White House, National Security Advisor Henry Kissinger confessed to his own mixed feelings about the Brandt diplomacy. Kissinger recognized the courage, and to some extent, the necessity of Brandt's policy, writing, "Brandt's wrenching decision to recognize the division of his country was a courageous recognition of reality."[10] But the overall strategy of using that recognition, as Kissinger described it, "as a means to achieve German *unity* by building good relations with the East and turning the Federal Republic into a magnet for Eastern Europe," made him nervous.[11] In his memoirs, Kissinger discussed his fears and remarked that "the question in our minds was which side of the dividing line would in fact be the magnet. We feared that over time, at first imperceptibly, the Communist world would wind up in the stronger position."[12]

Of course, America had its own détente policy, and the prime architect was Kissinger himself. German governments at times were wary about this U.S.-Soviet détente, as, for example, in 1977 when Chancellor Schmidt delivered a famous speech in London warning about the implications of U.S.-Soviet strategic arms agreements for NATO deterrence.[13]

In 1979 a series of Soviet adventures, including the invasion of Afghanistan, led the United States to abandon détente. President Jimmy Carter withdrew the strategic arms treaty from Senate consideration and embarked on a major defense buildup. The Reagan administration repudiated détente even more directly.

The Germans were unwilling to join the United States in burying détente, a divergence that led to what was perhaps the deepest period of crisis in postwar German-American ties. The aforementioned Euromissile dispute was part of that crisis. Another source of tension among the allies was the West European plan to join the Soviets in building a natural gas pipeline from Siberia to Western Europe. Reagan administration officials criticized the project harshly, charging that it would provide the Soviets hard currency for the military buildup while engendering West European dependence on Soviet energy supplies, which the Soviets would use for purposes of political blackmail.

These specific Reagan administration complaints about West German policy became embedded in a broader strategic pessimism about Western Europe: a fear that the West Europeans in general, and especially the West Germans, were in danger of being "Finlandized." Soviet strategic power had cowed the Germans into submission, it was alleged; just as Kissinger had worried fifteen years earlier, West Germany was nominally a member of NATO, but determined above all not to offend Moscow. Many American (and it should be added, French) analysts returned to the historical theme of Rapallo, and claimed to discern in that 1922 German-Soviet cooperation treaty an inclination for Germany to "turn its face toward the East and relink its fate with Russia's."[14]

German elites found these combined Rapallo/Finlandization analyses to be false at best and, at worst, deeply insulting. German governments saw themselves balancing a wariness about Soviet intentions with a determination to preserve the gains of East-West diplomacy. They saw détente as a natural West European vocation and the only sustainable long-term policy for easing the dilemmas of their divided continent. Germans could already see the concrete gains in terms of increased contact between citizens of the divided halves of their nation. The Kohl government, far from repudiating its predecessors' *Ostpolitik*, emphasized it as a political counterweight to the NATO arms buildup.[15]

Shared Burdens in a World Economy

A third source of traditional German-American tensions during the cold war originated in the area of economic relations. These tensions were not limited to the problem of bilateral economic relations, but included the role both of these major economic powers played in the functioning and management of a world economy. In fact, the broad debate over economic relations also included military topics—the so-called burden-sharing debate about distributing financial responsibilities for NATO defense.

In the immediate postwar years, the lines of responsibility were fairly clear. The United States emerged from World War II as the world's single economic superpower, as Paul Kennedy writes, "Among the Great Powers, the United States was the only country which became richer—in fact, much richer—rather than poorer because of the war."[16] It possessed two-thirds of the world's gold reserves, half of the world's total manufacturing production, half of the world's shipping, and produced one-third of the world's exports. The traditional European powers, by contrast, were economically exhausted and, in the case of the defeated Fascist nations—Germany, Italy and Japan—literally destroyed. "German national income and output in 1946" writes Kennedy, "was less than one-third that of 1938, a horrendous reduction."[17]

In addition to its immense wealth, the United States also possessed a political leadership that was capable of appreciating the dangers posed by this artificial maldistribution of world resources. Europe's economic misery, in some cases actual starvation, was seen in Washington not only as a tragedy in its own right but also as a potent political threat: West European Communist parties were on hand and ready with their own "solution" to the crisis. Partly to pre-empt this Communist solution, the United States announced its Marshall Plan of aid for the reconstruction of European economies. In the western zones of occupied Germany, a harsh but very effective currency reform also helped to provide the conditions for economic recovery. That recovery turned out to be dramatically successful throughout Western Europe, and nowhere more so than in West Germany itself.

It should have come as no surprise that this European (and Japanese) economic recovery meant also the *relative* economic decline of America. Indeed, it was the conscious purpose of U.S. policy. It posed difficulties of adjustment, however.

The first of these difficulties culminated in the currency crisis of 1971 with a dollar devaluation that can be seen, in retrospect, as the end of the fixed exchange-rate system established at Bretton Woods. The dollar had come under mounting pressure throughout the late 1960s (partly because of federal government spending for the Vietnam War). Leading figures in the new Nixon administration argued that the dollar was overvalued and represented a structural trade disadvantage for the United States. Although such a disadvantage might have been seen as reasonable in the 1950s, U.S. officials considered it unjustified now that Germany and Japan had rebuilt and established powerful export economies. In 1971, in fact, the United States registered its first trade deficit in this century.

The Nixon devaluation did provide an immediate improvement in America's trade deficit, but it was short-lived. The United States enjoyed its last trade surplus in 1975. With the Reagan military buildup and tax cuts, the process accelerated—the United States doubled its national debt in Reagan's first term.[18]

The political reaction to these developments has focused on the seemingly permanent trade imbalances with Germany and Japan and three areas of complaint. The first complaint has concerned trading practices themselves, although most of the criticism here has been directed against Japan, since it is generally acknowledged that Germany has kept its markets quite open.

The second complaint concerned monetary and (more generally) demand-management policies; in this case, American criticism was directed against Germany as well. The Carter, Reagan, and Bush administrations have all argued that as the world's preeminent exporter, Germany has a responsibility to pursue lower short-term interest rates as a stimulant to domestic demand. The Germans, with a central bank renowned for its monetary conservatism, have generally resisted these proddings. It is often said that these differing monetary philosophies stem from different historical experiences. The Germans, it is said, are fixated on the ruinous hyperinflation of the 1920s, and determined above all never to sacrifice the stability of the deutsche mark. American politics, in contrast, is still influenced by the terrible unemployment of the 1930s Great Depression. Like all clichés, this one should not be accepted uncritically, but it probably does help explain some of the persistent irritation between Washington and Bonn.

A third American complaint has concerned the high level of U.S. indebtedness. Many argued that U.S. defense spending was driven principally by the military commitment to Europe. About 60 percent of U.S. defense spending resulted from these European commitments, according to one Pentagon report.[19] Ever more frequently during the Reagan administration, voices in the U.S. Congress accused Europe of enjoying a free ride, and urged the Europeans to share more of the burden.

In West Germany there was little sympathy for these complaints. The arguments about monetary policy suggest to many Germans that America has still not learned the lesson of the 1970s: that there was no permanent tradeoff between employment and inflation; economic prosperity cannot be purchased at the price of monetary instability.

As for burden sharing, Germans pointed out that the French and Germans together, with a much smaller combined population, field ground forces roughly 80 percent as large as the Americans.[20] There are, moreover, different kinds of burdens not expressed in defense budgets—for example, Germany has military conscription while the United States does not. More fundamentally, German commentators argued that global economic imbalances stem from many causes; the United States must take the blame for many of them, e.g., profligate tax cuts and an inadequate educational system.

The End of the Cold War

By 1985 these three basic sources of German-American tensions—in military security, *Ostpolitik*, and the structure of macroeconomic relations—had become long-standing and familiar features of the transatlantic landscape. Many observers viewed them as permanent and even quite acceptable given the fundamental solidarity between the United States and the Federal Republic of Germany—a solidarity that would be forever perpetuated by a continued Soviet threat, or so it seemed.

Then Mikhail Gorbachev took over the Soviet leadership. Within a few short years the international system, the map of Europe, and (as an important corollary) the nature of German-American relations had been utterly transformed.

This is not the place to try to summarize all of the revolutionary changes that the Gorbachev reform program inspired in Europe. Suffice it to say that until 1985, the optimists—such as supporters of the Brandt *Ostpolitik*—had imagined at best a slow and gradual loosening of Communist societies and an even more gradual blurring of Europe's division. What happened instead was a wildfire of peaceful revolutions, equal in significance and greater in immediate impact to the European revolutions of 1848. The fire spread from the Soviet Union to Poland (already the scene of open mass resistance to the Communist model), to Hungary (with its tradition of relative economic liberalism), and finally to the ostensible East European strongholds of Communist orthodoxy—including the German Democratic Republic. Suddenly in the fall of 1989, German unification became a real prospect.

The opening of the Berlin wall was followed by a year of further astonishment. In late 1989 Chancellor Kohl unveiled a ten-year plan for German unification. Eleven *months* later Germany was unified. This year of German unification was also critical, and altogether positive, for German-American relations. Other West German alliance partners, notably France and Britain, showed unease about the pace of events and appeared unimpressed by German arguments that it had to move fast in reaction to a virtual hemorrhaging of emigrating East Germans.

U.S. officials, in contrast to the French and British, showed no such unease or suspicion. Weeks before the opening of the wall, America's ambassador to Bonn, Vernon Walters, predicted that Germany would be reunited with U.S. support. Events soon proved him right on both counts.

For their part, Bonn officials insisted that a united Germany would remain a member of NATO. Many analysts doubted that the Soviet Union would accept German unification under circumstances that meant, in effect, its most important ally joining the opposing camp. Some respectable analysts argued further that expecting the Soviets to acquiesce in such an arrangement was unreasonable and, given the end of the cold war, unnecessary. Bonn persisted. At a July 1990 meeting in the Caucasus, Chancellor Kohl won Gorbachev's assent—once more to the world's astonishment. The Germans promised that after the Soviet withdrawal, no foreign troops would be stationed on former East German territory. Germany also promised a massive aid program, including financing the relocation of troops to the Soviet Union. The Soviets agreed that full sovereignty for the united Germany included the right to remain in NATO.

Thus, even after the Soviet Union of Stalin had given way to the Soviet Union of Gorbachev, a German-American strategic and political partnership was reaffirmed by both sides. The European settlement proposed by Schumacher and Kennan four decades earlier, with a neutral Germany as its centerpiece, was once more firmly rejected. The German-American axis of Adenauer and Acheson was again embraced.

After the Euphoria

In the wake of these events, there were euphoric visions of a "new world peace order." The United States would continue leading an Atlantic community in close and amicable partnership with the newly sovereign Germany and strengthened European Community. European economic integration, the opening and development of Eastern markets, and the "peace dividend" would all provide a welcome new spurt of prosperity. With the aid of this prosperity plus the end of East-West antagonism, it would be possible to give more serious attention to the problems of the Third World. The Soviet Union, enjoying steady progress toward political democracy and market prosperity, would prove a peaceful and cooperative junior partner in the new order.

However, it soon became apparent that the scale of economic disaster in Eastern Europe and the Soviet Union was even greater than previously imagined. These disasters had immediate political ramifications. In the Soviet Union in 1990 Foreign Minister Eduard Shevardnadze's resignation speech was the most dramatic among numerous signals of the Soviet Union's possible return to dictatorship. Ethnic conflicts and turmoil raised the specter of civil war in the Balkans or Eastern Europe. On top of it all, there was war in the Persian Gulf.

These crises naturally led politicians and analysts to wonder about the stability of the transatlantic alliance, and a note of pessimism came into discussions of the central German-American linchpin of that alliance. A mixture of fears have been expressed. They include:

- A return to Rapallo: that is to say, a close and intimate Soviet-German partnership that undermines NATO unity.

- Increasing trade and macroeconomic frictions, and a greater willingness to fight for narrow national economic interests, now that the Soviet threat no longer imposes unity. Already in 1987 many commentators blamed the global market crash on American and German inability (or unwillingness) to coordinate their interest-rate policies. The Bundesbank interest-rate hike during the winter of 1991—in apparent response to inflationary pressures from the East—reminded some critics of that 1987 misadventure.
- The diversion of capital to eastern investment, with deleterious effects on world capital markets (and on the financing of U.S. deficits).
- The diversion of German attention and resources away from European integration, effectively stalling the whole European project.
- The threat of an oversized Germany upsetting the political and economic balance within the EC.
- A controversy over German conduct in the Gulf War with the charge that Germany may be "turning inward," preoccupied with burden of integrating the five new states while maintaining its high living standards in the West. For German-American relations, the Gulf war was too short and U.S. casualties too low to provoke very deep resentment at Germany's purely financial contribution. However, the war serves as a dramatic prelude to a historic German debate about the nation's future military/political role. There is clearly a temptation (reinforced by the nation's post-Hitler antimilitarism) to continue enjoying economic might while avoiding world political responsibilities. Some critics argue that if Germany succumbs to that temptation, consequences for U.S. ties would be grave.

Just as before, the Germans have a corresponding list of criticisms. First of all, say many Germans, the world needs to make up its mind about what it wants from Germany—is it more worried about a return to German militarism or a shirking of German military responsibilities? Second, there should be a greater recognition of the burdens that Germany is already shouldering. Aid to the Soviet Union is helping to bring about a strategic revolution favoring the West: the complete withdrawal of Soviet troops from their threatening position in central Europe. Third, there is a concern that the United States, as a society, does not yet grasp that its continued role of world leadership requires it to restore its own economic vitality by bringing its fiscal accounts into order, improving its savings and investment rate, and, above all, improving its educational system.

Finally, the Germans and other Europeans fear that a strategically overburdened and resentful America will withdraw its troops and retreat into neo-isolationism. Of course, U.S. leadership of the coalition against Iraq makes it difficult to argue that America is eager to give up its world military role. A more subtle concern is that a U.S. troop withdrawal from Europe would make inter-European relations more problematic. France, it is said, finds Germany less intimidating and therefore easier to engage in intimate economic/political relations because U.S. troops exercise a symbolic restraint on German ambitions. Likewise, small countries like the Netherlands may very well be more comfortable with America's NATO leadership than they would be with French or German leadership.

Future German-American Relations

Not all these anxieties can be valid. Some of them are clearly contradictory: in the tumultuous months since the opening of the Berlin wall, some pessimists have warned about excessive German power; others have worried about German weakness.

Moreover, these anxieties are grounded in the past. That is only natural, but any fair assessment must recognize at least the possibility that the international system has undergone a fundamental change. This is most obviously the case with regard to Germany.

The necessity for analysis to free itself from historical concepts that are no longer relevant applies especially to the Rapallo idea and the disputes and anxieties associated with Germany's *Ostpolitik*. Despite Kissinger's fears, it was the Western side of the iron curtain that exerted an irresistible pull on the East, not the other way around. West Germany never budged from the Western community and there is little reason to fear that it will do so in the future.

This is not to deny that a new, more intimate Soviet-German partnership could create some irritants in Germany's relationship with America and its European allies. For reasons of history, geography, and wealth, Germany is the most obvious Western partner for promoting Soviet economic restructuring and peaceful integration into the world community. And if the Soviet Union truly returns to dictatorship and confrontational international relations, then disunity between Germany and America becomes a threat. Clearly, however, the lesson of the past twenty years is that such tensions can be managed. To put it in crude terms, Germany *can be trusted* to conduct a responsible *Ostpolitik* under difficult conditions.

Paradoxically, the likely end of a direct Soviet military threat will introduce an element of extra challenge into the future of German-American relations. For, as argued at the outset, this means an end to the centrality of the U.S.-German strategic relationship. Most troops will be leaving Germany. Yet the future of Europe remains uncertain, subject to instabilities and conflicts. The German-American relationship remains an important source of stability. More than in the past, that relationship must be a conscious political choice.

Notes

1. David P. Calleo, *The German Problem Reconsidered: Germany and the World Order, 1870 to the Present* (Cambridge: Cambridge University Press, 1978), chaps. 1–3.
2. Richard Barnett, *The Alliance* (New York: Simon and Schuster, 1983), chap. 1.
3. George Kennan, *Memoirs: 1925–1950* (Boston: Little, Brown, 1967); *Memoirs: 1950–63* (Boston: Little, Brown, 1972), *passim*.
4. John L. Harper, forthcoming biographical work on Roosevelt, Kennan, and Acheson.
5. Alfred Grosser, *The Western Alliance: European-American Relations Since 1945* (New York: Vintage, 1982), pp. 190–199.
6. Grosser, ibid.; and Coral Bell, *Negotiation From Strength* (New York: Knopf, 1962), *passim*; Willy Brandt, *People and Politics* (Boston: Little, Brown, 1978), chap. 1.
7. Helmut Schmidt, "The 1977 Alastair Buchan Memorial Lecture," *Survival* 20 (January–February 1978).
8. David N. Schwartz, *NATO's Nuclear Dilemmas* (Washington, D.C.: Brookings, 1983), *passim*.
9. W. R. Smyser, *Restive Partners: Washington and Bonn Diverge* (Boulder: Westview, 1990), p. 58.
10. Henry Kissinger, *Years of Upheaval* (Boston: Little, Brown, 1982), pp. 146–147.
11. Ibid.
12. Ibid.
13. Schmidt, "Alastair Buchan Memorial Lecture."
14. Smyser, *Restive Partners*, p. 89.
15. See Angela Stent, "The One Germany," *Foreign Policy* (Winter 1990-91): 53–70.
16. Paul Kennedy, *The Rise and Fall of the Great Powers* (New York: Random House, 1987), p. 358.
17. Ibid., p. 365.
18. David P. Calleo and Dana H. Allin, "Geostrategic Trends and the World Economy," in *Australia and the World*, ed. Desmond Ball (Australian National University, 1990); *Economic Report of the President: 1985*, pp. 345, 351; IMF, *International Statistics Yearbook: 1984* (Washington, D.C.: IMF, 1984), p. 595.
19. Richard Halloran, "Europe Called Main U.S. Arms Cost," *New York Times*, 20 July 1984.
20. IISS, *The Military Balance: 1988–1989* (London: International Institute for Strategic Studies, 1989).

PART TWO

Political Issues

4

European Integration and the German *Länder:* Lost Competence or Found Opportunity?

Jon M. Appleton

The federally structured and organized state, where sovereign bodies are unified under one centralized authority, has a long history in Western civilization.[1] Of the more than 170 political systems in the world today, fewer than 25 have been created along Federalist lines.[2] The Federal Republic of Germany (FRG) is one of them. Today, the growing economic and political integration within the European Community (EC), however, may be threatening the delicate separation of powers embodied in the FRG.

Naturally entwined in the process of European integration is the transfer to the EC of a large degree of the decision-making authority and legislative competence of individual member-nations. Although this entails a certain loss of sovereignty for the central governments of these nations, it carries added meaning for the FRG because it is the only federal republic within the EC. The sixteen German states (*Länder*) have no direct representation in the EC administration in Brussels. As such, they may face a situation where long-term policies and laws that directly affect them will be adopted with minimal consideration of their legitimate interests. In other words, as the EC assumes more responsibility and competence, this not only signals a loss of sovereignty for the German federal government (the Bundesstaat or Bund) but also represents a direct challenge to the *Länder*'s domestic law-making and administrative capacities.

Yet many observers believe the centralized "superbureaucracy" emerging in Brussels will be unable to manage the practical administration of the EC.[3] They argue that this would best be undertaken by subsidiary regional administrations throughout Europe. With their years of practical experience and complex administrative infrastructures, these regions are arguably the only bodies truly capable of establishing functional contacts with one another, of learning to overcome cultural differences, of administering the detailed EC directives and regulations, and of cooperating to solve problems in critical areas such as economics, science and technology, transportation, environmental protection, and research and development. Recently, this concept of regional cooperation and low-level administrative integration (commonly referred to as the "subsidiarity principle") has gained momentum in EC negotiations and might eventually emerge as an integral component of both the impending political and monetary unions.[4]

In the context of this debate, the EC's efforts to create an internal market has ignited in Germany a dramatic constitutional crisis as the *Länder* struggle to balance the prospect of lost competence and political weight with the potential opportunity to emerge as integral European actors. What, then, is the challenge facing the *Länder*? In what specific areas is the EC Commission infringing on their competence? What are the options facing the *Länder*? Will they become merely low-level administrative functionaries of a centralized EC or might European integration instead offer them a unique opportunity to increase their visibility and political might?

This chapter will focus on the effect of the EC process on the German domestic political balance. If the subsidiarity principle is eventually adopted so as to offer the *Länder* a truly institutionalized role within the EC, then the structural framework for analysis will undoubtedly be altered. However, the issues discussed below and the means of recourse available to the *Länder* will still remain important facets of the trilateral EC-Bund-*Länder* relationship.

The Constitutional Framework of the Modern Federal System

Contrary to what many observers may believe, the formation of the Federal Republic after World War II was not simply dictated by the Allies. Admittedly, a federal structure was the preferred solution sought by the occupation forces (especially by the Americans). But federalism was also consistent with German history, "directly in line," writes Fritz Ossenbühl, "with the goals of the German authors of the Constitution at the time."[5]

The roots of German federalism go back at least as far as the seventeenth century, following the Treaty of Westphalia's failure to produce a unified Germany. With the nation-state then emerging as a viable political unit throughout Europe, Germany remained a general grouping of sovereign territories. The notion of coexisting sovereign territories loosely organized under one central authority, first institutionally embodied in the *Rheinbund* of 1806, has predominated throughout German history. The retention of independent authority by the individual states or regions has remained an integral part of each German regime.[6]

In the modern German Federalist system, responsibility and competence are divided between the Bund and the *Länder*. As Gottfried Dietze explains, the founders of the Federal Republic, "having experienced the most dangerous combination of centralized power and majority rule [under the Nazis], ... saw in decentralization and control of the political branches of government complementary means for the protection of freedom."[7] The adherence to a separation of powers has been embodied in the German equivalent to the U.S. Constitution, the *Grundgesetz*, or Basic Law, of 23 May 1949. The actual "statehood" of the German *Länder* is not defined specifically but is instead intermittently addressed throughout the entire document. Nevertheless, taken as a whole, the Basic Law does offer, as Ossenbühl asserts, "a long list of distinctive features which give the Federal Republic of Germany its own unique characteristic as a federalist state."[8]

The first mention of federalism is found in Article 20(1), which declares "the Federal Republic is a democratic and social federal state."[9] The philosophy behind the creation of *Länder*, districts, and municipalities is expressed in Article 28 as the fundamental need for representation of the people at all political levels. The municipalities have been granted the right to form their own self-administrative bodies and are independently responsible for governing those matters directly affecting the local community. In contrast, the Bund is responsible for assuring that the rights and responsibilities of each level of government are carried out in a constitutional manner. Each state has the right to draft its own constitution, but the constitutional order within the *Länder* "must reflect the fundamental republican, democratic, and social goals espoused in the Basic Law."[10]

The continued existence of the *Länder* is protected in the "perpetuity guarantee" of Article 79(3), which declares that any amendment to the Basic Law affecting "the division of the Federation in *Länder*" is "inadmissible." No doubt an attempt to guarantee that the events of 1933 never be repeated, this article raises an insurmountable barrier to changes in the underlying structure of the federal system. Interestingly, while the fundamental survival of the *Länder* is assured, their continued existence in their current form remains unprotected. According to Article 29, it would be possible to alter the borders of the *Länder* so that they might be completely disbanded or joined with others. But, as Heinz Laufer points out, extreme changes producing, for example, just two *Länder* (i.e., North Germany and South Germany), could clearly cause Article 79 to be revoked to prevent such a move.[11]

In addition, the Federal Constitutional Court has inferred from the Basic Law a "quality of statehood" that all *Länder* inherently possess, irrespective of any express delegation from the Bund.[12] The court has articulated three distinctive features of statehood: (1) "minimum state competence" in certain core areas that may not be assumed by the Bund; (2) "constitutional autonomy," whereby the *Länder*, at a minimum, retain the freedom to determine their own organizational structure; and (3) "financial autonomy," which guarantees that the *Länder* continue to receive their respective shares of the total tax revenues.[13]

The Role of the *Länder* in the German Government

Tangible participation by the *Länder* in the government of the Federal Republic occurs at two distinct levels: (1) direct representation in the federal law-making process through the second chamber of the German legislature, the Bundesrat, and (2) independent law-making competence and responsibility in certain core areas that have been reserved for the *Länder*, such as social and cultural policy.

Participation in the Federal Process

The distribution of power between the Bund and the *Länder* is embodied in Article 30 of the Basic Law. Here the primary, although not exclusive, administrative role of the *Länder* is explained: "the states are solely responsible for performing the state functions, so long as the Basic Law does not say otherwise."[14] This role is somewhat more explicitly articulated in Article 83, in which legislation is generally deemed a federal responsibility, while the *Länder* are seen as responsible for the administration of federal laws.

Through the Bundesrat, the *Länder* have obtained a certain degree of compensation for their limited legislative responsibility. Comprised of three to six representatives from each of the directly elected *Länder* governments, the Bundesrat is an integral actor in initiating, revising, and approving federal legislation and is useful in incorporating *Länder* interests into federal policy. Where proposed legislation has a "special bearing on state interests" (amendments to the Basic Law, bills that affect state finances, or ones that alter the *Länder*'s administrative sovereignty), the Bundesrat has absolute veto power. In the case of these so-called consent bills, this veto power confers to the Bundesrat significant political might; between 1969 and 1983 more than 50 percent of all bills introduced required Bundesrat approval.[15] Although the role of the Bundesrat is not so pronounced in other areas, its contributions are essential in the passage of all federal legislation.

In addition, the Bundesrat serves as an official link between the federal and state governments. Because members of the Bundesrat are not directly elected, but are instead sent and recalled on a rotating basis by the ruling party of the individual *Länder* governments, state parliamentary elections are of nationwide significance.

Independent Legislative Competence

Although primarily assigned an administrative role, the *Länder* are not merely administrative functionaries of the Bund. In specific core areas, they have implicitly been granted certain, albeit limited, independent law-making competence and sovereignty. Article 70 confers to the *Länder* the right to legislate in all areas not expressly granted to the Bund. Those areas exclusively reserved to the Bund include foreign policy, defense, citizenship and passports, control of the currency, toll and taxation, train and air transportation, and the regulation of the legal relationship between the Bund and the *Länder*.[16]

In certain other areas (including, among others, criminal law, political refugees, and economic policy) the Bund and *Länder* exercise "concurrent legislative powers."[17] This notion of "concurrent power" is somewhat misleading; the *Länder* have the authority to act independently only so long as the Bund has not acted. The Bund may act in these areas when (1) the legislation of one state may unduly influence the Bund or the other states; (2) the matter cannot be effectively handled through state legislation; or (3) the maintenance of the legal or economic unit requires legislation encompassing the territory of more than one state.[18]

Because of the extensive authority conferred to the Bund by these three bases for federal power, actual *Länder* competence has traditionally been limited to the domain of "cultural sovereignty." This realm encompasses the two primary policy areas of education and culture. Understandably, the *Länder* have a significant interest in protecting their influence over these areas; education and cultural policies are often important economic factors that have a direct impact on the competitiveness and attractiveness of the individual states.

The Impact of the European Community

The Länder's *Legal Status Within the EC*

The challenge that European integration poses to the *Länder* is grounded in the legal framework of the EC-*Länder* relationship. Significantly, the role of the German *Länder* as sovereign, self-administered political units with their own constitutionally protected realm of minimum competence has never been formally recognized by the EC Commission.[19] They therefore have no direct input into the promulgation of EC regulations, directives, guidelines, or recommendations.

The obvious practical barriers to institutional participation on the part of the hundreds of existing European regions[20] almost certainly mean that the German *Länder* will never achieve the level of recognition they want. Ossenbühl has gone so far as to call the position of the *Länder* in the EC integration process completely "hopeless." The fundamental existence of the *Länder*, he argues, is no longer an internal constitutional issue for the Federal Republic but is instead fully dependent on the process of European integration and the decision-making structure in Brussels.[21] As will be discussed below, the *Länder* are not without the means to defend their autonomy.

The Challenge Posed by the EC

The *Länder* recognized the potential threat of European integration right after the Treaty of Rome was ratified. In 1957 the Ministerpräsident (governor) of North Rhine–Westphalia warned the Bundesrat that the *Länder* could eventually be completely shut out of the law-making process and reduced to "purely administrative bodies."[22] Over the years, the soundness of this original warning has been demonstrated; in spite of the economic role primarily envisioned for the EC, it is clear that the path toward unification has not been limited to the economic sphere.

Nevertheless, until recently, significant infringement by an EC Commission with limited authority remained minimal. Today, however, some five years after the signing of the Single European Act (SEA) in February of 1986,[23] it is apparent that the EC is well on its way to not only economic but also political and social unity. A representative of the German Bund has called the SEA "the most important and fundamental project for changing and extending the existing community constitution since the conclusion of the Treaty of Rome and a meaningful stage in the further development of an economic, monetary and, in the long run, European union."[24] The act has laid the foundation for European integration. Of particular interest in the SEA are the following amendments and additions to the original EC treaties:[25]

1. the commitment to the creation of the borderless "Internal European Market" by 1 January 1993 (Treaty of Rome, Article 8[a], as added by Article 13, SEA);

2. the introduction of the principle of qualified majority vote to facilitate the assimilation of discrepancies in the legal and administrative frameworks of the member-nations (Treaty of Rome, Article 100[a], as added by Article 18, SEA);
3. the recognition that the foreign policies of the respective member-nations within the European realm must be coherent (Article 30, SEA);
4. the granting to the European Council of the authority to implement by majority vote minimum requirements for the gradual improvements of the working environment of member-nations (Treaty of Rome, Article 118[a], as added by Article 21, SEA);
5. the creation of a legal framework for cooperation in environmental protection (Treaty of Rome, Article 130 [R-T], as added by Article 25, SEA); and
6. the granting to the EC Commission of the power to implement directly directives adopted by the Council (Treaty of Rome, Article 145, as amended by Article 10, SEA).

Simply put, the EC now has not only the framework within which to enact binding regulations and guidelines that affect the very heart of the twelve EC member-nations, but it also has the political impetus and a pressing timetable for change. In this context, the German Basic Law offers the *Länder* little protection. Anticipating Europe's eventual political unification, the authors of the Basic Law expressly reserved for the Bund the right to "transfer sovereign rights by law to intergovernmental institutions."[26] In a 1986 decision, the German Federal Constitutional Court ruled that this provision allowed the FRG's legal order to be altered so that the country's "exclusive jurisdiction . . . over its national territory is withdrawn and room for the direct validity and applicability of law from another source is opened up."[27]

Concrete Areas of Infringement

In recent years, the EC has begun to act in numerous critical areas of *Länder* competence, including voting rights, health law, construction law, disaster protection, culture, public service, transportation, forestry, environmental protection, and employment law. Because of the administrative nature of these areas, it is not so much the Bund that sacrifices power, but instead the individual *Länder*. Education policy has perhaps been most affected. Since 1987 alone, the commission has produced dozens of general proposals, communications, resolutions, guidelines (which must be integrated into domestic law in each member-nation), and directives (automatically binding) in this critical *Länder* domain. Some of the more noteworthy measures include:

1. "Guideline for Universal Regulation of the Recognition of University Diplomas" (ABI. L 19/16 from 24 January 1989; BR-Drs. 546/87);
2. "Communiqué Regarding General and Professional Education in the EC," touching on all areas of the educational system (text not yet published, BR-Drs. 281/88);
3. "Conclusion of the EC Council as to Continued Professional Education," outlining a common EC plan for action (ABI. C 148/1 of 15 June 1989, BR-Drs. 152/89);
4. "Working Document of the Commission regarding the social dimension of the Internal Market," listing general and professional education as two of the critical instruments for harmonizing social policy (14 September 1989, SEC 88114);
5. "Proposal for the Promotion of Innovation in Education" (Council Document: 9145/88; BR-Drs. 533/88); and
6. up to ten individual programs promoting mobility and cooperation between the educational systems (including the LINGUA Program for the promotion of foreign language skills, the ERASMUS Program for the promotion of mobility among university students, and the Petra Program for the preparation of youth for adulthood and careers).

Typically, the EC has justified these actions as necessary and legitimate steps for removing manifest barriers to trade. While the assimilation of education policy within the EC is a necessary step in the forging of the internal market, from a legal standpoint this incursion into the realm of education has tenuous support in the EC treaties, the resolutions of the European Council, or the EC Education Action Program initiated in 1976. Whereas Article 49 of the Treaty of Rome does foresee cooperation in expediting freedom of movement of the workforce, this does not allow the EC to enact blanket regulations concerning such matters as recognition of university and professional diplomas or innovation in general education policies.[28] Furthermore, although Article 128 of the Treaty of Rome empowers the EC Commission to develop general principles for implementing a common vocational training policy, the EC has interpreted this provision in a broad manner. Some feel the EC has overstepped its bounds through the institution of general promotional programs. According to Ingo Hochbaum, "the Commission is certainly wrong if it claims to find in Article 128 an instrument for developing an [independent] educational policy."[29]

The Options for the *Länder*

Although EC integration clearly poses an identifiable threat to the *Länder*, the outlook for the German states in practice may be less bleak than it appears. After all, it may be impracticable to assume that an administrative body such as the EC, with fewer than 15,000 employees (of which one third are involved strictly in language services), could truly assume the dominant legislative and administrative roles in a European community with 320 million inhabitants.[30] This may become even less feasible in the future if additional nations are admitted to the EC. In addition, a number of affirmative measures are available to the *Länder* by which they might maintain, or even strengthen, their position vis-à-vis both the Bund and EC.

An Increased Domestic Role for the Bundesrat

On a purely national level, if the Bundesrat as a whole were to assume a more active role in the German federal legislation process, certain fundamental *Länder* interests could be protected irrespective of the developments in Brussels. European Community regulations are instantly applicable to member-nations and need not be transformed into national law; however, EC directives must be implemented by the member-nations through domestic legislation. Thus, the practical impact of EC directives on *Länder* interests will be shaped largely by domestic German law. A more active Bundesrat could therefore play a pivotal role in fashioning the resulting German policies, which the *Länder* must then administer.

In the past, however, the Bundesrat has never achieved the influence of which it is capable. Instead, it has served largely as a public forum for political posturing among the *Länder*. From its inception in 1949 until 1987, the Bundesrat has withheld approval on fewer than forty federal bills and has submitted just ten bills to the "Mediation Committee," a permanent joint congressional committee empowered to submit nonbinding compromise proposals when there are differences of opinion on the contents of legislation up for passage.[31] Yet today, it is just this body that needs to assume a leading role. One possible impetus for change may be the recent swing in the Bundesrat majority from the ruling Christian Democrat party (CDU) to the opposition Social Democrats (SPD).[32] As a true opposition to the CDU-led parliament and the Kohl administration, the Bundesrat may now be in a position to assume a more pronounced role in the German legislative process.

Furthermore, as the formal representative of *Länder* interests to the Bund, the Bundesrat could take on a more significant role in shaping German EC policy. This potential avenue for influence was enhanced by the 1987 Bund-*Länder* pact, which included a guarantee from the Bund that the Bundesrat be given the opportunity to adopt a formal position on all EC proposals that may be of interest to the *Länder*.[33] According to Article II(1) of this pact, the Bund must inform the Bundesrat in writing of all plans or proposals of the EC that "affect the legislative competence of, or are of significant interest to, the *Länder*" as soon as these proposals are communicated to the federal government. In those instances where proposed EC legislation concerns a domain exclusively reserved to the *Länder*, the Bund may disregard the position of the Bundesrat only "for imperative reasons of foreign policy or integration policy" and must provide the Bundesrat written grounds for this decision.

In practice, however, this so-called Article II Procedure has yet to bring any dramatic change. Although there are no official statistics on the tangible impact of the Bundesrat on positions ultimately adopted by the Bund, the influence of the *Länder* has been minimal at best.[34] The Bundesrat meets just fourteen times a year and is not well suited to reaching rapid majority positions. This problem is compounded by EC procedures, which typically entail long-term negotiations involving twelve often disparate perspectives. The speed with which negotiating postures must be modified frequently precludes consideration of state interests. Furthermore, even if the *Länder* are promptly informed of pending EC legislation, this information must first be analyzed by each of the individual *Länder*, then debated in the Bundesrat committees, and finally a unified position adopted by the Bundesrat. The EC Commission may have already convened by the time this process is completed.[35]

If the *Länder* hope to utilize effectively the Bundesrat to advance their interests, they must secure immediate, direct access to working drafts of EC documents. In addition, the Bundesrat will remain little more than a peripheral organ for influencing EC policies unless the *Länder* learn how to reach unified positions much more rapidly. Somewhat ironically, therefore, in order to protect their collective sovereignty vis-à-vis the EC, the *Länder* must be willing to compromise a degree of that sovereignty with respect to the other *Länder*. Because of the diverse political and economic character of the *Länder*, this may prove difficult.

Increased Direct Influence of the **Länder** *in Bonn*

A second approach by which the *Länder* could protect their interests would be to circumvent the often clumsy Bundresrat and seek instead to increase their influence with the federal government directly in Bonn. This might be accomplished either through direct participation by *Länder* representatives in the German contingent to the various EC committees, or via informal contacts in Bonn, e.g., through political lobbying.

As a result of negotiations between the governors of the *Länder* and the Bund in 1963, *Länder* representatives attained the right to participate directly as part of the German delegation on EC committees in those instances where: (1) the Bund lacks qualified officials to act in a certain area; (2) the state members are necessary for achieving the optimal negotiation result in Brussels; or (3) the course of negotiations directly affects the *Länder*.[36] Although all appointed *Länder* members remain formally bound to act as representatives of the Bund, participation on federal committees nevertheless gives them a forum for voicing their own concerns; it also provides an effective mechanism for slowing the pace of developments that are seen to affect adversely the *Länder*.

The issue of lobbying in Bonn requires little mention here, but it should not be underestimated as a potentially viable tool for promoting *Länder* interests. In the past, direct communication between the Bund and the state representatives has often been a one-way street. Whereas the Bund has immediate access to information, *Länder* representatives feel that, "although they have the direct administrative expertise," they are hard-pressed to keep informed of the events in Brussels.[37] Without adequate information, the *Länder* are unable to play a significant role in influencing policy; both formal and informal ties will play a critical role.

Direct Participation by the **Länder** *in Brussels*

Since the state of Bavaria first opened its Brussels "Information Office" over five years ago, the *Länder* have found it increasingly appealing to establish direct channels to the EC. First officially recognized as a right of the *Länder* in the 1987 Bund-*Länder* pact, direct representation in Brussels affords much quicker access to critical information and may provide the *Länder*, as well as the Bundesrat as a whole, the opportunity to review and comment on EC proposals before any final decisions are reached.

Today, all of the *Länder* (as well as some non-German regional governments) have recognized the value of direct representation in Brussels.[38] The Baden-Württemberg office, headed by Winfried Baur, is presently expanding from three to fifteen employees. As Baur points out, in Brussels the *Länder* are "both legal and political 'nobodies,' [so] everything must run on a personal level."[39] The earlier the *Länder* know about pending developments in Brussels, the more influence they will have over the resulting policy.

Baden-Württemberg: A Regional Approach

Largely in response to the threat posed to the *Länder* by European integration, the state of Baden-Württemberg recently initiated a political/

public relations offensive aimed at altering the international framework for EC integration. This approach incorporates the subsidiarity principle and advocates the emergence of certain dominant "regions" throughout Europe as an alternative to an increasingly centralized Europe. Through the decentralization of decision making and implementation authority within the EC and the coexistence of the supranational, national, and subnational levels of government, major German *Länder* such as Baden-Württemberg could actually stand to gain a measure influence within the EC mechanism.

In this context, Baden-Württemberg envisions the eventual formulation of a true "United States of Europe" arranged into dozens of confederated autonomous regions, complete with a European constitution and regional and communal councils. From the German perspective, this would serve not only to solidify the role of the *Länder* but also to incorporate into the integration process the democratic principles of federalism, direct representation, and self-determination.[40]

For Baden-Württemberg, the focus on "regional politics" is also a pragmatic response to the very real threat not only of lost political competence but also of adverse economic repercussions. A heavily industrialized, high-technology-oriented state in which almost 40 percent of jobs are directly or indirectly dependent on export, Baden-Württemberg understandably has strong interests in maintaining continued access to certain markets and retaining a certain degree of visible autonomy within the EC.

Baden-Württemberg's policy of "regionalism" must be understood as serving at least three functions: (1) to reform the existing state administrative structure so as to smooth the impending transition to an integrated Europe; (2) to create binding economic, political, and cultural ties with other similarly situated, highly industrialized regions; and (3) to raise the self-consciousness of these other regions to the point where they will assert their right to participate in the EC process, irrespective of their present lack of domestic legal competence to act as independent bodies. It is only when other regions within the EC begin to demand the right of representation in the EC mechanism that any form of institutional role for the German *Länder* is conceivable.

In Baden-Württemberg, regionalism has taken a number of forms, including increased emphasis on educational programs targeting European issues, enhanced relations with the *Länder* representatives to the EC parliament, expanded use of the information office in Brussels, and intensified cooperation with other European and non-European regions. In the last five years, Baden-Württemberg has founded a number of bilateral and multilateral partnerships with other similarly situated industrialized regions. One such partnership, designated "The Four Motors of Europe," encompasses the French region of Rhône Alpes, the Spanish region of Catalonia, the Italian region of Lombardy, and the German state of Baden-Württemberg. Each of these regions is economically strong, has an outstanding economic infrastructure, and has great potential in the areas of research and technology.

Established on 9 September 1988, this multilateral partnership is aimed at enhancing communication systems, augmenting direct transportation routes, intensifying cooperation between universities and research institutions, fostering closer cooperation in the economic and financial sectors, promoting exchange in the fields of art and culture, increasing joint foreign economic and political aid programs, and conceptualizing and developing a series of common exhibitions with the theme "The Four Motors of Europe."[41] Since 1988 these goals have been partially realized through numerous exchange programs, university partnerships, technology symposiums, business seminars, and the establishment of direct air and train connections.

Although the policy adopted by Baden-Württemberg should be recognized foremost as a political maneuver designed to improve its image, international profile, and economic contacts, the concept of a decentralized "Europe of the Regions" does in fact appear to provide a viable alternative to continued centralization and decreased direct representation in the promulgation of EC laws. This would also be a logical development in light of growing nationalist sentiment worldwide, which has manifested itself in the breakup of the Soviet Union and civil war in Yugoslavia, among others.

A Borderless Europe in the Future?

The prospect of a borderless Europe unquestionably offers the EC member-nations a multitude of economic, cultural, social, and political opportunities. The German *Länder* will not be unaffected by these positive developments. In the state of Baden-Württemberg, in particular, a borderless Europe accords the following advantages: (1) direct access to a tremendous export market, (2) probable lower energy costs through increased competition with neighboring energy producers, (3) an avenue for an enhanced transportation network, (4) more strict environmental regulation in bordering territories, (5) improved educational opportunities, particularly as they relate to foreign languages, and (6) prospects for supranational cooperation in the area of innovation and technology.

A unified Europe, however, will not be without its costs for the *Länder*. Where a national entity is committed to sacrificing portions of its sovereignty, and that entity is comprised of not only one centralized government but also of sixteen independent administrative units, some authority previously vested in these units will have to be sacrificed. In Germany, this means that the role of the sixteen *Länder* will inevitably be compromised to some extent by the process of European integration. They must therefore actively seek to maximize the potential benefits of a borderless Europe, while minimizing encroachments on their autonomous administrative and legislative competence.

Notes

1. The notion of a "mixed government" with shared competence dates as far back as the writings of Plato and Aristotle. See Winston U. Solberg, *The Federal Convention and the Formation of the Union of the American States* (New York: Liberal Arts Press, 1958), p. xxii.

2. Understandably, this limited club of federally organized nation-states claims as its members primarily those countries with the greatest territorial expanse and population masses such as Argentina, Brazil, Canada, the Federal Republic of Germany, India, the Soviet Union, and the United States.

3. "Berichterstattung von Herrn Staatssekretär Fleischer zum Vier Motoren," 8 February 1990, Staatsministerium, Baden-Württemberg (hereinafter cited as "Berichterstattung").

4. Conversation with officials at the Staatsministerium, Baden-Württemberg, 22 January 1990.

5. Fritz Ossenbühl, "Föderalismus nach 40 Jahren Grundgesetz," DVB1., 15 December 1989, p. 1230.

6. The sovereign character of the German territories was also embodied in the 1814 Deutscher Bund, the 1848 Constitution proposed by the national assembly in the Paulskirche, the 1866 Norddeutscher Bund, and the 1871 German Reich.

7. Gottfried Dietze, *The Federalist* (Baltimore: Johns Hopkins University Press, 1960), p. 353.

8. Ossenbühl, "Föderalismus nach 40 Jahren," p. 1231.

9. German Grundgesetz, Article 20(1) (hereinafter cited as GG).

10. Ibid., Article 28(1-3).

11. Heinz Laufer, *Das Föderative System in der Bundesrepublik Deutschland*, Bayerische Landeszentrale für politische Bildung (München: Stephan Heller, 1987), p. 66.

12. BVerfGE 1, 14 (34); 60, 175 (207).

13. Ossenbühl, "Föderalismus Nach 40 Jahren," p. 1231.

14. GG, Article 30.

15. *Handbuch des Bundesrates 1988/1989* (München: Bundesrat Public Relations Office, 1989), pp. 242–243.

16. GG, Article 73.

17. GG, Article 72. A catalogue of twenty-four different areas in which these concurrent powers exist can be found in Article 74. For further discussion of the interaction between the *Länder* and the Bund, see Helmut Klatt, *Baden-Württemberg und der Bund* (Stuttgart: W. Kohlhammer GmbH with Baden-Württemberg Landeszentrale für politische Bildung, 1989), p. 27.

18. GG, Article 70.

19. The *Länder* role is not recognized in the 1951 treaty that established the European Coal and Steel Community nor is it mentioned in the 1957 treaties creating the European Economic Community (Treaty of Rome) and the European Atomic Energy Community. The more recent EC treaties also do not acknowledge the existence of sovereign German states.
See Treaty Instituting the European Coal and Steel Community, signed 18 April 1951, (261 U.N.T.S. 140). The original six member-nations were Belgium, France, Federal Republic of Germany, Italy, Luxembourg, and the Netherlands. See also Treaty Establishing the European Economic Community, 25 March 1957, (294 U.N.T.S. 2) and Treaty Establishing the European Atomic Energy Community, 25 March 1957, (294 U.N.T.S. 259).

20. Although no other EC member-nation has federal states, each does have regional governments with varying degrees of competence and authority. In France, for example, there are 22 regional and over 37,000 communal governments.

21. Ossenbühl, "Föderalismus Nach 40 Jahren," p. 1237.

22. Quoted in Michael Borchmann, "Bundesstaat und europäische Integration," p. 588.

23. Single European Act (SEA), OJ No. L 169/1 (officially entered into force on 7 January 1987).

24. Quoted in Borchmann, "Bundesstaat und europäische Integration," p. 600.

25. Ibid., pp. 600–604.

26. GG, Article 24(1).

27. BVerfGE of 22.10.1986 - 2BvR 197/83 (Solange-Beschluß II), NJW 1987, 579.

28. Although Article 57 of the Treaty of Rome empowers the commission to develop guidelines for the mutual recognition of diplomas and examinations, this power is expressly confined to the context of self-employed workers.

29. Ingo Hochbaum, "*Länder* Souveränität und Verfassungsmässige Rechte als Grenzen der Gemeinschaftsrechts" (Paper presented to the EC Law and Education Convention, European Institute, Florence, November 1987), p. 5.

30. Staatsministerium, *Baden-Württemberg im Europäischen Binnenmarkt* (Stuttgart: Druckhaus Waiblingen, 1990), p. 79.

31. *Handbuch des Bundesrates*, p. 44.

32. On 21 April 1991 the SPD won a majority of seats in the state parliament of Rheinland-Pfalz. With this victory, SPD-led states achieved a 37-31 majority in the Bundesrat.

33. BGBl.II S.1102f, 17 December 1987.

34. From 1987 to 1989 there were just eight instances where the resulting EC policy has met or surpassed the formal position adopted by the Bundesrat. See "Erfahrungsbericht der Bevollmächtigen der *Länder* beim Bund" (Working Document of the Baden-Württemberg Ministry of Justice, 4/24/90).

35. This process may take up to six weeks; EC documents are handed over to the affected federal ministry, forwarded to the Bundesrat, distributed to the *Länder*, and finally debated in the Bundesrat. Ibid., p. 10.

36. Borchmann, "Bundesstaat und europäische Integration," p. 593.

37. Conversation with officials at the State Representation of Baden-Württemberg to Bonn, 8 May 1990.

38. One non-German region has already established a representative office in Brussels, the French partner region of Baden-Württemberg, Rhône Alpes.

39. Conversation with Wilfried H. Baur, head of the Information Office of Baden-Württemberg in Brussels, 29 January 1990.

40. *B-W Report*, p. 81.

41. "Berichterstattung," p. 2.

5

Momper at Germany's Dawn

John Meakem

> *It was a cold, grey morning still, but the earth was lit with the clarity which follows rain.*
> —John Le Carre[1]

> *It [Berlin] is a new city, the newest I've ever seen.*
> —Mark Twain[2]

West German politicians like those in many other European countries tend to concentrate their attention on their professional responsibilities, while the many ceremonial functions are handled by the elected head of state, the federal president.[3] In contrast, U.S. officeholders tend to mix their ceremonial and functional roles to a much greater extent, frequently for strategic purposes.

This helps to explain why the "governing mayor of [West] Berlin" has never been just another mayor, or Bürgermeister. In addition to administering the largest German city, he also inherits the legacy of resistance to the East which since 1945 has defined not only the city but also in many ways the entire Western alliance. In this sense, the office has been much more American than any other in West German politics.

Not surprisingly then the position has often been a stepping-stone to national prominence as it has been for Ernst Reuter, Willy Brandt, and Richard von Weizsäcker. This also helps to explain why a number of West Berlin mayors have come from other parts of Germany (e.g., Brandt and von Weizsäcker). This said, the position has its drawbacks too. As Thomas Habicht writes, when it comes to comparatively mundane local issues, "almost all Berlin's Mayors since Willy Brandt (1957 to 1966) have had to fight the reproach from their political enemies that they have 'withdrawn'."[4]

Mayor from March 1989 to December 1990, Walter Momper (SPD) had a rare opportunity to reap substantial political benefits from 9 November

1989 to 18 March 1990—a period of time that saw East Germany's borders open and the first free election in the German Democratic Republic (GDR). During this extraordinary period, with so many official moments requiring his presence, Momper became a fixture in the German media. Furthermore, 10 November 1989 coincided with the start of Berlin's turn at presiding over the Bundesrat, so that the mayor was also frequently in Bonn as chairman of the upper house. Finally, the 1990 GDR election offered still more chances for the spotlight to shine on him because Berlin was a natural focal point during hustings in which he was hardly the only West German politician to campaign heavily.

That all this would promote Momper from local politician to national figure was perhaps inevitable. One observer claimed that "Momper knowingly used the spirit of Germany's hour,"[5] while another noted that "when it comes to always having new initiatives for the unifications of Germany and Berlin, there is no one faster than Walter Momper."[6] In any event, while it would be much fairer to describe his actions as those of an aspiring politician, it was not hard to realize that he wanted Germany's dawn to be his own as well.

Despite his immediate success, Momper's tactics had three significant and less successful consequences. First, they led him to contradict his previously critical positions concerning the Western alliance. Second, they brought his own personal rivalry with Chancellor Helmut Kohl to an unusually tense level. Third, they gave short shrift to his alliance partner, straining his coalition's stability. Combined, they set the stage for his clear defeat in the 2 December 1990 municipal elections.

West Berlin's Red-Green Coalition

West Berlin has had a long tradition of left-leaning politics, but its January 1989 election brought a coalition to power that was particularly testy toward the Western alliance. Indeed, as events in East Germany began to climax in the second half of 1989, the coalition became more and more of an anachronism. Its fate can be illustrated by Walter Momper's rise and fall.

Born in 1945, Momper is a native of the SPD-oriented Bremen area; he moved to Berlin as a student in the 1960s. Climbing to the top of the Berlin SPD, he made a red scarf his political trademark while living in Kreuzberg, the "alternative" section of the city. A regular participant in protests against the three Western allies overseeing Berlin, he became particularly well known during the Reagan administration for his public references to the president as a "wild-shooting cowboy." In early 1989 he had also stated that "only with two equally legal German states was a

TABLE 5.1 The Municipal Elections of 29 January 1989 (in percentages)

Party	1st Vote	2nd Vote	No. of Seats
SPD	41.7	37.3	55
CDU	40.2	37.7	55
AL	11.1	11.8	17
Republican party	1.2	7.5	11
FDP	3.5	3.9	0

Note: 1,220,423 voters participated in these elections, with a turnout of 79.6 percent. There were a total of 138 seats, with 70 required for a majority.

Source: Presse- und Informationsamt des Landes Berlin, 1990.

European peace order possible."⁷ Contentious as these words might sound to American ears, they were very much in line with sentiments in West Berlin before the GDR started to crumble. But early in 1989, the results of the municipal elections hardly encouraged Momper to move toward the center (Table 5.1). Both of the largest parties, the CDU and SPD, suffered setbacks in these elections. Further, the FDP, the usual partner of the party obtaining a plurality, failed to receive the 5 percent of votes necessary to be represented in the city's House of Representatives. The two winning parties were on the fringes: the Republican party, often characterized as antiforeign and neo-Nazi; and the Alternative List, essentially the Berlin branch of the Green party, usually associated with its environmental and disarmament (including anti-NATO) positions. Both cleared the 5 percent hurdle for the first time.

In order to unseat CDU mayor Eberhard Diepgen, Momper was obliged to ally himself with the AL when all parties shunned the Republicans. Subsequently, the coalition's 13 March statement of accord acknowledged that "many look at red-green (SPD-AL) cooperation with skepticism, even worry" while seeking to reassure the public as well as the Western allies by declaring that "democracy and tolerance, social justice and ecological reason will be the leading ideas of the new policies." The AL received three of the sixteen posts in the Berlin senate, or cabinet—Women, Family, and Youth; School, Career Training, and Sport; and City Development and Environment. Walter Momper became mayor.

That others were *not* reassured became patently clear in May 1989 during the visit of President George Bush to Bonn. It was a tense moment in U.S.–West German relations because of the decision over modernizing the Short-Range Nuclear Force (SNF) missiles stationed in the Federal Republic. In a breach of protocol that received considerable attention in Germany, Kohl refused to invite Momper to the state dinner given in Bush's honor.

As the Borders Opened

One could say that the mayor got his revenge on 10 November 1989 just hours after East Germany opened its borders. Although most of the celebrating was nonpartisan, West Berlin's official festivities in front of the Rathaus Schöneberg took on an embarrassingly anti-Kohl air. The crowd warmly welcomed speeches by Momper, Willy Brandt, Hans-Dietrich Genscher, and Berlin parliamentary president Jürgen Wohlrabe, but whistles on national television were conspicuous when the chancellor took his turn at the rostrum. To an extent, the incident was the Berlin CDU's own fault. It had hastily drawn supporters to its own rally in a different part of town.[8] Chancellor Kohl nevertheless held his host responsible.

Beyond this immediate friction, the speeches given by Kohl and Momper that day embodied the differences that would characterize the CDU and SPD all the way up to the GDR elections: the CDU thanked the Western allies for their support and took a confrontational stance toward the East German Communist regime, pushing the goal of unification (albeit a bit haphazardly); the SPD hesitated to embrace unification, took a confrontational stance toward the Kohl government, and insisted on a bipartisan approach to the matter (which had underlined SPD powerlessness). It was also much more willing than the CDU to work with GDR officials on logistical issues prompted by the turn of events. In this respect, it is important to note that both parties' public positions and goals evolved considerably over the following months in response to the GDR's rapid deterioration and the growing inevitability of unification.

The New City

Yet for all parties, the turn of events made it possible for "Berlin to dream of Berlin"[9] and a promising future. Reflecting the city's long-repressed ambitions and interests, Berlin politicians on both the left and right began calling for it to become the capital, an Olympic site, and so forth. As one observer put it, "the atmosphere in the streets ... is that of a monarch whose restoration to the throne [is] inevitable."[10]

But Momper claimed the monarch was broke. To CDU protests, he maintained that his coalition had inherited a poor fiscal standing and was therefore unable to respond to the tremendous strains being placed on the city's infrastructure. In the first weekend alone, more than 1 million visitors visited Berlin, and the East Germans as well as international visitors continued to come, with all the obvious implications for city services. On 16 November, he went before the Bundestag to ask for emergency supplemental aid for work on subways, roads, and bridges in addition to Bonn's already hefty annual grant (about half the city government's budget). On 9 January 1990 DM 400 were appropriated.

At this time, Momper also started pressing to win full voting rights for West Berlin's representatives in the Bundestag. As condition of the Four-Power Agreement on the governance of East and West Berlin, West Berlin's parliamentarians in Bonn had had voting privileges only at the committee level, but not on questions facing the entire Bundestag. In addition to limiting the city's influence in general, this had particularly meant that West Berlin had no voice in the voting for chancellor—and Momper clearly wanted to increase the anti-Kohl vote before the December 1990 federal elections. Given the developments of 1989, French, British, and American officials eventually agreed that the status of Berlin—as always, cast against the larger light of East-West relations—should enter a new phase. Thus, in a victory for the mayor, full voting rights were extended in June 1990—though the whole question became moot when the full unification of the two Germanies was enacted the next fall.

Another Momper initiative, the Regional Committee, rapidly came into being following a 2 December 1989 meeting with GDR interim prime minister Hans Modrow. Consisting of representatives from the governments of East and West Berlin as well as from those of East and West Germany, the committee's purpose was to decide matters relating to the practical functioning of the rapidly changing Berlin and surrounding Brandenburg areas. With its inaugural session on 22 December, the Regional Committee broke new ground as the first intra-German governmental authority.

The new committee was not without its problems. In the first place, its actual agenda stretched well beyond its stated logistical aims (border crossings, medical services, garbage disposal, etc.). With fifteen working groups virtually corresponding to the senators in the municipal administration, its scope really approached that of a regional government. Despite this, it had not been formed with direct public consent and lacked direct accountability to voters. Finally, opponents charged that the committee was really a ploy of Momper's to lessen Bonn's influence over Berlin—and that East German officials were all too willing to bring a more pliant SPD mayor to the table.

Aiding the GDR

Be this as it may, with the coming of the New Year GDR officials were the ones holding the weak hands. Across both Germanys, the mood was shifting from the euphoria of November and December 1989 to concern for the coming elections in the East. GDR prime minister Modrow, seen before the fall of 1989 as one of the brightest hopes for "reform from within," now came increasingly to be thought of as the electoral candidate representing the well-organized, well-funded old regime. Opposition groups, which had earlier been no more than grass-roots organizations unprepared for electoral battle, became increasingly serious contenders as they started forming alliances with the major West German parties. Though Modrow in many ways retained his own personal popularity, economic malaise and a general crisis of confidence in his government ensued, especially as many influential members of the SED (Socialist Unity party, or Communist party) resigned their party positions. By late January, there was serious doubt as to whether the Modrow government could even survive until the originally announced election date of 6 May. Thus, bowing to pressure, he declared on 28 January that elections would be moved up to 18 March, and for the meantime invited opposition leaders to participate in his government.

In sync with these rapid developments, sending immediate, transitional aid to the GDR became a major issue in the Federal Republic. Kohl flatly refused to consider aid before a democratically elected government was in place, giving his final no during Modrow's visit to Bonn in mid February. If anything, the Bonn coalition, especially CSU finance minister Theo Waigel, went out of its way to play up the economic woes of the GDR government. SPD officials countered that the humane and nonpartisan approach would be to provide short-term, practical assistance.

Momper put this sentiment into action when the Berlin House voted on 8 February to grant the city of East Berlin DM 25 million for housing rehabilitation. Yet, despite the SPD-AL majority, his motion still had trouble passing. First, a question was raised about the propriety of giving aid at the time, when not only a new GDR but also a new East Berlin government would soon be elected. Second, West Berlin's own fiscal problems made such a donation questionable. Finally, the influx of GDR refugees had made West Berlin's own housing shortage even worse; withdrawing funds from his own housing budget was not something Momper could do gracefully.

The Momper Plan(s)

Momper's ideas found a warmer reception outside Germany. In recognition of the changes under way, he made quickly scheduled visits to Paris, London, and Washington to "report in" to the Western allies. In a sense visits of protocol to friendly hosts, they also provided Momper with opportunities to start making a name for himself abroad.

Just as Kohl had set the tone for intra-German debate in November with his "ten-point plan," in London the mayor addressed the situation as it stood in February. With his own "nine-point plan," he sought a peaceful, nonthreatening transition for a united Germany in its relations with the NATO countries and the USSR. In his view, after German political unity, an interim period should follow during which the territory east of the Elbe River would be demilitarized and put under the control of the Four Powers in much the same way the current regime was overseeing Berlin. At the same time, allied control in West Berlin could be phased out because the new situation made the city's "semicolonial" status no longer necessary. Then, after combined German elections, the former GDR could be fully incorporated into the Federal Republic in terms of currency, legal status, and social programs. Subsequent negotiations of the Conference on Security and Cooperation in Europe (CSCE)—perhaps in Berlin as the first official seat of the organization (Prague has since been chosen)—could incorporate German developments in forging a durable European peace order.

Naturally, CDU opponents took issue with Momper's premises and proposals, accusing him of wanting to introduce an unnecessary transitional phase that, if anything, would hamper and/or obstruct the goal of unification. Yet if nothing else, his plan was cleverly designed to appeal to West Berlin voters: it offered some of the city's positive aspects as models for administering the GDR but promised to end some of the drawbacks, even suggesting Berlin as the site of a multinational organization.

Momper further elaborated his ideas in a Berlin press conference on 12 February, immediately following Kohl's trip to Moscow. One issue on the table was the ambiguity of the FRG constitution regarding the integration process: Article 23 demanded only accession of the federal states to the Federal Republic; meanwhile, also applicable was Article 146, which required the drafting of an entirely new constitution on the completion of German unity. While most conservatives advocated use of Article 23, many on the left were leery of it and what they considered to be the uncertain social and environmental ramifications of an unduly hasty unity. However, with prevailing division always a local reality in Berlin, Momper took exception to the national SPD and reaffirmed his advocacy of Article 23.[11] (See also Articles relating to Unification in Appendix 2.)

Kohl had proclaimed his Moscow trip a great victory, with Mikhail Gorbachev giving him the green light to press for exactly this sort of quick unification. Still, the mayor chose to stress that "the most important result of the trip" was the ensured participation of the Four Powers in the unification process (to be defined that week in Ottawa as "Two plus Four") as a means of ensuring stability and guaranteeing the interests of other European countries. Quick unification was fine, but he welcomed anything resembling a limitation on what he considered to be Kohl's cavalier behavior.

In this spirit, Momper additionally proposed a joint Bundestag/Bundesrat committee that would work with—or perhaps in practice against— the chancellor on intra-German issues. To the mayor, this would give West

Germany's regional governments, who often had to implement and foot the bills of GDR-oriented programs, more input in decisions affecting their operations. He hoped it would also prompt more federal aid to the regions, made possible (here he dangled an idea that often appealed to his constituency) through a halving of the Bundeswehr.[12]

On 26 February he launched another trial balloon in an effort to increase his influence on the unification process. Without consulting the other parties in the West Berlin House, he proposed a stability-ensuring "timetable for the step-by-step reunification of Berlin." Following the East German elections, representative members of the West Berlin House and the newly elected GDR legislature from East Berlin would meet as a democratically elected body to oversee all of Berlin. At first, this group would supervise the work of the Regional Committee and help to prepare for East Berlin's first democratic municipal elections on 6 May. Thereafter, the East and West Berlin municipal parliaments could work together— their voting power based on relative populations of the two halves of the city (2 million in the West and 1.3 million in the East)—toward the unification of the two city administrations, a new city constitution, and a new election law. Together they would also determine a representative for a United Berlin, who would directly supervise all these processes.

This last proposal had two problems. First, the legal feasibility of bringing together differing levels of government from separate states was awkward, despite the interrelationship between East and West Berlin under the Four Powers Treaty. Second, though Momper was quick to point out that the "representative for a United Berlin" was to lack executive authority, he, as the head of government in the more populous half of the city, was directly in line to assume the position. That Momper would have his eye on becoming the first mayor of a reunited Berlin was understandable, but with this particular proposal he was getting a bit ahead of himself.

Momper in Washington

Momper's Washington trip from 26 to 28 February was well-timed. Coincidentally, Kohl had met with Bush at Camp David just forty-eight hours before Momper arrived in the capital. The meeting had ended on a sour note as, to the alarmed dismay of U.S. and world opinion, Kohl refused to guarantee the Oder-Neisse line as the future eastern border of a united Germany. Bush himself understood that the chancellor's hesitancy stemmed from concern for the more conservative members of the Bonn coalition, although it simultaneously strained relations with the more centrist FDP. Nevertheless, Momper suddenly found himself addressing the surprisingly large and well-informed community of German experts in Washington, one which was both eager to learn more about the current situation and hungry for some words of reassurance.

The mayor left them happy through his public addresses and private meetings with Bush, Secretary of State James Baker, and Secretary of Defense Richard Cheney (who, in a gesture the mayor considered very flattering, asked for a meeting upon hearing he was in town). Though predicting that NATO would develop into a more politically oriented body, he still stood firmly for German membership in the alliance and the continued presence of allied troops in Berlin. As Ralf Georg Reuth writes, "he turned around—quite quickly—from being a vehement SPD polemicist of "Two Germany" dogma and made himself, using the weight of the mayoral position, into Berlin's advocate of German unity . . . presenting himself now as an old friend of the United States."[13]

This said, Momper hardly missed the opportunity to dig into Kohl. He mocked the chancellor while affirming the Oder-Neisse border and noted that Willy Brandt's *Ostpolitik* had de facto acknowledged the border in 1970. With his fluent English and low-key style, he was also a good match for his American audiences, especially in contrast to the chancellor, who speaks no English. Consequently, the mayor received minimal interrogation on either his past record, his or the SPD's more ambiguous NATO policy (as a joint East and West German SPD delegation visiting Washington a few days later thoroughly was), or even his success in canceling the annual allied military parade in West Berlin. In short, his trip was a considerable success, both in reassuring Washingtonians and in boosting his own standing at the chancellor's expense.

This latter fact did not go unnoticed at home. *Der Spiegel* noted that "On March 1, one day after meeting with Bush for 30 minutes in Washington, Momper met with Kohl for 2 hours in Bonn."[14] The tête-à-tête had the trappings of a showdown, and much could be read into their joint statement afterwards on the importance of keeping the unification process of the city of Berlin linked to that of all Germany. In other words, it was a nonaggression pact with regard to both Kohl's hurried push for unification at the national level and Momper's local, eclectic barrage.

As it turned out, the mayor's initiatives had little chance to get too far off the ground anyway. Over the next few weeks, the final lead-up to and fallout from the GDR election would dominate the scene. And, afterwards, things would be much different.

The GDR Election

By this time, Momper was not the only one whose stock seemed to be rising; for several reasons, the East German SPD seemed set to do very well at the polls. First, it was generally assumed that East Germans, brought up on Marxist-Leninist dogma, would take much more naturally to social democracy as a midpoint between Eastern and Western approaches. Second, the SPD-East had a clear headstart because it had

TABLE 5.2 Results of the GDR Elections of 18 March 1990

Party[a]	Percent of Votes	Seats in Parliament
CDU	40.9	164
SPD	21.8	87
PDS (former SED)	16.3	65
DSU (CSU equivalent)	6.3	25
FDP	5.3	21
18 other parties	9.4	38
Total		400

[a]A party did not have to receive a minimum share of the vote in order to be represented.
Note: There were 11,538,313 voters, with a participation rate of 93.22 percent.
Source: Berliner Morgenpost, 20 March 1990.

formed its alliance with the West German SPD well before three conservative parties had allied themselves with the West German CDU/CSU coalition. Third, Kohl's aggressive policy of pursuing a quick union (or as Hans-Jochen Vogel derisively described it, an "Anschluss, . . . as though it were his own private affair"[15]) had discomforted many, especially as the German media devoted more and more attention to the possible social consequences of unification.[16] Fourth, the conservative alliance also had an inherent flaw, it included an East German Christian Democratic party (Lothar de Maiziére's party), which had kowtowed to the SED for forty years as one of the token "bloc" parties in opposition. Finally, in the last week of the campaign, the leader of one of the other two parties in the conservative coalition was forced to resign after having admitted to collaboration with the East German secret police. Accordingly, polls generally predicted the SPD would receive 40 to 50 percent of the vote, and the conservative coalition twenty to twenty-five percent.

So it was a big surprise when the actual results gave the conservative coalition a clear majority (Table 5.2). The election results prompted considerable self-questioning among Social Democrats. Later developments have shown that their initial concerns—i.e., for the social consequences of unification—were truly important but were not given the top priority by the voters at that time. Instead, East Germans apparently voted to ensure unification first and worry about the details later. The SPD had neglected the bottom line.

> Yet Momper was still off target in his reaction to the vote: I am very happy . . . the SPD in Berlin and . . . the Brandenburg area on March 18 achieved a better result than in the South [where the vote was heavily conservative]. I think it has something to do with the people near West Berlin being better informed about the West than in other areas . . . and on

the other side West Berlin was always closer to the mentalities and developments in the GDR.[17]

To be sure, the Berlin area's left-leaning tradition predates the postwar division. It could be easily maintained that those residing in East Berlin, core of the GDR regime, had long lived in a deeper ideological dreamworld than other East Germans; conversely, it may be that many in West Berlin, disillusioned with the West, had grown accustomed to being a bit more apologetic toward the GDR than was merited. More obviously though, East Berlin also housed the greatest concentration of Honecker regime apparatchiks. While voting for the PDS was most clearly in their own interest in the face of the coming unity wave, some may have also reasoned that a strong SPD might be more positively disposed to them once the inevitable reprisals came.

The SPD-AL Coalition in Limbo

"Celebrating" its first anniversary just before the GDR election with a press conference on 14 March, West Berlin's governing coalition also found itself engaged in self-questioning. Momper acknowledged that he did often find the AL difficult ("One must discuss every detail with them for an unbelievably long time," he had once quipped)[18] but nonetheless described the situation as "much more stable than you all think" and spoke of the coalition's "success amid the most trying of circumstances."[19]

As one commentator put it, the AL had much more trouble finding a silver lining: "Since the turning point in the GDR there has been a smashing change in the Rathaus Schöneberg. The AL, which concentrates on local and ecological issues, now feels that it has lost its influence. And the SPD is increasingly realizing that the big problems facing Berlin and its surroundings are hardly up to the AL to decide."[20] The AL, like the West German Green party, maintained a "hands off" policy toward the GDR, continuing to respect its sovereignty as separate from that of West Germany. In practice, this meant the AL and Greens refused to campaign in the East or to supply campaign funds to East German political groups. It also meant that the mayor could afford to downplay the AL and its priority issues, such as the eight-week-long strike of the city's public daycare workers in early 1990. As the left-leaning *Tageszeitung* described it, "King Momper stands in high popularity and is satisfied, the Alternative List has difficulty breathing but sees no alternative to its continued existence in alliance with the SPD."[21]

In fact, there remained the possibility that the AL would regain an important role in local politics as priorities shifted toward the many awkward issues involved in the laying out of a reunited Berlin, especially concerning the future of Potsdamer Platz. Nevertheless, the coalition's future was at best unclear, as was that of its SPD leader.

Future Role?

In any society, a relatively large number of prospective politicians may show promise of one day rising to national or even international prominence. However, relatively few enjoy turns of events that give them chances to accede to such levels, and of this group only an even smaller number make good. Indeed, perhaps the toughest test comes once events stop going their way, for then they must truly stand on their own.

In the mayor's case, as *Der Spiegel* wrote, "just over a year ago, Momper was the chief of the SPD-party in the Berlin House, not much more than a discouraged party's candidate. Not a few of the Socialists on his ticket wanted him off the ballot. . . . Now he stands with all doors opened before him."[22] From 9 November to 18 March, he tried to live up to the moment, walking through as many of these doors as possible, as well as trying to build a few more of his own. On the surface, things went so well that "no German politician has come from zero to the top so quickly."[23] Following the assassination attempt on the SPD chancellor candidate Oskar La Fontaine, he was even considered a possible substitute candidate.[24]

Yet it was hardly certain that Momper would be able to maintain his position once the doors started closing. Criticism within Berlin, where "he is at his most controversial," was rife, with talk of his authoritarian behavior toward staff[25] and remarks from fellow legislators about his "overly high sense of self-esteem."[26] Further, despite his success, Momper had yet to break into the ranks of the SPD's leading figures (Brandt, Vogel, La Fontaine, Rau, etc.).[27]

Now that the December 1990 election is past and the sun has gone down on Momper, he has the opportunity to put his talents to the true test.

Notes

1. John Le Carré, *A Small Town in Germany* (London: Pan Books, 1969), p. 282.

2. Mark Twain, "The German Chicago" (1892), as reprinted in *The Complete Essays of Mark Twain*, ed. Charles Neider (Garden City, N.Y.: Doubleday, 1963), p. 87.

3. Of course, officially there has not been a "West" German politician, much less a "West" Berlin mayor since unification on 3 October 1990, but there was during the time in question.

4. Thomas Habicht, "Die Gunst der deutschlandpolitischen Stunde hat Momper zu nutzen gewusst," *Handelsblatt*, 1 March 1990.

5. Habicht, "Gunst der deutschlandpolitischen Stunde."
6. Michael Ludwig Müller, "In der Uni Leipzig sprach Momper über die Einheit," *Berliner Morgenpost*, 18 March 1990.
7. Ralf Georg Reuth, "Des Regierenden Bürgermeisters richtige Schlüssel," *Frankfurter Allgemeine Zeitung*, 3 March 1990.
8. Interview with Martin Hanz, Bundeskanzleramt, 27 November 1989.
9. Wolf Jobst Siedler, "Berlin Träumt von Berlin," *Stern*, 18 March 1990.
10. Giles Merrit, "Here Comes Berlin, a Capital Again," *International Herald Tribune*, 19 April 1990.
11. See Appendix 2 for the relevant constitutional articles.
12. Material on this period is based on a press release of the 12 February 1990 press conference.
13. Reuth, "Regierenden Bürgermeisters."
14. "Schal global," *Der Spiegel*, 5 March 1990.
15. Hans-Jochen Vogel, press conference in Berlin, 13 March 1990.
16. Subsequent German commentary has generally neglected to bring up what might have been one of an American's first concerns: why did the East and West German presses fail to describe the electorate correctly in the weeks leading up to the election? Although this would require a more systematic study, my own impression in January and February was that, at least on television, a disproportionate amount of time was devoted to the question of social implications. At the same time, the huge crowds turning out to watch Kohl speak in the GDR, much less the very tangible pro-unification atmosphere on the streets of Leipzig and Dresden, seemed to receive conspicuously short shrift. Had unification itself become too boring a story? (Editors' note: There have also been serious questions about the methods employed to conduct interviews and gather data in the GDR for the misleading pre-election polls in March 1990.)
17. Harmut Moreike and Kai Pramann, "Berlin grenzenlos," *Neue Berliner Illustrierte*, 20 April 1990.
18. "Walter Momper: Meine drei Träume," *Bild Zeitung*, 25 January 1990.
19. Brigitte Grunert, "Momper: Koalition mit der AL 'viel stabiler als alle dachten'," *Tagesspiegel*, 13 March 1990.
20. Müller, "In der Uni Leipzig."
21. Kordula Doerfler, "Das rot-grüne Fachwerkhaus Berlin," *Tageszeitung*, 15 March 1990.
22. "Schal global," *Spiegel*.
23. Harry Ristock, as quoted in Marianne Heuwagen, "Von Null nach oben mit einer Krone aus Pappe," *Süddeutsche Zeitung*, 10 March 1990.
24. *International Herald Tribune*, 26 April 1990.
25. Heuwagen, "Von Null nach oben."
26. Müller, "In der Uni Leipzig."
27. Habicht, "Gunst der deutschlandpolitischen Stunde."

PART THREE

Economic Issues

6

German Monetary Union: The Inevitable Experiment

Melinda Hargrave-Kanzow

In the early fall of 1989 the Bundesbank (German Central Bank) was worried about mounting inflation. The annual rise in prices stood at about 3 percent, a relatively high level for the Federal Republic. The economy was booming. Factories were operating at capacity. The trade surplus was attaining record highs. Profits were soaring, and pending wage negotiations threatened to pressure prices even higher. All these conditions worried the monetary policymakers in Frankfurt. Little did they suspect that within months the picture would change completely, and inflation would loom ever larger as the Federal Republic embarked on a massive economic experiment: the injection of a world currency into an economy saddled by forty years of central planning.

Although 9 November 1989, the day the Berlin wall was breached, was marked as a historic date in the halls of the Bundesbank, no one was contemplating economic and monetary union. The main concern was how to help the East Germans help themselves—using their own marks. By early spring 1990 the policy had altered drastically. Politics dictated the pace of change as Bonn announced plans to introduce the deutsche mark (DM) into the German Democratic Republic (GDR). Although the Bundesbank was definitely hesitant about pursuing such a move, it could do little to stop the political momentum. If Bonn thought currency union was necessary, Frankfurt would have to make it possible.

Thus a big monetary experiment began. Currency union represented the first step in uniting the two Germanys. It was not just a symbolic act; it promised immense economic, political, and social consequences. Worries about inflation and interest rates took on new dimensions as the Bundesbank and many other economic analysts, both inside the Federal Republic and abroad, grappled with the idea of introducing a strong Western currency into a crippled Eastern economy.

Early 1990—The Policy Develops

Catalytic Events

Two catalytic events in early 1990 forced Bonn to consider offering the deutsche mark to the East Germans. First, the refugee problem was becoming acute. In early January up to two thousand East Germans were crossing the border daily to take up life in the West. It was predicted that .5 million to 2 million refugees would come over to the Federal Republic by early 1991. Something had to be done to stem the tide because the Federal Republic could not absorb that many people without severely straining an already tight housing market and exacerbating unemployment rates. Politicians from all parties seized the idea of currency union as a solution. They argued that the promise of deutsche marks would give East Germans who remained in the East the buying power and improved economic outlook that the refugees sought in the West.

The second catalytic event was the East German parliamentary elections slated for March 1990. All the parties in the Federal Republic were deeply involved in the campaign in the East. As the drama developed it became apparent that a vote for the Christian Democratic Union (CDU) or the Social Democratic party (SPD) was really a demonstration of support for the leaders of those parties in the West. The implications for the united German elections in December 1990 were not lost on the Western politicians. They quickly saw the rewards to be reaped by sponsoring currency union. Thus as the campaign heated up, the debate was not whether the East Germans would obtain deutsche marks, but rather when and under what conditions.

Several weeks before the East Germans went to the polls, Chancellor Helmut Kohl hinted that his government would structure a swift currency union with a rate of one east mark for one deutsche mark, a 1:1 conversion. The hints certainly played a role in handing Chancellor Kohl's party, the CDU, a surprisingly overwhelming victory at the East German polls.

Concrete Proposals

The first concrete proposal for economic and monetary union emerged from the Bundesbank. Not long after the East German election, the press leaked the plan for a 1:1 conversion for savings up to 2,000 east marks and a 2:1 conversion for wages, pensions, and savings above 2,000 east marks, with some financial compensation to cushion the removal of state subsidies.[1] The Bundesbank plan, much less generous than the campaign hints of Chancellor Kohl, reflected the bank's concern that union on a 1:1 basis would unleash high inflation and cripple many East German firms.

Politics, however, controlled the turn of events once again. On 23 April 1990 Chancellor Kohl proposed a specific plan that was to become the basis of negotiation for the treaty guaranteeing economic, monetary, and social union that entered into force on 1 July 1990. Under the government's plan, East German wages, pensions, and savings up to 4,000 east marks would be exchanged for deutsche marks at 1:1. Savings above 4,000 east marks would be converted at 2:1; East German corporate debt would also be converted at 2:1.

In the weeks that followed, the governments in the East and West negotiated the plan. As the East Germans had very little bargaining room, the treaty signed in May 1990 differed little from the plan first proposed by Chancellor Kohl.

The Consequences of Currency Union

Bringing the deutsche mark to the five new states of the Federal Republic has brought significant changes to the German economy. Because the German economy is closely linked to other Western economies, the economic and monetary union has had international ramifications.

The proposed currency union was largely met with skepticism. When the government announced the plan, German interest rates began rising while the stock market slid downward. But soon the euphoria of full German unity overshadowed the pessimists, and both the deutsche mark and the stock market recovered as markets contemplated the long-term economic consequences of the opening in the East. Several months after economic and monetary union was in place, however, the true magnitude of the problems in the East German economy became apparent.

Inflation

Most analysts expected the infusion of deutsche marks into the East to inflate the money supply by approximately 10 percent, an increase that the German economy "could absorb" without a significant jump in inflation. In reality, by the spring of 1991 the broad money supply (M3) had grown by nearly 20 percent.[2] As analysts had predicted, only half of this resulted from the monetary "overhang" (or excess supply that cannot be readily converted) in the five new states. The other 10 percent was produced by the fast pace of growth in the West German economy as well as the sizable increase in government spending in the aftermath of unification. Although money-supply growth may ease somewhat as eastern Germans find investments not counted in M3, the surge in spending power does not bode well for the future price index.

Luckily, advantageous conditions, including the highly valued deutsche mark and a jump in imports to meet extra demand, kept inflation from rising above 3 percent in the first ten months of the currency union. However, these conditions will probably not continue over the next few years. Since the end of the war in the Gulf, the deutsche mark has lost significant ground against all major currencies. The outlook on inflation is worsened, moreover, by the lower deutsche mark, combined with a series of slated tax hikes and imminent wage agreements. By the end of 1991 prices are expected to be rising at an annual rate of 4 percent—again, a high figure for the Germans.

The 1:1 conversion plan was, as Belgian finance minister Philippe Maystadt noted in early 1990, a bet that the future productivity of the new German states would increase quickly enough both to justify the overvaluation of the east mark and to avoid a big jump in inflation.[3] In effect, just the opposite has happened. Production in the eastern part of Germany, instead of rising, has fallen dramatically. Eastern GNP dropped 15 percent in 1990; 1991 could see a similar plunge.[4] At the earliest, growth is expected in 1992 in the new eastern states.

Despite the recession, spending power in eastern Germany has not necessarily fallen. Those who managed to retain their jobs have higher real wages because of the 1:1 conversion rate and pressures for their wages to rise to Western levels. The unemployed also have more spending power. Under the terms of the economic, monetary, and social union, unemployed easterners receive 60 percent (90 percent of their old wages) in deutsche marks.[5] The prospect of a stagnant economy is probably forcing most Germans to save more than they normally do, and prices for many basic goods are rising fast. Easterners, though, are generally financially better off now than before unification.

Capital Markets and Interest Rates

Closely related to the problem of inflation is the prospect that the expense of economic and monetary union, much of which will be financed through borrowing, will strain the supply of capital and thus push up interest rates. The costs of unification have turned out to be much greater than most observers expected at the time of the monetary union. This was mainly because few realized how crippled the GDR's capital stock and infrastructure were. Social adjustment benefits and environmental cleanup have already presented the government with big bills. The government's borrowing needs have therefore soared beyond the levels forecasted in early 1990.[6] With borrowing needs of DM 100 billion for 1990 and an estimated DM 140 billion (many expect this figure to be closer to DM 170 billion) for 1991, the German government is seeking to borrow five times more money than it did before unification, an amount that corresponds to 5 percent of German GNP.

Initially the German government had hoped to counter the costs of monetary and economic union with positive effects on the revenue side. But cuts in defense and in programs to support Berlin and former border areas have not brought a large amount of savings, especially when compared to the costs the government must pay. In addition, the anticipated rise in eastern German production, which would have generated extra tax revenues, has not yet materialized.

Capital Markets. During the first few months after currency union, the German bond markets have absorbed the extra public borrowing without any signs of major strain. In fact the German market has had enough funds so far to enable the country to remain a net exporter of capital. The markets could become more jittery in 1991 and 1992, however, if the economic situation worsens, forcing government debt to higher-than-expected levels.

Interest Rates. The government's financing plans and fears of inflation have kept interest rates high in Germany. The Bundesbank has not hesitated to hike rates when the inflationary pressure has become too great. In the fall of 1990 it nudged up its Lombard rate (the higher of its two rates), and in February 1991 it raised both the Discount and the Lombard rate. These increases, combined with the fall of the deutsche mark in currency markets, mean investors are demanding a risk premium for Germany. This premium will probably not slip before government borrowing slackens off and inflation abates somewhat. Most analysts do not expect either to happen before 1992 at the earliest.

Such a complicated scenario will make it difficult for policymakers in Frankfurt to navigate the economic shoals of the early 1990s. By law, the Bundesbank's primary goal must be price stability, and this has endowed the bank with a large amount of anti-inflation credibility. But by October 1991 the policy-making board of the central bank will receive five new members as a result of unification. The board's broader range of interests combined with the government's intention to keep the recession in the East as mild as possible will make it much more difficult for the Bundesbank to raise interest rates to fight inflation. Many members of the board will argue, however, that, in order to maintain its international reputation, the bank needs to fight postunification inflation just as seriously as it has in the past.

East German Firms

The most problematic consequence of economic and monetary union is its effect on East German firms. Many of them have gone out of business since the introduction of the deutsche mark. Many more have cut production and may have to close. A group of American economists has estimated that only one in ten eastern firms can remain competitive at the wage level prevailing several months after unification.[7]

Eastern firms have faced many hurdles as a result of the switch to deutsche marks. Although corporate debt in the five new states was halved in nominal terms when it was exchanged at the 2:1 rate, the ensuing debt service had to be financed with West German interest rates, which were much higher in real terms than east mark rates. They will probably remain relatively high well into 1992, which means corporate debt will continue to be a large burden, unbearable in many cases.

An additional blow was the immediate loss of customers after July 1990. Once easterners acquired deutsche marks, they bought Western products. Even firms that had a chance to become competitive in a free market had a difficult time adjusting to such a quick and dramatic change in demand. Whether or not buyers return to the few products still being made in the five new states depends on the speed and the amount of future investment in manufacturing.

Rising wages pose the most serious problem for eastern firms, and they also threaten the overall success of economic and monetary union. At first glance the 1:1 exchange rate, while an overvaluation of the east mark, seemed valid for converting wages because the equation yielded a match in labor costs and productivity. Eastern wages and productivity stood at about one-third the levels in the Federal Republic.[8] Since currency union, there has been significant wage convergence as eastern wages have risen 50 percent to 80 percent to catch up to western levels.[9] The increase in wages has not been spurred, however, by a corresponding improvement in productivity. The result has been economic collapse for many eastern enterprises in light of expensive labor costs. (West German wages are high by world standards.)

Skeptics of the 1:1 exchange rate predicted that high labor costs would inevitably result in a loss of jobs in the East. Others point out that wage convergence would also have happened at other exchange rates. With monetary union came the joining of labor markets in the East and West. This meant the pressures of free migration would force eastern employers to pay higher salaries to retain their skilled labor. Western labor unions have also played a role in stirring up wage demands in the five new states.

The rise in labor costs, a devastating consequence of the economic and monetary union, has forced many firms into bankruptcy and discouraged new investment, which is so desperately needed if the eastern economy is to start growing. Most firms in the five new states need to revamp their capital stock if they are to compete successfully on world markets. One study has estimated that DM 1.7 trillion must be invested in the East over the next ten years in order to bring productivity up to western German levels.[10] While labor remains overpriced, however, few investors are going to be willing to buy the machines and buildings that the East needs to become more efficient. The government will probably have to institute some type of policy such as a wage subsidy to neutralize labor cost convergence and to encourage investment.[11]

The problems outlined above have resulted in a large number of plant closings and reductions in output. In turn, unemployment and underemployment figures have jumped. By early 1991 9 percent of the labor force in the five new states was out of work. Nearly one-third was either unemployed or working short term. The outlook for the rest of 1991 and the beginning of 1992 remains bleak. Analysts predict that unemployed and short-term workers will constitute 30 percent to 50 percent of the workforce. An upturn may come in 1992, but many forecasters remain uncertain about how long the recession in the East will last, especially since growth in western Germany has begun to slow.

Despite the gloomy short-term predictions, there is reason to believe that once the bottom of the adjustment slump is reached, the economy in the East will begin to grow at quite a fast rate. The workforce is relatively well educated. Certain areas of East Germany, particularly the large cities of Dresden and Leipzig, have a long industrial tradition. The potential for services and tourism is large. Statistics on the number of new small businesses set up since economic and monetary union, while not dramatic, are evidence that entrepreneurial spirit exists. After the slump of the early 1990s is overcome, growth in the five new states could reach 7 percent to 10 percent annually.[12]

Consequences for the International Economy

Given the current interdependence of the world economy, the changes taking place in the German economy as a result of economic and monetary union have international repercussions. This is especially true for the European Community as the German economy and the deutsche mark are so closely tied to other West European economies. It is also true, to a lesser extent, for the United States and Japan, which have significant trade and financial dealings with Germany.

Capital Markets and Interest Rates

Perhaps the most important consequence for the world economy is what will happen to capital markets and interest rates as the situation in Germany first worsens and then becomes better. The needs of the Germans have so far had little effect on international capital markets. There has not been a significant movement of capital into Germany at the cost of other large borrowers such as the United States. Some analysts had feared that the German financing policy would squeeze the amount of funds available worldwide and thus cause a rise in interest rates everywhere. So far this has not happened, and rates have even fallen in some markets. However, the large rise in the German government's debt in 1991 and 1992 may begin to have the detrimental effect on international markets that analysts first feared.

Private investment over the long term in Germany may also begin to affect international markets. Despite the fact that Eastern Germany's economy was valued in a hard currency after July 1990, private investment there has been sluggish during the first few months after unification. Complications over property rights and rising wages have deterred potential investors. These conditions will have to change somewhat if the East is to attract the vast amount of private funds and know-how it needs to modernize.

If the outlook for Germany improves significantly in the 1990s while the government and the private sector are still borrowing large amounts to finance unification, high interest rates will attract more and more international funds to the German market. The deutsche mark will rise in value. With the combination of fiscal expansion, a tight monetary policy (a likely prospect, given Bundesbank philosophy), and what is perceived to be a low-risk environment for investment, the German economy would begin to resemble that of the United States in the early 1980s, with the effect that large amounts of world capital will flow there.

If the comparative value of the deutsche mark jumps up in the future because of greater capital needs, other countries may have to raise their interest rates to keep their currencies from depreciating too sharply against the German currency. Such a move could be recessionary for these countries and for the world economy in general, thus arousing political tensions between Germany and its major trading partners. If countries end up not defending their currencies against a rising deutsche mark, they would then import inflation as they pay higher prices for traded goods. In the first few months after unification, such a scenario has been avoided because the deutsche mark has lost value as the market has adjusted its judgment in light of the problems unleashed by economic and monetary union.

Movements in the value of the deutsche mark hold special significance for countries that have joined the Germans in the European Monetary System (EMS). Before July 1990 many EMS members were wary that the introduction of the deutsche mark, the currency to which the EMS is anchored, into eastern Germany would engender high inflation and destabilize the system. But such fears have abated. Indeed, the initial consequences of currency union have soothed tensions within the EMS. As the deutsche mark has lost value since the Gulf war, the pressure to realign exchange rates within the system has subsided. In addition, the surge in German imports has helped to alleviate big imbalances in EC trade accounts. However, the prospects of rising inflation in Germany (which will most likely be met by a hike in German interest rates) could revive tensions in the EMS. Many members would resent having to follow Germany's recessionary monetary policy in order to avoid downward pressures on their own currencies.

Uncertainty about the deutsche mark will make it more difficult for the European Community to use the EMS in working toward economic and monetary integration in Europe. The fallout from the German experiment—which Bundesbank president Karl Otto Pöhl described as "disastrous" in a March 1991 speech that sent a shock wave through currency markets—has certainly made many key players rethink the mechanics and timing of introducing a European currency. Although there have as yet been no formal plans to slow the process, Mr. Pöhl's warning will not be taken lightly. The Germans' preoccupation with their own economic problems as well as the weak political support for the EMS in the five new German states will also probably have a decelerating effect on the European unification process.

Trade and Growth

The initial consequences for world trade and growth as a result of economic and monetary union in Germany have been positive. Since unification, Germany has undertaken fiscal expansion and demand stimulation, policy moves long demanded by Germany's main trading partners. Although the change has been rather abrupt, many countries are satisfied with the economic stimulation provided by the surge in German imports. The erosion of the large German trade surplus has also been welcomed by the EC and the G-7 countries. As the problems resulting from German economic and monetary union become more complicated in the next few years, world reaction may be more skeptical if high government and trade deficits in Germany move the world economy into significant imbalance.

Consequences of Economic and Monetary Union

The consequences of German economic and monetary union are complicated. The final outcome will depend on the interaction of several variables. Will there be a significant rise in inflation in Germany? How much money will the government have to borrow to cover all the costs?

What will then be the effect on interest rates in Germany and worldwide? How will planned tax hikes affect economic growth? When will investment in the East pick up and thus bring economic growth to the five new states? How will international markets judge the events in Germany?

As of the spring of 1991, many observers, both in Germany and abroad, have expressed surprise at the extent of the economic upheaval in the wake of unification. As unemployment figures for the five new states soar to new levels each month, unrest in the East mounts. In the West, embitterment over the high costs of economic, monetary, and social union grows and can only become worse in the summer of 1991 when taxes are raised. In light of the prospect of deeper recession and accelerating inflation for 1991 and 1992, there is greater potential for tension between policymakers in Bonn and Frankfurt.

Many of the problems that have followed unification were foreseeable. However, in the euphoria that accompanied political unification, the prospect of problems was pushed into the background. Now that full union has been in place for several months, the real difficulties involved in this novel experiment have to be addressed.

The decision to proceed with rash economic and monetary union is a hotly debated topic in Germany at the moment. But it is a moot question. In the spring of 1990, it seemed to be the only way to prevent the turmoil caused by the massive western migration of East Germans. The immediate introduction of the deutsche mark was also the clear wish of East German voters in March 1990. The alternative would have been to seal off an economic zone in the East. This would have proved very difficult to accomplish and probably would have only delayed the pain of economic reform.[13]

As swift economic and monetary union was politically necessary, so was the 1:1 conversion rate. (Actually, the plan set out in the treaty yielded an average exchange rate of 1.8:1.) All major political parties were in agreement about the rate, although the Bundesbank and other economic analysts were skeptical. The main problem resulting from economic and monetary union has been the high level of plant closings and unemployment in the East. This is mainly due to rising wages, which would have also happened under other exchange rates.

In the months ahead, the debate is bound to shift from questioning the past to focusing on the future. Policy-making will be tricky in a country where a majority of the economy is dynamic and growing while a significant minority is stagnant but full of potential. The main challenge for Bonn and Frankfurt will be to balance the merits of stable currency and satisfied trading partners against the evils of a long-lasting deep recession in the five new states. Germany will certainly need an array of creative ideas to succeed in its inevitable experiment.

Notes

1. "Auch in der ehemaligen DDR muß das Bundesgesetz gelten," *Frankfurter Allgemeine Zeitung*, 3 April 1990.
2. Silvia Ascarelli and John Schmid, "Bundesbank's Issing: East German Problems Dramatized," *Dow Jones News Service*, 5 April 1991.
3. Philippe Maystadt, "Gefahr für die Nachbarn," *Die Zeit*, 11 May 1990.
4. "Don't Mention the Wall," *Economist*, 6 April 1991.
5. Allan T. Demaree, "The New Germany's Glowing Future," *Fortune*, 3 December 1990.
6. For a more thorough discussion of forecasts in early 1990, see Dresdner Bank Economics Department, Frankfurt. *Trends* (March 1990 and April 1990).
7. Editorial, *Financial Times*, 21 March 1991.
8. "The Ost Mark's Last Laugh," *Economist*, 28 April 1990.
9. "Don't Mention the Wall," *Economist*.
10. L. Lipschitz and D. McDonald, "German Unification: Economic Issues," IMF Occasional Paper 75. Cited in ibid.
11. "Don't Mention the Wall," *Economist*.
12. Demaree, "New Germany's Glowing Future."
13. Hans Willgerodt, "Gegen eine Dolchstoßlegende," *Frankfurter Allgemeine Zeitung*, 13 April 1991.

7

German Trade and Joint Ventures with the East

Cole Thompson

Germany does more business with Eastern Europe and the USSR than any other Western country. During the first six months of 1989, before the wave of revolutions in Eastern Europe and the collapse of the old East Germany, West German exports to and imports from these countries totaled $14.6 billion, roughly three times as much as the second- and third-place Western countries, Italy ($5 billion) and the United States ($4.4 billion).[1] This chapter will address the reasons German business has been so successful in penetrating Eastern Europe and the Soviet Union and what the opening of the East will mean for the German economy in the future.

The long-standing German predilection for *Osthandel*, or trade with the East, is driven by geography. Ethnic Germans, including many merchants, settled throughout Eastern Europe beginning in the thirteenth century; in fact, most of Poland's large cities were founded by Germans as focal points for trade. In seventeenth-century Moscow, the area reserved for foreign merchants was known simply as "the German quarter," and Germany itself extended until 1945 as far east as what is now Kaliningrad in the Soviet Union. The collective memory of that time lingers in the minds of Germans and may account in part for their continued desire for business in the East during the postwar era. This inclination to do business with member-states of a hostile military alliance has often aggravated the United States. Jörg Fuss explains the German perspective: "The recognition of common responsibility for the world forces us to cooperate, regardless of differing ideology and world views. . . . Basically the West has no choice: the economic policy of the Soviet Union has to be given trade and technological support. The U.S.A. still has to be convinced."[2]

The 1989 revolutions in the Eastern bloc countries promise to vindicate this view. The German business magazine *Wirtschaftswoche* put it this way: "From Warsaw to Sofia, the fruits of tirelessly cultivated contacts from previous years are ripening, giving the West German economy a tremendous leap over the American, French and Japanese competition."[3]

German Trade with the East

Up until the full impact in 1988 of Soviet president Mikhail Gorbachev's *perestroika* in the Soviet Union, the East was a market that seemed not worth the trouble to most Western firms. Daunting bureaucracies slowed the pace of business to a crawl, and the only way to make a profit in hard currency was to sell Eastern bloc products in the West (generally a losing proposition) or to persuade Eastern bloc planners to release some of their jealously guarded hard currency reserves. Despite these conditions, after the easing of cold war tensions, West German firms continued their industrial tradition and vigorously pursued *Osthandel*. West German trade with the East expanded to reach a high point in 1975 of 6.4 percent of its total German trade with the outside world.[4] German trade with the East then slackened, stabilizing in the 1980s at about 5 percent. The biggest partner for West Germany in the last two decades has been the Soviet Union, which accounted in a typical year for about 40 percent of German *Osthandel*, followed by East Germany with about 27 percent. West German success in the Eastern bloc since the end of the cold war rested on three practices: understanding of state-planned economies' reactions to outside firms; stubborn pursuit of personal contacts; and heavy and continuing support for *Osthandel* by federal and state governments in West Germany.

Understanding the reactions of state-planned economies to outside firms has been a long-term German practice and important to its success in the markets. Since the revolutions of 1989 and the demise of COMECON, or Council for Mutual Economic Assistance (formally dissolved in early 1991, for practical purposes in 1990), the countries of the Eastern bloc have been moving away from centrally planned economies. But we need to understand how the old planned economies worked to comprehend how German firms operated in those countries so well. Under the old order, economic activity in the Eastern bloc was defined in increasing detail from the top down, starting with the Communist party Central Committee in each country setting the areas of emphasis for economic growth in a Five-Year Plan. Demand for goods and services thus could not come from consumers or buyers of capital goods; rather, it came from the need of manufacturers or the national economy as a whole to fulfill the plan.

As a rule, these plans were never realized. In the Soviet Union, only the very first Five-Year Plan under Stalin in the early 1930s was fulfilled. Failure to achieve planned targets created a potential demand for imports.

Generally, officials in Eastern bloc countries sought to make up shortfalls by first going to other COMECON countries, then to Western suppliers.[5]

Accordingly, one of the keys to German success in penetrating Eastern bloc markets was its careful research in identifying shortfalls in each country's plan and then meeting them with German production. This was not as difficult as it might seem. Planned economies produce vast amounts of statistics, and with détente in the early 1970s Eastern bloc countries began to make much of this data available. But Germans found that statistical yearbooks and other sources were increasingly inaccurate as one went up the state planning hierarchy, because production figures were padded at each level. Yet statistics from economic institutes and banks tended to be reliable. Through careful study of planned and actual production figures in each country over time, German firms were able to identify shortfalls that were worth pursuing.[6]

As the volume of intra-Comecon trade increased in the early 1980s, German firms adapted and began to consider such trade in assessing each Eastern bloc country's potential need for German imports. One German consultant, taking advantage of the copious data from the East, simplified market analysis to a formula:

$$IfW = TN - OP + TE - EbI;$$

where: IfW = Imports required from the West (opportunity for German firms); TN = Total needs according to the Plan; OP = Own Production; TE = Total exports; EbI = Imports from other Eastern bloc countries.[7]

Disaggregating economic plans in this fashion was crucial, but could not of itself generate sales. Sales required patient cultivation of personal contacts, and this, more than any other feature of German business acumen, was the key to the Federal Republic's *Osthandel* success. German experience indicates that the human factor of doing business—currying favor of officials, endless small talk, the importance of amicable face-to-face meetings—is as important in Eastern Europe and the Soviet Union as it is in East Asian countries. Geography naturally helped West German firms; it was easier for them to attend trade fairs and symposia in the Eastern bloc. In some cases, these were the same trade fairs that German business executives had traditionally attended before the war. These events were the only practical way to make the all-important personal contacts with East bloc businessmen and trade officials. West German companies found it especially valuable to cultivate contacts within relevant trade and professional associations.

The third feature of West German *Osthandel*, a willingness to lean on government resources, may have been the biggest difference overall between German and American business. German government support came not, as one might expect, through especially generous subsidies or other financial arrangements to favor companies exporting to the East,[8] but through information. Since the early 1960s the Bundesstelle für Aussenhandelsinformation (Federal Center for Foreign Trade Information) has published a very wide range of detailed studies and synopses on all aspects of the Eastern bloc market, and has made these readily available to German companies. The Bundesverband der deutschen Industrie (Federal Association of German Industry) also prints monographs on Eastern markets and supplies practical advice. German companies interested in pursuing trade in the Eastern bloc were also urged to take up contact with officials from German embassies or consulates in the target country, as these officials devoted much of their time to cultivating commercially useful contacts with local national officials. German politicians also demonstrated a readiness to work for German trade with the Eastern bloc; a prime example was German chancellor Helmut Kohl's October 1988 trip to Moscow, which focused on increasing German trade with the Soviet Union. "Business and politicians work hand in hand in the East," is how one professor at a state-run export academy described West German policy toward *Osthandel*.

This policy of encouraging trade with the East was driven by Germany's unique political agenda governing relations with the Eastern bloc. The postwar division of Germany initially prompted a policy of nonrecognition of East Germany, in the hope that somehow the Communist German rump state could be brought back into the German nation on Western terms. Economic relations with the Eastern bloc were accordingly minimal, dominated by political desires not to strengthen the political (and potential military) enemy.[9] A key change came in the late 1950s, when West German politicians recognized that the division of Germany would persist. The opinion gradually took hold that the FRG had more to gain by fostering contacts with East Germany and preventing complete divergence of the two Germanies than by accepting as normal the existence of the "other" Germany. FRG *Osthandel* policies hinged on the recognition that because East Germany had been forcibly included in the Soviet bloc, relations with it could never, in principle, be any better than those with the Soviet Union. Mindful of its duties as a model member of the Western alliance, which effectively eliminated any scope for independent political initiatives toward the East, West German politicians saw trade as a politically acceptable way to achieve two goals: (1) expanding the web of contacts between the two Germanies and (2) demonstrating to the Soviets that good relations with West Germany were in the Soviets' material interest, thereby minimizing the likelihood that the Soviets would destroy those good relations by cutting off access to West Berlin.[10]

Under this new umbrella of legitimacy, West German trade with the Eastern bloc countries became an accepted, if arcane, area of export activity for West German firms beginning in the early 1960s. In the warmer political climate created by détente in the early 1970s and by Willy Brandt's *Ostpolitik* of "many small steps," West German trade with the East expanded to its 1975 high point. Until 1987 or so, this trade was dominated by large projects involving the biggest German firms. Companies like Krupp and Thyssen (both manufacturers of metal products) built turn-key factories or supplied material for showcase projects like the controversial Siberian gas pipeline. Small and middle-sized West German firms were not especially valued by Eastern bloc countries, as these did not fit in well with the national scale of Eastern bloc economic plans.[11]

In sum, the postwar history of German trade with the Eastern bloc through the late 1980s taught that success went to those companies, generally large, that found niches they could fill in the economic plans of Eastern bloc countries, established contacts with the central authorities (i.e., in the ministry relevant to their field), and then carefully cultivated them. The Germans also showed they had the patience so crucial to doing business in the East. German companies will no doubt profit from their accumulated banks of personal business contacts, for no matter how Eastern bloc economies evolve, the people will remain the same. The Communist parties in the Eastern bloc countries sought to co-opt the best and the brightest men and women in their societies, and these are the people West German business assiduously cultivated over the years. These same people will probably emerge at the forefront of the new economic elite under a free market system as well. Yet while the people remain the same, the economic landscape in the Eastern bloc is in upheaval, and *Osthandel* has taken on new shapes.

Joint Ventures with the East

After taking power as general secretary of the Communist party of the Soviet Union, Mikhail Gorbachev made it clear that an overhaul of the Soviet economy was central to his agenda. Consequently, the grip of central planners on the Soviet economy has loosened incrementally since the mid 1980s. The rest of Eastern Europe—most notably Poland—has reacted to the thaw by bounding ahead toward free markets. The problem that has arisen in all countries is that the political leadership has been scrapping the command and control structures that ran the Eastern bloc's economies, but economic environments compatible to market forces and investment are developing much more slowly. In theory, about 25,000 factories in the Soviet Union can now import and export goods without working through the previously mandatory state trade organizations. But the thicket of regulation in the Soviet Union is still dense, and as competencies and laws change, Soviet firms are not sure what is allowed and what is not. Worse, say some German firms, Soviet authorities do not seem to know what Soviet firms are allowed to do either. It took seemingly forever to get anything done when the central authorities had complete power, German managers grumble, but once a decision was made one could rely on it.[12] One German company seeking to start a cooperative project in the Soviet Union's Kola Peninsula had to visit seven different ministries, and then two local agencies.[13]

Despite the deepening chaos in the Soviet Union and gloomy economic forecasts in Eastern Europe, one aspect of the economic transition in the East has aroused great interest in the Western business world: joint ventures. Founded as a new company according to local laws, a joint venture has two owners, an Eastern bloc firm and a Western one. Their hybrid nature is symbolic of the huge effort by Eastern bloc countries to cross over the gap between their old command economies and the market economies of the West. Joint ventures allow Western firms access to the potential advantages of the East: a huge underserved consumer market and cheap labor and materials. Eastern bloc countries, for their part, hope that joint ventures will revitalize their economies and fill critical gaps in production. Profits from hard-currency sales—the ultimate goal of most joint ventures—are split according to ownership share. In the longer term, Eastern bloc countries hope joint ventures will by osmosis bring their managers and workers up to par with the West. It is not yet clear whether German companies expanding into the East will do so primarily through joint ventures or through fully German-owned operations, but since the operational problems can be expected to be the same, lessons drawn from experience with joint ventures are useful predictors of future German efforts.

The Eastern bloc countries have emphasized their desire that joint ventures produce goods, not services. The Soviets have announced their preference for joint ventures founded to build machines, make chemicals, and make consumer goods, especially food products. Characteristically, the Soviets expressed the desire that joint ventures would increase the proportion of Soviet-manufactured goods suitable for international markets from 29 percent to 80 percent by 1990.[14] Driven by the increasingly severe economic problems of socialism, Eastern bloc countries have one by one passed laws allowing their combines and factories to enter into joint ventures with Western companies. Maverick Yugoslavia was first in 1967, followed by Hungary in 1972, Poland in 1976, Bulgaria in 1980, Czechoslovakia in 1986, and finally the Soviet Union itself on 13 January 1987.[15]

Not surprisingly, the Germans have been in the forefront of joint venture activity in the Eastern bloc. In the Soviet Union about 3,000 joint ventures had sprung up by early 1991, and (categorized by nationality) the Germans have one of the largest shares (about 10–15 percent of all such Soviet ventures).[16] Similar situations prevail in other Eastern bloc countries; in Hungary, often seen as most receptive to Western firms, a majority of the 2,500 or so joint ventures are owned by German or Austrian firms.[17] By examining the three German joint ventures in the East widely regarded as the most successful to date, one may discern the forms that German business activity in the Eastern bloc is increasingly likely to take as that region's economic transition unfolds. All three ventures are in the Soviet Union, and all three manufacture what Soviet officials consider priority goods.

Homatek. The first of these model joint ventures, Homatek, is owned 55 percent by the Soviet partner Ordshonikidze and 45 percent by Heinemann AG, a publicly traded but small German company that builds machines and technical installations. Occupying about 250 square meters of space in the Ordshonikidze factory in Moscow, the Homatek produces machine tools that are sold to Socialist bloc countries. The basic machines are built by the Russians. Crucial high-quality components are delivered by the Germans and assembled into the basic machine by Russian technicians who have been trained at the Heinemann factory in Germany. The resulting machine tools are not as good as Western models, but offer good value for the money: only the German-supplied components, which greatly boost the quality of the product, need to be paid for in hard currency. The German partner is prohibited, however, from converting ruble profits into marks, so most of Homatek's profits are worthless for Heinemann.[18]

January Uprising/Liebherr. The second model joint venture is owned 40 percent by Liebherr, a German construction equipment manufacturer, and 60 percent by the Soviet heavy crane combine "January Uprising" in the Black Sea city of Odessa.[19] The venture is ambitious, aiming to produce 700 heavy truck-mounted cranes per year by 1992—as much as the total annual production of such cranes in West Germany. Interestingly, the truck mounts are demobilized Soviet Army SS-20 missile launchers. The venture plan calls for almost 100 percent of the crane components to be imported from Liebherr initially. As the venture is in a high-priority field from the Soviet standpoint, the imported Liebherr components are to be paid for in hard currency—obviously a lucrative feature of the venture for Liebherr. With time the Soviets are to produce an increasing percentage of the crane components at the assembly site in Odessa, starting with structural members, then graduating to transmission and hydraulics. The most sophisticated 10 percent of components—electronic safety devices—are to be permanently imported from Liebherr. Soviet technicians in the venture are flown for training to Liebherr's factory in southern Germany, and a staff of six to ten Liebherr technicians is to ensure the quality of work done in Odessa. Because Soviet internal demand for mobile cranes is intense, no exports are foreseen. If someday the Soviets insist on exporting the venture's cranes, they must be sold through Liebherr's sales organization.[20]

Lenvest. "Lenvest," the third model joint venture, is owned 40 percent by the well-known German shoe manufacturer Salamander, and 60 percent by the Soviet shoe combine called "Proletarian Victory." It produces 1 million pairs of shoes annually at its factory in Leningrad. Extraordinarily successful—Soviet consumers wait in line up to four hours to buy shoes from the sales room next to the factory—the venture has set up a second factory in the city of Vitebsk, also producing 1 million pairs of shoes annually. Combined production of the two plants is planned to increase to 10 million pairs of shoes annually by the year 2000. Both plants are profitable, although profits are in untransferable rubles. Unlike the other two ventures, no materials are imported from the West. Considerable effort is put into the welfare of the plants' workers—free lunches and help with long-term loans are provided—and workers' pay is tied to performance. The performance of Soviet workers in the venture, according to Salamander managers, is quite good.

Lessons Learned in Trade with the East

These three joint ventures, and other more or less successful German ventures in the East, are cited repeatedly by the cottage industry of *Osthandel* consultants in western Germany as examples of what German businesses should and should not try to do in the East. Thus, the lessons learned by Heinemann, Liebherr, and Salamander can be expected to influence greatly other German firms looking to the East.

The experiences of these firms makes it clear that successful German ventures have been the product of willingness to invest enormous amounts of time and work through seemingly never-ending barriers—frustration is still a large part of doing business in the Eastern bloc. As an example, a rule of thumb for German companies operating in Czechoslovakia has been that a cooperation agreement takes several months to complete, but a joint venture agreement takes several years. Experienced German business executives warn strongly against immediately trying to set up a joint venture, the most ambitious move possible into Eastern markets, warning that a joint venture should be the culmination, not the beginning, of cooperative projects.[21]

The Germans have found that the business culture in the East has not changed, which can be expected to give German firms, experienced in the ways of the Eastern bloc, an intangible advantage over other Western firms. Amicable small talk during negotiations continues to be vital to success, and the more successful German ventures in the East have been marked by good personality fits between the main partners. Reiner Lang, German manager for the Homatek machine-building venture in Moscow, attributes much of that venture's success to his friendship with the Soviet manager, Nikolai Tshikiryov.[22] Small gifts, especially alcohol, continue to be absolutely essential (and genuinely appreciated by those living in pinched economies).

With the increasing freedom of access to information in the East, Eastern bloc negotiators have become harder bargainers. They tend to know a lot about Western products in their field and want top-quality products from the West. German firms have learned not to attempt to sell outmoded goods in the East, according to one *Osthandel* expert. The Germans have also learned to take pains to avoid hints of Western arrogance—managers in the Eastern bloc countries are all too aware that they are among the losers of one of history's greatest rivalries. A midsized German manufacturer came up with the following list of qualities needed by those seeking trade with the new East: (1) a lot of time; (2) a lot of understanding: (3) endurance; and (4) a good stomach (included, apparently, because of traumatic experiences with Eastern bloc food).[23]

Gerhard Wacker, chief of the Salamander shoe concern, has stressed the following lessons, confirmed by other German firms and *Osthandel* consultants: (1) the Western partner must have an exact idea of the negotiations' objective from the very beginning; (2) cost and benefits should be constantly calculated; and (3) breakthroughs in negotiations should immediately be put on paper (letters of intent, etc.).[24] On average, according to one *Osthandel* expert, German experience has been that only one out of every seven attempts to conclude a deal with an Eastern bloc partner succeeds.

The contracts that are born of successful negotiations with Eastern bloc partners are as a rule surprisingly thick, booklike documents. As one German consultant puts it, Eastern bloc firms attempt to protect themselves through such contracts against "everything, but literally everything" that might happen to them as a result of their deal with the Western company.[25] That consultant recommends taking advantage of the increasing confusion in Eastern bloc countries over which laws are in force to fight fire with fire, and turn contracts into a quasi-legal code that include detailed German demands and requirements. As an example of the detail German firms have found necessary, the German machine-building company Schiess AG in its joint venture agreement with a Soviet combine (which took two years to negotiate) specified the number and type of electrical outlets in the assembly hall.[26] The Germans have also learned to respect some of the detailed specifications of Eastern bloc partners as making good business sense under local conditions. The very detailed directions in contracts with the Soviets on how goods are to be labeled and packaged are in fact important to observe, as it is not unusual for freight in the Soviet Union to spend one year's storage under open skies.[27]

By far the single biggest problem German firms have had with joint ventures in the East is deliveries of all kinds: materials and subassemblies come too late or not at all, and quality is poor. Also, German firms have found their joint ventures are often charged much higher rates for raw materials, electricity, and water than local state-run factories.[28] The best solution seems to be getting raw material and component sources under control of the joint venture/cooperative management. The Homatek machine-building joint venture plans to build up several subassembly plants around its main assembly site to preclude reliance on state suppliers. Salamander is contemplating building its own tannery in the Soviet Union so that its two shoe-building plants there can rely on getting decent leather. Ironically, German firms seeking to set up shop in the Eastern bloc thus seem destined to replicate much of the Eastern bloc's Socialist-style "vertically integrated" manufacturing, in which factories make even their own nails and screws, rather than risk relying on deliveries of the same. This is spectacularly inefficient, but in the East there seems to be no alternative.

German experience indicates that there should be at least one manager from the Western firm on site to keep operations rolling, as local supervisors sorely lack initiative.[29] The work ethic of Soviet and Eastern European workers can be quite variable—German firms have found that it takes some time to instill Western standards of attention to speed and quality, but once there, the Eastern bloc workers are good.[30] A key discovery German firms have made is that pay is often not the best motivator in the Eastern bloc. People have more money than opportunities to spend (hence the large overhang of personal savings in Eastern bloc countries, especially the Soviet Union),[31] and material rewards such as clothing and food are of key importance. Salamander gives its joint venture employees 50 percent discounts on the venture's shoes,[32] and Homatek gives its key Soviet employees, such as the sales manager, a Volkswagen Passat car if they reach management goals.[33] Salamander has also found that deliveries and the pace of construction of new facilities can be greatly accelerated by giving shoes from the joint venture to the workers concerned.[34]

One problem that has yet to be solved by any joint venture is how to earn hard currency profits, and solving this will be the key to the success of future German–Eastern bloc joint ventures. Axel LeBahn, the Deutsche Bank's expert on the Soviet Union and Eastern Europe, estimates that for most joint ventures 15 to 30 percent of the venture's total production must be sold on world markets to earn enough hard currency to pay for imported Western components, licenses, salaries of Western employees in the venture, and other costs.[35] So far no German–Eastern bloc venture has achieved this ratio, but the German government's Center for Foreign Trade Information has suggested a possible solution. Since November 1989 the Foreign Trade Bank of the Soviet Union has been holding hard-currency auctions, during which Soviet firms can bid in rubles for lumps of Western money. It seems likely that joint ventures will be allowed to take part in these auctions. The center therefore proposes a two-pronged strategy for German-Soviet joint ventures: using German marks or dollars supplied by the Western partner, the joint venture can auction off hard currency for very large amounts of rubles. These rubles can then be used by the joint venture to pay its bills in the Soviet Union. The second prong of the strategy is to use the ruble profits allocated to the Western partner to bid for hard currency at the state-sponsored auctions.[36] The resulting reduction in profits is huge. At the end of 1990, these auctions have pegged the ruble's worth at one forty-fifth its official Soviet exchange rate value against the mark.[37] But this strategy would allow German firms to transfer joint venture earnings out of the Soviet Union in the form of marks or dollars— key to making ventures viable over the long term. Similar arrangements should be possible in other Eastern bloc countries as well, and additionally, the Eastern bloc countries seem increasingly convinced of the need to make their currencies readily convertible, sooner rather than later.

An important consideration for German firms now contemplating joint ventures in the Eastern bloc is therefore whether the goal is to earn hard currency directly by sales on the world market or indirectly through hard-currency auctions. The latter seems more promising. It is unlikely that products made in Eastern bloc countries will be able to compete with those from other cheap labor regions such as Asia for some time.[38] Also, the traditional markets for Eastern bloc exports (Africa, other poor regions) have become more competitive. The demand for goods of all kinds within Eastern bloc countries, however, promises to be high for a long time owing to the pent-up purchasing power represented by the high level of personal savings in most of the Eastern bloc. Consumer goods of any quality should do especially well, as such goods have been missing from Eastern European and Soviet shelves for almost half a century. The experience of Salamander's shoe-producing joint venture confirms this. Without one kopek for advertising, says Salamander chief Gerhard Wacker, "the shoes sell themselves" as fast as the joint venture can make them.[39]

As the spheres of competency in the East will become more and not less confused in the near future, German companies will probably follow the advice of *Osthandel* consultants and follow a two-track approach to dealing with the authorities: get contacts and approvals at both central and factory levels. The day will probably come when it will be possible to deal only with company managers as in the West, but for now the need to curry favor with central-planning ministries remains.[40]

German companies have found that considerable training of local national workers is necessary, as is heavy marketing and accounting support (accrual accounting, the standard in the West since the 1930s, was unknown in planned Eastern bloc economies). On the plus side, German firms have found that Eastern bloc engineers are frequently very good and may offer the opportunity to add considerable value to a product for relatively little cost.

In terms of which countries now offer the best opportunities for German firms, there seems to be a consensus among German businessmen and consultants that endeavors in the Soviet Union have the highest risk of failure, despite the shining examples of Homatek, Liebherr, and Salamander. In mid 1990, two and one half years after joint ventures were made legal, only 10 percent of all joint ventures founded with the Soviets were operating, and very few of those were actually profitable.[41] The most promising countries, according to German estimates, will continue to be Hungary (enthusiastic government support) and Czechoslovakia (solid industrial tradition), and it is here that German efforts will probably be concentrated. Volkswagen's purchase of the respected Czech car maker Skoda, for $6.6 billion—by far the biggest move by any Western firm into the East—would seem to confirm a German focus on Czechoslovakia and Hungary and may be a harbinger.[42]

Prospects for the Future

The prospects for the future of German business in the countries of the Eastern bloc are clearly excellent. Personal contacts and experience will continue to be critical for Western firms doing business there, and here the Germans have a competitive edge that will not easily be made up by other Western countries. As it has for seven centuries, geography will make it comparatively easy for the Germans to do business in the East, and, other factors being equal, shorter distances will give German companies permanent cost advantages over other Western firms. This proximity will yield other less quantifiable advantages, such as the already widely acknowledged adoption of German as the language of business in Eastern Europe. It is also not unlikely that the Eastern bloc countries may end up filling German industry's need for low labor cost plants, much as Southeast Asia serves Japan and the *maquiladora* factories of northern Mexico serve the United States. This would help German industry fix one of its biggest disadvantages relative to other industrial countries: its very high cost of labor. In short, the past German strategy of patiently tending trade and cooperative agreements and joint ventures in the East may thus pay off very well.

German *Osthandel* will also benefit from the economic union of East and West Germany. East German industry has collapsed at an alarming rate since economic union in late 1990, but the legacy of East Germany's role in COMECON brings the best possible contacts with the rest of the Eastern bloc. Indeed, extensive German trade with Eastern Europe and the Soviet Union will probably be mandatory. The Soviet Union made its approval of German unification contingent on Germany's assumption of East German export obligations to the USSR. These are substantial: in 1989 the Soviet Union procured 18.6 percent of its machines, 29.4 percent of its ships, 29.6 percent of its locomotives, and 55 percent of its cold storage and air-conditioning equipment from East Germany. Chancellor Helmut Kohl has agreed in principle to make these deliveries.[43] Theoretically, this could more than double the proportion of trade with the Eastern bloc (excluding eastern Germany) from the 4.9 percent of total trade for the old West Germany to 10.8 percent of the unified German economy. According to *Capital*, a German magazine, the opening of Eastern Europe will over a period of years boost Germany's proportion of trade with the East even higher, to about 20 percent of total trade (although that proportion has not changed in 1990 over 1989, due to the weak buying power of Eastern bloc economies in 1990).[44]

Yet Germany's drive into Eastern European markets, mandatory or not, may also harbor some serious dangers for the German economy over the long run. A study done by two researchers from Germany's highly respected Stiftung für Wissenschaft und Politik at Ebenhausen, the economist Achim von Heynitz and the political scientist Hans W. Maull (who has also been an advisor to Chancellor Kohl) makes two worrisome predictions. First, the rebuilding of East Germany, and to a lesser extent the rest of Eastern Europe, will suck up huge amounts of capital that otherwise would have gone into keeping western German industry in fighting trim.[45] Although the five new *Länder* (states) of former East Germany will yield great benefits once brought up to Western standards of productivity, much of the initial investment in rebuilding—widely estimated at about $700 billion—will be "lost" on pollution controls, propping up collapsing buildings, overhauling rail lines, and other expenses not connected with production.

Second, the consumers of the Eastern bloc will be for the foreseeable future very easy to satisfy. According to the Maull study, Soviet and Eastern European consumers want products that are sturdy and serviceable, whereas North Americans and Asians increasingly demand products using the latest technology and tailored to fit market niches as those niches arise. With some 300 million not-too-particular customers in the East hungering for products that are "good enough," German industry is likely to withdraw increasingly from competition in the most demanding global markets and concentrate on mass production of plain, unsophisticated products for the unsophisticated and largely captive markets of the East. The logical outcome, Maull warns, is a serious erosion of German competitiveness on world markets—the habitual key to German prosperity.[46]

Clearly, western German industry should heed these warnings and continue to focus on the hardest, most competitive markets, regardless of how easy it may be to unload goods in the East. A logical solution would be for it to continue to concentrate on Western markets, and for eastern Germany to continue to produce most of the goods destined for Eastern bloc countries. This could buy the time that eastern German industry needs to bring itself up to West German standards. It seems Chancellor Kohl is encouraging just such a policy by subsidizing eastern German exports to former COMECON countries and thus keeping at least some orders coming in to factories in former East Germany.[47] If this policy is to work without immense subsidies, the present artificially high cost of labor now in eastern Germany must be reduced, painful as this would be. Eastern bloc customers can no longer afford to buy eastern Germany's products, now that they must pay in deutsche marks, and the German government should not interfere if eastern German wages drift downward to find their natural level.

Yet, whatever the circumstances under which German goods are produced for the Eastern market, one important question remains: how will the Eastern bloc countries pay for these goods? All, with the exception of Romania, are already heavily indebted to the West, and further borrowing is an unrealistic option.[48] Although German firms will figure prominently in any economic renaissance in the Eastern bloc counties, Germany cannot on its own rebuild the economies of the Soviet Union and Eastern Europe. The Eastern bloc countries must ultimately begin to integrate their economies into the European Community (EC)—as Hungary, Poland, and Czechoslovakia will do in the early to mid 1990s, through treaties of associate membership in the EC[49]—and find something they can produce that Western Europe will buy.

Yet it seems it will be a very long time before Eastern bloc industry will be able to compete outside of its own region, even with Western help.[50] Furthermore, that help may come only in small amounts for many years—the European Bank for Reconstruction and Development, opened by Western countries in April 1991 to spur recovery in the Eastern bloc, is now slated to invest only $6 billion until 1995.[51] Even German business executives admit that Eastern bloc countries, viewed as manufacturing sites, do not offer quite the same cost advantage as other parts of the world. It also seems extremely unlikely the Eastern bloc countries will have competitive services to offer to the rest of the world.

The only alternative is agriculture. The prewar pattern of trade in central and Eastern Europe—whereby the Germans traded finished goods for agricultural products from Eastern Europe and the Soviet Union—would, if resurrected, hold the best hope of keeping Eastern bloc economies healthy enough to buy German exports to the East and goods from joint ventures or other manufacturing plants with German participation. Eastern Europe and the Soviet Union are still relatively better suited for agriculture than densely populated Western Europe. The Eastern bloc countries could, and should, become the breadbasket of a broadened European Community. German business could then expect to find many consumers there willing and able to pay for German goods.

But to make this possible, the EC's Common Agricultural Policy (CAP), which governs and protects Western European agriculture, must be reformed. As an example of the present problem, the 1989 trade agreement between the EC and Poland forces that country to pay heavy tariffs on a long list of food products, including ducks, geese, sausages, flour, cabbage, preserved potatoes, and leather[52]—just the products which the Poles might be expected to be able to produce and trade efficiently with the West.

Germany, as the single most powerful voice in the European Community, holds the key to opening Europe to Eastern bloc food exports. However, German farmers have enjoyed considerable protection under the CAP, and Germany's politically potent farming lobby has forced even normally free-market minded Chancellor Kohl to oppose any reforms to CAP. But Kohl and other German politicians may soon have no choice but to champion free trade in agriculture from the Atlantic to the Urals, for if the Eastern bloc countries cannot export their agricultural products to the West, they will wind up exporting economic refugees instead—primarily to Germany. The sooner the German government stands up to its domestic farming lobby, therefore, and pushes for elimination of agricultural quotas and subsidies in the European Community, the better. The flow of agricultural goods from East to West that such a reform would bring would go a long way toward allowing Eastern bloc countries to pay their way in the evolving single European market. That, in turn, would make possible a boom in *Osthandel* that could fuel vigorous growth in Germany—Eastern Germany as well as Western—through the end of the century.

Notes

1. "Osthandel des Westens," chart No. 8112 from Globus Kartendienst (Postfach 700769, 2000 Hamburg 70).

2. Jörg Fuss, "Situation der Ost-West-Beziehungen und Wirtschaftliche Perspektiven aus deutscher Sicht," in materials for presentation at the 1990 *Osthandel* seminar at the Export-Akademie Baden-Württemberg in Reutlingen, 30 March 1989.

3. "Die Kunst des Mikado," *Wirtschaftswoche*, N. 15, 6 April 1990, p. 92.

4. Fuss, "Situation der Ost-West-Beziehungen."

5. Heinz Matzeit, "Marktforschung für Ostblockländer," in materials for presentation at the 1990 seminar on *Osthandel* at Export-Akademie Baden-Württemberg in Reutlingen, p. 2.

6. Matzeit, "Marktforschung," pp. 5–8.

7. Siegfried Anysas, "Exportvorbereitung im Ostgeschäft," Mitteilungen der Bundesstelle für Aussenhandelsinformation no. 10.209.85.000 (pamphlet from FRG Office of Foreign Trade Information), July 1985, p. 3.

8. Wilhelm Schäfer, "Die Osthandelspolitik der Bundesrepublik Deutschland in ihren institutionellen Rahmenbedingungen und Entscheidungsprozessen" (Ph.D. diss., Department of Economics, Freie Universität Berlin, 1979), pp. 250, 256.

9. Schäfer, "Die Osthandelspolitik," p. 10.

10. Angela Stent, "Soviet-West German Relations under Helmut Kohl: Continuity or Change?" in *Economic Relations with the Soviet Union—American and West German Perspectives*, ed. Angela Stent (Boulder: Westview, 1985), pp. 28–30.

11. Anysas, "Exportvorbereitung im Ostgeschäft," p. 9.

12. "Neigung zur Nostalgie," *Wirtschaftswoche*, N. 15, 6 April 1990, p. 102.

13. *Capital* (November 1988), p. 42.

14. Dirk Holtbrügge, "Joint Ventures in der UdSSR," *Außenwirtschaft* 3–4 [pub. by Schweizerisches Institut für Außenwirtschafts-, Struktur-, und Regionalforschung, at Hochschule St. Gallen, Switzerland] (December 1989), p. 135.

15. Marian Malecki, "Joint Ventures," *Osteuropa Wirtschaft* (September 1989), p. 225.

16. "A Realistic Assessment of German-Soviet Economic Relations," *Economist*, 20 April 1991, p. 62.

17. *Hungary Country Report*, from Economist Intelligence Unit/Business International, 1990, N. 4, p. 20.

18. "Ich komme mir vor wie Sisyphus," *Spiegel*, N. 30, 25 July 1988, pp. 72–74.

19. "Liebherr Management," *Manager* (January 1988), p. 117.

20. *Manager* (January 1988), pp. 117–23.

21. *Manager* (4 April 1988), p. 199.

22. *Spiegel* (25 July 1988), p. 73.

23. Correspondence dated 20 April 1990, from Thomas Heinemann, general manager of A. Heinemann K.G. (a metal-working firm in Rensburg, Germany).

24. "Viele Tips aus erster Hand—Salamander-Chef Wacker über die Erfahrungen im Handel mit der UdSSR," *Die Stuttgarter Nachrichten*, 3 May 1990, p. 17.

25. Fuss, "Situation der Ost-West Beziehungen," p. 8.

26. "Kontrolle ist besser," *Industriemagazin* (September 1988), p. 163.

27. Dieter J.G. Schneider, *Das Sowjetunion-Geschäft: Rechtliche Vorschriften, Marktsituation, Geschäftsabwicklung* (Wiesbaden: Gabler, 1990), p. 117.

28. Pamphlet from Außenhandelsdienst der Industrie- und Handelskammern und Wirtschaftsverbände, 29 March 1990, p. 10.
29. Holtbrügge, "Joint Ventures," p. 140.
30. Ibid., p. 141.
31. "How to Help East Europe," *Financial Times*, 7 January 1991, p. 10.
32. "Ein Stück von Lenins Träumen," *Spiegel*, 29 October 1989, p. 190.
33. *Spiegel*, 25 July 1988, p. 72.
34. "Lurchis Abenteuer bei den Kosaken," *Stuttgarter Zeitung*, 3 May 1990, p. 21.
35. "Erfahrungen bei Joint Ventures in der UdSSR," *Nachrichten für Außenhandel* [daily newsletter published by the Bundesstelle für Außenhandelsinformation, Köln], Newsletter no. 247, 21 December 1989.
36. "Erfahrungen bei Joint Ventures in der UdSSR," *Nachrichten fur Außenhandel*, no. 247, 21 December 1989.
37. "Reine Umrubelei," *Wirtschaftswoche*, 23 November 1990, p. 149.
38. Holtbrügge, "Joint Ventures," p. 145.
39. "Lurchis Abenteuer," p. 21.
40. Heinz Matzeit, "Neue Entscheidungsstrukturen in COMECON-Ländern," in materials for presentation at 1990 seminar on *Osthandel* at Export-Adakemie Baden-Württemberg, Reutlingen, 23 February 1989, p. 3.
41. "Neigung zur Nostalgie," *Wirtschaftswoche*, no. 15, 6 April 1990, p. 109.
42. "Eastward, Ho! The Pioneers Plunge In," *Business Week*, 15 April 1991, p. 51.
43. Rainer Hübner, "Der Preis der Einheit," *Capital*, April 1990, p. 112.
44. Ibid., p. 112; information on trade proportions from German Information Center, New York.
45. Hübner, "Der Preis der Einheit," pp. 110–16.
46. Ibid., pp. 110–16.
47. "Die Retter kommen aus Moskau," *Wirtschaftswoche*, 15 March 1991, p. 10.
48. "Trends der Woche," *Wirtschaftswoche*, 11 January 1991, p. 13.
49. "French Encouragement for Warsaw Plan to Join EC," *Financial Times*, 9 April 1991, p. 2, and "Hungary at Impasse on Brussels Farm Trade," p. 6.
50. From conversations with American and German trade representatives at the Leipzig Frühjahrsmesse (Spring Trade Fair), 1990.
51. "Bankrolling the Rebirth of the East," *Business Week*, 29 April 1991, p. 45.
52. "Geese, Plucked and Drawn," *Wall Street Journal*, 24 April 1991, p. A14.

8

East German Firms in the New Germany

J. Henrike Garkisch

The currency union of 1 July 1990 between the two Germanys catapulted eastern German firms into a difficult situation; many are at present almost certainly doomed. Germany now faces the monumental challenge of transforming the centrally planned economy of the former German Democratic Republic (GDR) into a market economy. For the past forty-five years the state had full control over who produced what for whom at what price. Monopolies were isolated from the pressures of competition, and the state regulated the right to foreign trade. All this has changed. No longer will firms be forced to relinquish their profits to the state. No longer will the state then arbitrarily decide which firms get to benefit from the reinvestment of a portion of these profits.

Firms in eastern Germany must now reorient their thinking toward making decisions based on profit and investments in the larger context of a competitive international marketplace. They will have to relearn every aspect of doing business, from accounting to marketing. For most firms, the task of surviving in the West as members of a discredited and antiquated industrial structure will prove difficult and painful. Their struggle is compounded by their vastly different internal conditions. They lack the focus that firms normally have in a free-market economy.

The government and, indirectly, the electorate can choose to completely do away with the old firms or to rebuild selected ones. In either event, they need to have a thorough understanding of the old firms. The political, economic and social stakes in the rebuilding of eastern German firms are so great that failure to think carefully about these issues would be very costly and even potentially deleterious to the German economy as a whole.

The Currency Union: Implications for Eastern German Firms

Even as the first wave of euphoria swept through the Germanys beginning in November 1989, politicians, bureaucrats, business executives, academics, and others were drawing up plans for the economic and political remaking of the GDR. By late spring 1990, each month brought gloomier news of just how catastrophic its economy really was, and the public in the FRG become more vocal about how this would affect their taxes.

The original plans for an economic union of East and West Germany (devised by the Economics Ministry) called for massive reforms in the GDR to be followed by the introduction of the deutsche mark (DM) there at the end of 1992. The reforms proposed for the GDR were typical of proposals for other Eastern bloc countries switching over to market economies: state subsidies had to be slashed, banking and capital markets had to be established, and possible convertibility of the east mark had to be considered.

Three months after the "fall of the wall," Chancellor Helmut Kohl found himself forced into action much sooner than expected. To the dismay of the many government officials managing the unification efforts, Kohl announced early in February 1990 that he would pursue economic union between the Germanys on a speedier timetable. Painfully aware of the December election, Kohl knew that the political pressures would hardly be diminished by the much-publicized prospect of higher taxes, rising inflation, and the added fallout from economic union. In the other Germany, the daily exodus of more than 2,000 East Germans was already stripping the GDR of all economic hope. Aside from acting on the basis of perceived and real constitutional and political mandates, West German leaders found themselves forced into granting quick aid and promises of more assistance to persuade East Germans to stay at home instead of flooding into West Germany by the thousands. Around 85,000 people had arrived by mid-February 1990, joining 343,000 who had arrived in 1989.

The announcement of the currency union to be established 1 July 1990 was made on 12 April, and was greeted with mixed reactions throughout the Germanys. A formal currency union between the two states would be a de facto economic union. Difficult questions about how and at what rate 170 billion GDR marks would be exchanged had seemed merely hypothetical weeks before, but they soon became the issue of the moment. For the GDR, the decision was almost entirely at the discretion of West Germans. The basic debate was between Kohl's desire, on the one hand, to placate the East Germans by converting their marks to deutsche marks at a 1:1 ratio, and the Bundesbank's overriding interest on the other to control inflation by converting at a much lower rate. In the end, it was agreed that individuals would be able to exchange up to 4,000 DM (children less, pensioners more) at a 1:1 ratio. Prices and wages were to be converted at the same rate, and debts would be converted at 2:1.

Although the precise fate of wages, prices, industries, and a host of social issues was then uncertain, there was little doubt that the East German economy would collapse after the currency union. Productivity in East Germany was less than half of that in West Germany, and its goods had little appeal in the marketplace. Also, industrial subsidies were to be stopped immediately after the currency union. In anticipation of the collapse of the East German economy, the West German government would either have to prepare for a flood of refugees or need to help to reorganize the East German economy.

In the wake of the currency union, the East German government divided regional ventures and the 170 *Kombinate*, state-owned conglomerates, into units resembling Western firms. More than 8,000 "firms" emerged from this process and passed into the ownership of an independent government agency called the Treuhandanstalt, whose mandate was to privatize the East German firms and to do so quickly.

The East German economy had, by most accounts, been the most successful of the Eastern bloc economies. Although inefficient and problem-riddled, it was not the fiasco that, for instance, the Polish economy had become by 1989. Many people were therefore hopeful, in 1989 and early 1990, that, with extensive initial aid from West Germany, many of the firms would be salvageable.

Defining East German Business Entities and Their Environment

The East German Firm

Firms in a market economy consist of owners, management, and labor. The firm also has obligations to other entities, including the government and creditors, but these entities do not normally take part in the basic decisions of the firm. Owners usually invest in a firm for the purpose of earning a profit. Management is obliged to represent the interests of the owners in the day-to-day operations. Labor acts to maximize its own return from the firm, sometimes in cooperation with management. This basic structure determines the motivations of most actors in for-profit firms. This basic structure is absent in many eastern German firms.

The Communist ideal posits state ownership of firms. The state was to represent the interests of all citizens, to whom the firms belonged in theory. Management was responsible for meeting the goals set by the government. Labor's interest was theoretically represented by the state, since the state and labor were, again in theory, seen as one and the same.

As one Communist regime after another crumbles, the issue of ownership is proving much more difficult to resolve in practice than it was to explain in theory. Resolving who owns the means of production in the former GDR is a difficult social and political issue; as long as the question remains unresolved, the survival of these firms is unlikely. The issue of ownership was muddled when the currency union was moved up several months before the actual unification of the two Germanys occurred on 3 October 1990. Only after the political union could investors be assured that their investments would fall under the laws of the Federal Republic of Germany (FRG) defining private property.

Before the question of ownership was resolved these firms would continue to flounder, even as wards of the Treuhandanstalt. Similarly, management's role of serving the interests of the owners in the day-to-day operations is muddied. The Treuhandandstalt, initially with a staff of around one thousand, could offer only minimal guidance to the firms as it searched for investors to buy them.

Privatization, the key to resolving the ownership issue, has proceeded less smoothly than had been hoped. Funds were grossly insufficient; by mid-1990 the Treuhandanstalt had met only 41 percent of the credits for which firms in need had applied. In addition, there were allegations that the agency had favored former Communist officials at the expense of new entrepreneurs.

Business Challenges of East German Firms

Since 1974 the East German economic policy was one of *Abgrenzung*, or of making its economy completely self-sufficient. The economy was heavily oriented toward industry, as were all the Eastern bloc economies. Two-thirds of the economy's industry had been in manufacturing, energy, and mining. One-third of all products were exported, mostly to COMECON countries.[1] The success of individual firms in the market economy would depend not only on the health of the business sector in which they were involved but also on the ability of the employees to adapt to a market economy by meeting the demands of the market.

Demand. Demand for products from East Germany decreased radically after July 1990 for two reasons.[2] First, Eastern consumers dramatically changed their buying habits when Western goods became available to them. Some GDR food-production facilities, for instance of chocolates and other sweets, were forced to shut down production before the currency union because demand collapsed when West German confections entered the market. Poor-quality East German products were responsible for this shift in consumer behavior. Moreover, many of East Germany's initial capital and consumer needs could largely be met by the previously idle capacity of West German firms. The second reason that demand fell was that many of the COMECON markets were collapsing as well. In the face of ruble inconvertibility, the Soviet Union could no longer afford to purchase many East German products for hard currency. Also, Eastern Europe and the Soviet Union, faced with having to make hard-currency purchases in East Germany, could choose higher-quality products at comparable prices in the West. The demand for steel from the state-owned eastern German steel producer, for instance, fell dramatically in 1990; its products were three times as costly as those of West German firms.[3]

With short warning, East German firms were thrust into competition with firms that could produce better products at lower prices. Many were faced for the first time with the bewildering task of setting prices that reflected the costs of and demand for their goods. They found themselves completely mismatched with their new marketplace; the firms were individual units composing a massive structural industrial imbalance in eastern Germany.

Inputs. Even during the best of times, shortages had frustrated both factory line workers and consumers in the GDR. Many East German producers depended on the Soviet Union and other COMECON countries for raw materials, which were obtained through barter. This barter system was fundamentally disturbed when East German firms began to sell their products for hard currency. In addition, the East German supply of human capital was eroded by the massive outmigration of workers both before and after unification. Many young, skilled workers left their positions in the East for promises of greater security and wealth in the West. Finally, the capital investment needs of many East German firms were enormous.

By the late 1980s the East German economy was nearly hobbled by the condition of its industrial infrastructure. The last major capital investments had been made in the 1970s, and the factories had been slowly crumbling. The environment had suffered catastrophic damage, and additional investments would be required to prevent further environmental harm. Many firms operated with outmoded technology, crumbling physical infrastructure, and low morale. The firms themselves did not have the means to invest in themselves. The decision to invest had previously been the state's, and it would now fall to the new owners. For some investors, the condition of the physical plants made investment unthinkable.

Regulation. While many West Germans recognized that standards in East German industry could not immediately equal those in the West, the government found the environmental standards of some Eastern firms too abysmal to support under any costs. The environmental burden, more than any other, would likely doom much of East Germany's heaviest, dirtiest industry.

Of course there are a myriad of other types of regulations, and exceptions to them, with which the firms will have to comply. Increasingly, these regulations will originate not only in Germany but also in the offices of the European Community.

These "normal" business challenges alone would be enough to assign many of these decrepit firms to the dustbin of economic history. Combined with the fundamental problems of internal definition, these challenges to profitable business are in most cases insurmountable without massive outside help.

Policy-Making and the Demise of East German Firms

In late June 1990 the *New York Times* observed that a number of predictions were accompanying the anticipated currency union: "Forecasts of what this might wreak run the gamut from dire predictions of widespread unemployment and social upheaval to prophesies of a second 'German miracle,' an economic boom fed by the injection of 16 million more hungry, hard-driving Germans into the powerhouse West German economy."[4] Theo Waigel, the West German minister of finance, claimed with a marked lack of exuberance that "no one could forecast the effects of the economic, currency and social union of the two Germanys."[5]

The West and East German governments ran the risk of, in essence, signing the death warrant of East German industry when they agreed to the form and timing of their currency union. The new German government implicitly accepted some of the responsibility for managing the economic catastrophe that would undoubtedly follow the currency union. Massive unemployment in the East would be politically, economically, and socially unacceptable in the East and West alike.

Gerhard Pohl, East German economics minister, had estimated that 30 percent of firms making the transition from planned to market economy would be able to compete, 50 percent would need major changes to survive, and 20 percent would go bankrupt.[6] Given the first appalling economic indicators, Pohl's estimates will probably turn out to have been optimistic.

By mid-1990, 60,000 new firms had been established in East Germany. West German economics minister Helmut Haussman predicted that 100,000 more would be established within the next six months, and that this would result in 100,000 new jobs.[7] Industrial production, though, fell by more than 15 percent in June and by more than 40 percent in July 1990. The East German GNP shrank by more than 4 percent in the first six months of 1990.[8] Prior to the currency union, Bonn had estimated that unemployment would reach a maximum of 440,000 by late 1990 in East Germany. Official unemployment figures had already reached a level of 223,000 in the first two weeks after the monetary union, and unemployment predictions for early 1991 were revised to 1 million or more.[9] Dietmar Mueller of the East German Economics Ministry warned in 1990 that of eastern Germany's 9 million workers, 3 million could expect to lose their jobs.[10]

While there was much interest in establishing new firms in eastern Germany and this offered the long-term prospect of employment opportunities, the old firms still formed the major part of the economy. Formulating policies for these "old" firms would prove to be a large undertaking.

Eastern Germany is not making a "fresh start"; rather, it is desperately trying to build on the still-smoldering ruins of the past. All the Eastern European countries face a vast array of burdens from their past, including trade commitments to other economically and politically floundering members of what was COMECON, environmental catastrophes, large numbers of former Communists who may be vital to any economic rebuilding effort, and the privatization of state property whose ownership is still an open question. Resolving the issues of the past would make policy formation for eastern German firms a challenge of unknown dimensions.

The government was forced into accepting the role of taking preliminary responsibility for running the East German firms and of figuring out what to do with them. The government's concern is not, of course, primarily the well-being of the firms. Rather, it is interested in seeing its macroeconomic goals met, including low unemployment, a solid tax base, and minimal inflation. Since the government provides welfare of some sort to unemployed Germans and suffers the political consequences of unemployment and the economic consequences of supporting a large group of people not contributing to the country's economy, the government maintains an active interest in the fate of the eastern firms.

Perhaps the easiest cases of privatization are those of approximately 12,000 smaller firms that were nationalized after 1972. Half of these firms had already been reprivatized by July 1990. These were offered to their former owners for sale. The more than 8,000 firms produced by the breakup of the large state-owned conglomerates (and which employed 5.5 million of eastern Germany's 9 million workers) would be much more difficult to privatize.

Although, as we have seen, the government quickly established an agency, the Treuhandanstalt, to keep the firms afloat by providing credit and to sell them to private investors, the government still sets the basic parameters that determine the future of these firms. The Treuhandanstalt is completely dependent on the government for financing and for the precise definition of its mandate. It cannot significantly alter the general macroeconomic setting of western Germany or Europe, nor can it alone determine the country's industrial policy. The Treuhandanstalt was initially charged mainly with finding buyers for the firms and trying to make estimates of the real value of the firms.

Proclaiming initial estimates of $400 billion in sales of firms, the Treuhandanstalt had by April 1991 privatized fewer than 100 larger companies and about half of the smaller ones for a sum of DM 9 billion.[11] Clearly, the initial value estimates had to be revised and the premises reevaluated.

The fate of old and new firms in eastern Germany is of crucial importance to the level of public-sector spending that can be maintained in the years to come. This spending is vital to infrastructure development such as telecommunications, power, and transportation facilities, which is of great importance in attracting investment, and to the provision of social services, especially to the unemployed. Before 1990 the East German state raised 75 percent of its revenues by taxing the state-owned companies; in 1991 these taxes would become corporate profit taxes.[12] Since the level of tax revenue from firms would sink dramatically as firms entered the market economy, alternate sources of revenue for government spending would be necessary. The West Germans would be needed to help in the bailout. Although Kohl had promised no new taxes and assumed that the costs of unification would be covered by the revenue generated by increased economic growth, he was forced to publicly change his policies by 1991.

Before November 1989 West Germany was already spending DM 5 billion per year on its relationship with East Germany.[13] Future assistance levels can be expected to be many times this amount. Predictions run as high as a total of more than DM 500 billion.[14] Estimates of direct capital required from government banks and businesses for the former GDR range from $10 billion and up.[15] Between January and mid-February 1990, the West German government had doubled the sum it allotted for aid to East Germany and other East European countries to $4.9 billion. This sum represented deficit spending for West Germany and was financed through government borrowing; in 1990 $70 billion in bonds were sold to create funds to help eastern Germany rebuild. The sum may be expected to grow dramatically. By June 1990 the estimates of the cost of unification through 1991 had reached $69 billion; in September 1990 the cost estimates had already jumped to $104 billion.[16] In 1990 the German budget deficit had exploded from the $11.3 billion budget deficit Bonn had posted in 1989 to more than $70 billion.[17] The German government began in 1991 to look toward tax increases in the western part of the country to finance the further spending.

Just as vital as the sums of money that will flow from western to eastern Germany, though, will be the rate at which the ownership of the old eastern German firms is defined. Those aspects of the firms that may make them attractive to Westerners, such as access to Eastern markets, diminishes as the firms race toward financial disaster.

Politicians and voters could only guess at the impact the decision for a quick monetary and political union of the two Germanys would have on the survival of firms in eastern Germany. Clearly the union was to represent a step into the unknown and many factors contributed to the decision. The ultimate impact on the firms of the former GDR will be felt throughout all of Germany for some time to come.

Notes

1. Ferdinand Protzman, "Germany's Speed on Unity Is Impelled by Slide in East," *New York Times*, 7 August 1990, p. A7.
2. "Into the Vortex," *Economist*, 30 June 1990, p. 6, Survey.
3. Barbara Rudolph and James Graff, "The Big Merger," *Time*, 9 July 1990, p. 77.
4. Serge Schmemann, "Warily, East Germany Stores Itself Away," *New York Times*, 27 June 1990, p. A1.
5. "Hard Times Discounted," *New York Times*, 27 June 1990, p. A4.
6. "Industrial Waste," *Economist*, 30 June 1990, p. 12, Survey.
7. Serge Schmemann, "East Germans Gaze Ahead, Hopefully," *New York Times*, 1 July 1990, p. Y6.
8. Ferdinand Protzman, "Business Shuns a Falling East Germany," *New York Times*, 20 September 1990, p. A1.
9. Ferdinand Protzman, "Germany's Speed on Unity Is Impelled by Slide in East,"*New York Times*, 7 August 1990, p. A7.
10. David Lawday, "Germany Takes a Big Gamble," *U.S. News & World Report*, 2 July 1990, p. 29.
11. "So Much To Do, So Little Time," *Financial Times*, 9 April 1991.
12. Shawn Tully, "Doing Business in One Germany," *Fortune*, 2 July 1990, p. 81.
13. "D-mark Day Dawns," *Economist*, 30 June 1990, p. 4, Survey.
14. "Down the Rapids," *Economist*, 30 June 1989, p. 21, Survey.
15. David Fairlamb, "Bonanza or Boondoggle?" *Institutional Investor* (February 1990), p. 118.
16. John Templeman and William Glasgall, "'Whatever It Costs, We Have No Option'," *Business Week*, 8 October 1990, p. 53.
17. John Rossant and Jonathan Levine, "Kohl Is In a Race Against Time and Money," *Business Week*, 3 December 1990, p. 51.

PART FOUR

New Technologies and Public Policy Issues

9

Private Broadcasting in the Federal Republic of Germany

Barbara Reilly

In contrast to its largely commercial counterpart in the United States, the German broadcasting industry has long been dominated by public broadcasting corporations financed through a combination of users' fees and advertising revenues.[1] While American television programs on privately owned stations—financed solely through advertising revenues—are renowned for their relentless commercial interruptions, the public broadcasting corporations in Germany are permitted to advertise only in "blocks" between programs for a total of twenty minutes per day.[2] In addition, German public programming is subject to review by supervisory boards, whose members are drawn from different fields and ideally represent the most significant elements of the entire demographic spectrum (i.e., educators, representatives of the various religious denominations, unions, industry, and political parties).[3] These supervisory bodies are designed to ensure balanced programming, in which all significant societal groups have a chance to air their views, or, at least, to have their concerns and interests addressed.[4]

Prior to 1981 private broadcasting was virtually unknown in the Federal Republic of Germany. In that year, for the first time in Germany's postwar history, the Federal Constitutional Court (Bundesverfassungsgericht) recognized the right of the individual states, or *Länder*, to grant broadcasting licenses to private companies.[5] Advertising revenues were to be the sole source of financing for the commercial broadcasters.[6] Although not permitted to share the users' fees with the public stations, the commercial broadcasters were also not required to adhere to the strict programming standards governing their public competitors.[7]

From the start, commercial broadcasters were relegated to cable and satellite transmission, based on the widely held belief that the frequencies required for terrestrial (airwave) transmission were extremely scarce and thus could not satisfy the needs of public broadcasters, the military, and commercial broadcasters simultaneously.[8] Although additional terrestrial frequencies were subsequently "discovered," they could not satisfy the demands of all would-be broadcasters. Thus, the greatest possibility of expansion for the private broadcasters continues to be in the field of cable and satellite transmission.

German broadcasting over the last ten years has been tumultuous. While public broadcasters have attempted (often unsuccessfully) to protect the best piece of the broadcasting pie for themselves (e.g., "global contracts" for sporting events), commercial broadcasters have been seeking access to terrestrial transmission or any other means of capturing a share of the public broadcasters' audience. During this period, the Federal Constitutional Court has recognized the existence of a "dual system" of broadcasting in which even the commercial broadcasters have a responsibility to provide a minimum level of programming quality. The precise definition of this responsibility, however, continues to evolve in recent Court decisions.

This chapter will discuss the recent developments in German broadcasting against a backdrop of Federal Constitutional and High Court decisions that opened the way for commercial involvement in radio and television and continue to mold these commercial participants' role in the German broadcasting industry.

History and Structure of the German Broadcasting Industry

Since its inception in 1923, German broadcasting has been subject to state oversight and, during certain periods, to state control.[9] The necessity of state supervision of the broadcasting media (which also exists in the United States through government agencies such as the Federal Communications Commission) follows naturally from the belief that a broadcasting license enables one to influence public opinion through the rapid dissemination of information and opinion to a large viewing (or listening) audience. By the same token, broadcasters fulfill certain "public functions," such as news broadcasting, thereby justifying state oversight.

During the Weimar Republic (1919–1933), the German broadcasting industry was made up of eight regional private companies.[10] Private companies were permitted to broadcast chiefly because the *Länder* did not have the financial means to produce their own programming.[11] In 1925 these regional companies were merged into the Reichsrundfunkgesellschaft (RRG).[12] The Reichspost (National Post Office) acquired 51 percent of RRG's shares and the remaining 49 percent were kept in private hands until 1932, when the private shares were transferred to the *Länder*.[13] One year later, the RRG was integrated into the Propaganda Ministry (Reichsministerium für Volksaufklärung und Propaganda),[14] and broadcasting became a tool of the government.

After the war, the occupying powers took control of all broadcasting media.[15] Decentralized public broadcasting corporations modeled after the British Broadcasting Corporation (BBC) were established to ensure that radio and television, rather than serving the interests of the government, be placed at the disposal of society at large.[16] The American model of predominantly private broadcasters was out of the question in the newly established and still war-ravaged Federal Republic.[17]

The postwar developments set the stage for the gradual evolution of the German broadcasting industry as it exists today. At present there are nine regional public broadcasting corporations in western Germany (Landesrundfunkanstalten), governed by the laws of the individual *Länder* and treaties among them.[18] The regional corporations are linked together in the Standing Conference of German Public Law Broadcasting Corporations (Arbeitsgemeinschaft der öffentlich-rechtlichen Rundfunkanstalten Deutschlands [ARD]).[19] Together, the regional broadcasters produce broadcasting shown nationwide on the first television channel (Erstes Deutsches Fernsehen). They also produce regional television programs, normally seen on the third television channel, and count among their members the two radio broadcasting corporations, Deutsche Welle (Voice of Germany) and Deutschlandfunk, established under federal law.[20] There is, in addition, a second television channel (Zweites Deutsches Fernsehen [ZDF]), which is produced by the *Länder* and broadcast nationwide.[21]

The ZDF evolved in its present form as the result of a 1961 Federal Constitutional Court decision, which clearly established the *Länders'* ultimate responsibility in the broadcasting realm.[22] Prior to this decision, the federal government, under Chancellor Konrad Adenauer, had attempted to establish a second television channel, under federal law, to compete with the regional public broadcasting corporations.[23] Because the Basic Law does not expressly vest the *Länder* with responsibility for broadcasting, the federal government reasoned that it would be acting within its concurrent powers in establishing a broadcasting facility.[24]

The Federal Constitutional Court ruled that the federal government's actions were a constitutional infringement of the *Länders'* reserved powers.[25] According to Article 30 of the Basic Law: "the exercise of government powers and the discharge of government functions shall be incumbent on the *Länder* in so far as this Basic Law does not otherwise prescribe or permit." The Court reasoned that broadcasting, long a government, or "public," function in Germany, was clearly within the competence of the *Länder*. Given that this competence had not been exclusively entrusted to the federal government, the federal government was not authorized to establish a broadcasting corporation without the involvement of the *Länder*.[26] Shortly thereafter, ZDF was organized pursuant to an agreement among the *Länder*.[27]

The public broadcasting corporations are supervised by advisory boards composed of representatives of Germany's most significant political, social, and religious groups.[28] Representatives of the Catholic and Protestant churches, the major political parties, union and employer organizations, newspaper publishers, journalists, and educators are among those making up the ZDF television council.[29] The councils of the ARD member stations are similarly organized. Council members confer on program content in their attempts to arrive at a balanced program offering.[30]

The Federal Constitutional Court reaffirmed the necessity of these councils in its first television decision in 1961.[31] Owing to the scarcity of frequencies and the tremendous start-up and fixed costs associated with broadcasting, market access was seen as necessarily restricted and safeguards as especially important in assuring the constitutionally guaranteed freedom of expression.[32]

The Arrival of Private Broadcasters on the German Broadcasting Scene

Private broadcasters did not arrive on the scene in postwar Germany until 1981. In that year, the Federal Constitutional Court ruled that a Saarland law allowing for the granting of broadcasting licenses to private companies did not, in principle, violate the Basic Law.[33] While conceding that private companies are entitled to broadcast, the court outlined a series of safeguards to ensure "pluralism" as well as balanced and impartial programming.[34] The court distinguished between *Binnenpluralismus* (internal pluralism) and *Aussenpluralismus* (external pluralism), the former requiring that the channel itself present a full spectrum of program offerings from differing perspectives and the latter allowing the channel to represent one particular perspective as long as other competing stations with complementary views can ensure diversity.[35]

In 1986, the court indicated that private broadcasters were subject to less stringent standards in making programming decisions than the public broadcasting corporations and that the program offerings of the private broadcasters could properly be examined under an "external pluralism" test.[36]

In a recent decision concerning the broadcasting law of North Rhine–Westphalia, however, the Federal High Court ruled that the *Länder* can require private broadcasters to conform to the internal pluralism standard as long as such conformity does not significantly hinder or threaten the existence of the private broadcasters.[37]

In the wake of the court's 1981 decision, the *Länder* negotiated and, in 1987, enacted a new broadcasting treaty (*Rundfunkstaatsvertrag*) allowing for the establishment of private broadcasting companies to compete with the public stations. Up until the time this "enabling" legislation was enacted in 1987, private broadcasters had failed to assert a significant presence on the German broadcasting scene.[38] In addition to the significant capital costs entailed in broadcasting, two obstacles prevented the large-scale entry of private broadcasters into the German broadcasting market. First, because airwaves do not offer unlimited capacity, satellite and cable transmission were the only viable alternatives to terrestrial transmission. However, the success of these technologies depends on the viewers' willingness to incur the additional expense associated with them. This inclination did not seem especially strong in German households until quite recently.[39]

A second obstacle to private companies' entry into the broadcasting market has been the defensive maneuvers undertaken by the public broadcasting corporations to prevent private companies from gaining a foothold in the television market.[40] An analysis of both of these obstacles is necessary to obtain an understanding of the current state of German broadcasting.

Terrestrial, Cable, and Satellite Transmission

Upon taking over power in 1982, the Christian Democratic Union (CDU) government pledged to take steps to encourage private broadcasting in Germany.[41] The Deutsche Bundespost (Federal Post Office and telecommunications authority), under the leadership of Christian Schwarz-Schilling (long an advocate of investment in the new technologies), pushed full steam ahead on its ambitious cable-laying project, in which a total of DM 1.5 billion were to be invested annually by the Bundespost, starting in 1983, for the installation of wideband cable.[42]

Apparently, the Bundespost failed to consider the proclivities of its potential cable subscribers until after thousands of meters of cable had already been laid. The West German television viewer, it seemed, already burdened with annual user fees for television and radio, was largely unwilling to part with even more marks for cable hookup, monthly cable fees, or cable-compatible television sets. In many cities more than 60 percent of the cables laid were never hooked up to individual homes or apartments.[43] Thus, initially, the cabling effort was somewhat of a fiasco. The last two years, however, have seen an increase in the number of cable hookups in the old western *Länder*.[44] The five new eastern *Länder* have also contributed significantly to this upward trend.[45]

In addition to its cabling effort, the Bundespost undertook a search for new terrestrial high frequencies in conjunction with the Bavarian Media Agency.[46] On the one hand, high frequencies have a limited range of transmission, which is disadvantageous for large-scale advertising.[47] On the other, the limited transmission range allows one frequency to be distributed among several broadcasters in close proximity to one another.[48]

As a result of this search, one or two unused terrestrial frequencies were discovered in almost every mid- to large-sized German city—a total of approximately seventy channels in all.[49] The new frequencies were, of course, hotly contested among the various applicants. Among the private companies, two had emerged as frontrunners: RTL plus and SAT 1.[50] Both of these stations argued that it was not economically feasible to broadcast from a few cities. Nationwide broadcasting capacity would be necessary to assure advertising proceeds sufficient to cover their high fixed costs.[51] The notion of sharing a station with other broadcasters was also rejected out of hand because it would lead to a "splintered" station image.[52] By and large, the newly discovered terrestrial stations have gone mainly to the two largest private competitors: RTL plus and SAT 1.[53]

RTL plus is a German-language television station broadcast from Luxembourg.[54] Originally terrestrially transmitted, RTL plus has been transmitted by satellite (European Communication Satellite [ECS]) and cable since 28 August 1985.[55] The station can now be seen throughout western Germany.[56] Bertelsmann AG, the world's largest media concern, has a 38 percent share in RTL plus through its subsidiary Ufa Film und Fernsehen GmbH.[57] Forty-six percent of RTL plus's shares are held by the Compagnie Luxembourgeoise de Télédiffusion.[58]

SAT 1 was the first private German satellite TV station. It was also first transmitted by the ECS on 1 January 1985.[59] Several powerful publishing personalities and production companies hold SAT 1's shares, including Leo Kirsch (40 percent through his company PKS), AV Euromedia (a subsidiary of Holtzbrinck Publishing House, with 15 percent of the shares), the newspaper consortium APF, and the Springer AG (holding 15 percent of the shares directly and 15 percent indirectly).[60]

Several smaller broadcasters have also emerged in the last several years. These include Tele 5, in which Tele München GmbH, CLT, the Italian Berlusconi Group, and the Capital Cities, an American broadcasting company, are shareholders.[61] In addition, Pro 7 has emerged as the successor of Eureka TV.[62] Forty-nine percent of its shares are owned by Leo Kirsch's son, Thomas Kirsch.[63]

Maximum advertising time for all private companies broadcasting in Germany is 20 percent of their daily broadcast time.[64] Generally, the private broadcasters have no internal supervisory council; however, they are subject to the supervision of the broadcasting authorities of the *Länder* in which they broadcast.[65]

To a greater or lesser extent, the private broadcasters' success depends on the acceptance of new technologies in Germany. Although a few of the larger private companies have managed to secure a place for themselves on the terrestrial airwaves, most have not been so fortunate. The future of smaller and medium-sized private broadcasting is tied to the development of satellite and cable capabilities—a slow-going process whose chances of success have only begun to look positive in the last few years.

Defensive Maneuvers of the Public Broadcasters

For the few private broadcasters who have made it to the big leagues (e.g., RTL plus and SAT 1), additional hurdles must be overcome before they can consider their positions somewhat secure. The public broadcasters, long entrenched as monopolists, or "cooperating oligopolists," in the German broadcasting market, had secured various "rights" for themselves over the years, which they attempted to retain even after the genesis of private broadcasting. One such "royal prerogative" was their right of first refusal for virtually all major sporting events taking place in Germany.[66]

In September 1985 the public broadcasting corporations entered into a so-called global contract with the top sports leagues in the Deutscher Sportbund (DSB). The contract gave ZDF and ARD the first shot at all national sporting events involving certain DSB members (and several nonmembers) in exchange for a lump-sum payment.[67] Sporting events not chosen by the public stations could then be offered to the various private bidders.[68] The public broadcasters were given up to five days before the scheduled event, however, to determine whether they would air that event.[69]

The Federal Cartel Office (Bundeskartellamt) ruled that the global contract violated section 18 of the German antitrust law by restricting the DSB members from determining how best to exploit their wares—in this case, sports programming.[70] The sports leagues were forced, under the terms of the contract, to first offer their programming to the public broadcasters, even where a higher bidder existed elsewhere. The decision of the Cartel Office was upheld by the Appellate Court (Kammergericht).[71] This decision was, in turn, in all major aspects affirmed by the Federal High Court (Bundesgerichtshof) in 1990.[72]

The global contract case was significant in several respects. First, it placed the public broadcasting corporations on the same footing as private broadcasters with respect to program procurement. No longer could ARD and ZDF hide their anticompetitive procurement practices behind a "public function" mask. Second, it established the authority of the Federal

Cartel Office to take steps against the public broadcasters for abuse of their economic power to the detriment of their private competitors. According to the Federal High Court, such federal intervention is not in conflict with the broadcasting authority of the *Länder*.[73]

Conclusion

The introduction of private companies into the German broadcasting market was surprisingly arduous in a country otherwise quite accustomed to healthy competition. Unlike the United States, where just about every industry is fair game for competition, Germans appeared apprehensive about full-scale, survival-of-the-fittest competition in broadcasting, especially television broadcasting. Thus it comes as no great surprise that private broadcasters in Germany are tightly restricted with respect to advertising time and program content requirements. The acceptance of the Federal Constitutional and High Courts of content-quality standards for private broadcasters suggests an unwillingness to let the market alone decide what is worth watching and what is not. The limits placed on advertising time even on private stations indicate that Germans are unwilling to open the floodgates to excessive advertising.

Whether or not competition between public and private broadcasters will ultimately benefit the viewing public remains to be seen. It seems clear, however, that the right of private broadcasters to exist alongside their public competitors is no longer a subject of controversy. Not only have the private broadcasters won the support of the courts and, to some extent, the legislature, but their popularity among viewers also seems to be increasing.

To the extent that viewers had hoped for rejuvenating competition between the new private broadcasters and the print media, there is bound to be some disappointment. Due to the high costs of establishing a broadcasting facility, many of the most prominent names in the German press and publishing fields, among them Bertelsmann and Axel Springer, are now exerting their influence in the newly established private broadcasting corporations. The presence of so many big names among the shareholders of the two leading private broadcasters have raised eyebrows and caused some concern that the concentration so evident in the print media field is extending its domain to private broadcasting.

The advertising limitations and content-quality standards imposed on Germany's private broadcasters make clear that, despite the introduction of private broadcasters, the German broadcasting industry will not follow in the footsteps of its counterpart in the United States. This thought is met with a sigh of relief by many a German and, perhaps, even an American or two.

Notes

1. See Wernhard Möschel, "Merger Control in Broadcasting in Germany," *World Competition* 13, no. 7 (1990): 69, at 71. Users' fees are the predominant form of financing for the public broadcasting corporations in Germany. The total revenue for ARD in 1988, for example, was DM 4.525 billion. Users' fees, paid annually by all owners of radios and televisions, accounted for DM 3.6 billion in proceeds in that year. DM 925 million was collected from television advertisers. The 1988 revenues for ZDF amounted to DM 1.521 billion. DM 873 million of that amount was drawn from users' fees and the remainder from advertising revenues (id., at 71).

2. *Rundfunkstaatsvertrag* (Broadcasting Treaty) of 3 April 1987, Article 3(3), reprinted in W. D. Ring, Medienrecht, looseleaf service (Munich: Franz Rehm Verlag, 1988), C-0.1 at 3.

3. See Federal Constitutional Court (Bundesverfassungsgericht) Decision (BVerfGE) 12, 1961, 205, at 261–63; NJW (*Neue Juristische Wochenschrift*) 1961, 547, at 553.

4. According to the Federal Constitutional Court, Article 5 of the Basic Law (guaranteeing freedom of expression) requires that all significant societal groups have some influence in determining program content and that the program contain some minimal level of fairness, impartiality, and reciprocal respect (for others' viewpoints).

5. BVerfGE 57, 1981, 295; NJW 1981, 1774.

6. See BVerfGE 73, 1986, 118 at 154. See also Gemeinsame Richtlinie der Landesmedienanstalten zur Durchführung der Werberegelung des Rundfunkstaatsvertrages vom 10. November 1988, reprinted in *DLM Jahrbuch* 1989/90, published by the Landesmedienanstalten (München: 1990), at 335.

7. BVerfGE 73, 1986, 118 at 155. See also Kübler, Die neue Rundfunkordnung: Marktstruktur und Wettbewerbsbedingungen, NJW 1987, at 2961.

8. W. Gellner, *Ordnungspolitik im Fernsehwesen* (Frankfurt: Peter Lang GmbH, 1990) at 43.

9. Ring, Medienrecht, supra n. 2, C-0.4 at 2.1.

10. Ibid.

11. Ibid.

12. Ibid. See also Gellner, *Ordnungspolitik*, at 29.

13. Ring, Medienrecht, C-0.4 at 2.1. Gellner, *Ordnungspolitik*, at 31.

14. Ibid.

15. Ring, Medienrecht; Gellner, *Ordnungspolitik*, at 35.

16. Ring, Medienrecht, 2, C-0.4 at 2.1; Gellner, *Ordnungspolitik*, at 36.

17. Ibid.

18. See Rundfunkstaatsvertrag, 3 April 1987, supra n. 2, C-0.1 at 1. The five new *Länder* (Saxony, Saxony-Anhalt, Brandenburg, Mecklenburg-Vorpommern, and Thuringia) resulting from Germany's unification are now forming regional public broadcasting corporations based on the West German model. The exact number of such corporations is not yet clear, given that several (of the relatively small) new *Länder* will almost certainly merge their broadcasting facilities. *DLM Jahrbuch* 1989/90, supra note 6, at 17.

19. See P. Schiwy and W. Schutz, *Rundfunkrecht* (Neuwied: Luchterhand Verlag, 1977) at 159.

20. The constitutionality of these two federally established radio broadcasting corporations is still a subject of some debate. The federal government based its authority in establishing the two radio corporations—both of which are broadcast outside of Germany—on its foreign affairs powers. The *Länder* have never challenged the establishment of these corporations in court. Id. n. 19.

21. See Gellner, *Ordnungspolitik*, at 40-41.

22. BVerfGE 12, 1961, 205; NJW 1961, at 547.

23. Ring, Medienrecht, C-0.4 at 6.

24. The Basic Law, ratified by the *Länder* of the Federal Republic of Germany in May 1949, provides the guiding legal principles with which all legislation and jurisprudence must conform. Ring, *Medienrecht*, C-0.4 at 6.

25. BVerfGE 12, 1961, at 243; NJW 1961, at 549.

26. Ibid.

27. Schiwy and Schutz, *Rundfunkrecht*. The establishment of ZDF was agreed by all the *Länder* in the Staatsvertrag from 1961.

28. See Rundfunkstaatsvertrag, Article 8 (1). See also Gellner, *Ordnungspolitik*, at 64-67.

29. Gellner, *Ordnungspolitik*.

30. Ibid.

31. BVerfGE 12, 1961, at 261-263; NJW 1961, at 553. This was the same decision in which the court ruled on the constitutionality of the federally established broadcaster which led to the establishment of ZDF.

32. Ibid.

33. BVerfGE 57, 1981, 295; NJW 1981, at 1774.

34. BVerfGE 57, 1981, at 324-26; NJW 1981, at 1776.

35. BVerfGE 57, 1981, at 325; NJW 1981, at 1777. See also Gellner, *Ordnungspolitik*, at 45.

36. BVerfGE 73, 1986, 118 at 159.

37. Decision reported in NJW 1991, 899, at 905. The North Rhine–Westphalian law required internal pluralism in private broadcasters' programming, albeit at a somewhat lesser standard than that required of the public broadcasting corporation for North Rhine–Westphalia. Id. at 905.

38. *DLM Jahrbuch* 1989/90, supra note 6, at 53. At the time the broadcasting treaty was ratified in 1987, the public broadcasting stations held 90 percent of the market share in homes where private broadcasters could only be received terrestrially (i.e., noncabled homes).

39. Interestingly, the new eastern *Länder* have shown a much greater interest in satellite and cable television than their fellow citizens in western Germany. Of 6.2 million households owning televisions in the former German Democratic Republic, approximately 3.2 million (about 53 percent) receive cable or satellite transmissions. In certain areas, for instance, New Brandenburg, almost 100 percent of the homes are cabled. *DLM Jahrbuch* 1989/90, supra note 6, at 18.

40. See Decision of the 6th Decision Division of the Bundeskartellamt re: global contract case, 1986.

41. Ring, *Medienrecht*, C-0.4 at 23. See also Gellner, *Ordnungspolitik*, at 206.
42. Ibid.
43. At the end of June 1989, for instance, 12.6 of the 25 million households with televisions in former West Germany were *anschließbar* (capable of being hooked up), whereas only 5.2 million households were *angeschlossen* (actually hooked up). Working Paper of the Federal Cartel Office for a session of the Working Group on Antitrust Law held on 3 and 4 October 1989, at 11.
44. As of 30 June 1990 the number of households in former West Germany that could be hooked up had increased to 15 million. 49 percent (7.25 million) of that number were actually hooked up. *DLM Jahrbuch* 1989/90, supra note 6, at 289.
45. See supra note 39.
46. Interview in 1988 with Herrn Nölkensmeier, Federal Cartel Office expert on the German broadcasting industry.
47. Ibid.
48. Ibid.
49. Ibid.
50. See Working Paper, supra note 43, at 9. W. Gellner, supra note 8, at 262.
51. Interview with Herrn Nölkensmeier, supra note 46.
52. Ibid.
53. Working Paper, supra note 43, at 9. W. Gellner, supra note 8, at 262.
54. Working Paper, supra note 43, at 9.
55. See M. J. Kim, Satellitenfernsehen in Europa (Frankfurt: Peter Lang GmbH, 1989) at 70. Since the beginning of 1988, RTL plus can be received terrestrially in a number of *Länder*.
56. See Kabelpilotprojekt und Versuch mit drahtlosem Rundfunk, Zwischenbericht des Kabelrates der Anstalt für Kabelkommunikation (Berlin: 1989) at 106.
57. Working paper, supra note 43, at 9. M. J. Kim, supra note 55, at 71.
58. Ibid.
59. See Kim, supra note 55, at 73. Since 1988, SAT 1 can be received terrestrially in about 2.8 million German households. Id.
60. Kim, supra note 55, at 73. Working Paper, supra note 43, at 9.
61. Kim, supra note 55, at 75–76. Working Paper, supra note 43, at 9.
62. Working Paper, supra note 43, at 9.
63. Ibid.
64. See Rundfunkstaatsvertrag from April 3, 1987, supra note 2, C-0.1 at 5.
65. Those private broadcasters whose programs can be received in several *Länder* are subject to the supervision of the broadcasting authority of one of the *Länder* in which they broadcast. RTL plus, for example, is supervised throughout the Federal Republic of Germany by the Broadcasting Committee for the Land Lower Saxony. *DLM Jahrbuch* 1989/90, supra note 6, at 59.
66. Decision of the Bundeskartellamt, supra note 40, at 6.
67. Ibid.
68. See §2.3 of the Decision of the Bundeskartellamt, supra note 40, at 8.
69. Ibid.
70. Ibid. at 5.

71. Decision of the Appellate Court (Kammergericht), reprinted in Wirtschaft und Wettbewerb/Entscheidungen der Oberlandsgerichte 4267 (WuW/E OLG) 1988.

72. Decision of the Federal High Court from March 14, 1990, No. KVR 4/88, reprinted in NJW 1990, p. 2815.

73. NJW 1990, at 2815.

10

Technology and the Competitive Advantage of Nations: The Case of Biotechnology

Richard W. Morris

In this era of intense economic competition among nations, the process of technology transfer is seen as key.[1] At the heart of this competition is a debate over the proper role of policy in determining the competitive position of nations. U.S. policymakers generally fall into one of two categories: (1) the interventionists, who favor policy to enhance or protect the competitiveness of specific industry sectors, and (2) proponents of laissez-faire, who insist on allowing the forces of free market to shape the destiny of nations, industries, or specific companies. While rejecting industrial policy, the adherents of laissez-faire more willingly advocate policy that maintains the openness of markets (antiprotectionism) and the availability of capital, believing that in an open system the best and strongest will survive.

Recently, this oversimplified dichotomy has given way to reality. Policymakers in the United States are reevaluating their positions in light of the tremendous industrial successes of Germany, Japan, and other developed nations. The increasing movement of newly industrialized nations to compete successfully in "niche" technology or other upscale markets is also being watched. Although Japan's industrial policies have spawned much debate, industrial policy in the Federal Republic of Germany (FRG) is no less significant.

Perhaps for these reasons the German policy on biotechnology—a highly regulated industry with tremendous economic potential—will enhance our understanding of the appropriate role of national industrial policy and the quest for competitive economic advantage. This essay therefore reports on the results of a three-month study on technology transfer in the Federal Republic, particularly on policy and life science R&D as viewed from the perspective of a federal policy-making agency, the Bundesministerium für Forschung und Technology (BMFT, Federal Ministry of Research and Technology). I shall try in this essay to (1) provide an overview of technology transfer in government-sponsored biotechnology research labs and technology-transfer centers, (2) identify general strengths and weaknesses in Germany's current technology-transfer system, (3) compare German technology-transfer practices with those in the United States, and (4) to recommend improvements in the BMFT's policy formulation.

Background

The commercialization of technology is important to the FRG. Within this broad discipline (where many other technologies may be transferred or commercialized) biotechnology poses unique regulatory, proof-of-concept, and scale-up problems in its transition to the marketplace. These problems will undoubtedly become more evident in the 1990s as international competition in the biotechnology industry pits researchers, companies, and even geographic regions against each other.

The FRG is rapidly preparing to address these issues. In a remarkable partnership with industry and regional governments that began in the 1980s, the German government has made consistently large investments to develop research excellence in the biosciences. All indications suggest that the FRG will continue to sustain these investments. The inevitable productivity of bioscientists working with these funds will undoubtedly place pressures on other biotechnology applications vis-à-vis the solution of real-life human problems and the creation of profitable business opportunities. These pressures are already being felt in the regulatory issues affecting recombinant DNA research. But shortly an abundance of commercially relevant biotechnology will soon place demands on Germany's private sector and technology-transfer centers to absorb and exploit these new developments.

In contrast to the country's highly visible, well-trained, and motivated basic research establishment, it is not clear that Germany is equally prepared to transfer its technology. In fact, the FRG's technology-transfer programs, particularly regarding biotechnology, call into question many larger economic and political issues, not the least of which are the regulation of genetic manipulation and animal research and Germany's international role as trading partner.

A Taxonomy of German Technology-Transfer Centers

It is difficult to make generalizations about the technology centers examined in this study because of the variety of services offered and consumed in the process. Borrowing from the U.S. example, however, we can propose a functional "taxonomy" for descriptive and comparative purposes. Most technology transfer centers in the FRG fit into one of four functional categories:

1. Applied or engineering research centers. These centers are devoted to serving the research, testing, and product-development needs of a client through contract research services performed in a disinterested manner with respect to the commercial viability or market performance of a particular product or service. The Fraunhofer Gesellschaft is the best example of this type of center, although the German universities seem to be increasingly willing to perform similar services.

2. Institutional licensing offices. These offices seek to protect the rights of institutions and individual employees vis-à-vis ownership of intellectual properties. They are typically components of university or research institution administration and emphasize the licensing of patents and copyrights. Few of these licensing offices operate on a full-time basis for the purposes of generating revenue for their parent institutions. (In fact, administrators at such institutions believed that to generate revenue from patents and trademarks would result in reductions in the amount of annual federal and state funds that they received.) These institutional licensing offices seemed to be large and well developed at the Kernforschungszentren (Central Research Centers) in Julich and Karlsruhe, but small and less active at other federal laboratories.

3. Consulting or information dissemination offices. These collect or produce economic and technological information and disseminate it for the purposes of economic development and business assistance. As information dissemination centers, these offices often deal with complex technologies and are often the first point of contact for entrepreneurs seeking technology-transfer assistance. However, they typically provide very few services directly to small or newly forming companies. Wirtschaftsförderung Berlin (Berlin Economic Promotion) provides an example of a technologically adept consulting and information dissemination office.

4. Incubators. These are physical facilities devoted to sheltering and providing basic business services at low cost to newly formed firms. The city-affiliated technology centers in Aachen, Heidelberg, and Karlsruhe fit into this category. The services provided are not specifically tailored to the needs of start up or technology based firms, although the facilities managers often attempt to recruit such firms as tenants. A relationship often develops between these "incubators" and local universities, but usually only as result of the proximity of the former to the latter.

Functional Aspects of the German Biotechnology Transfer System

Twenty-one of the thirty-three technology centers surveyed responded to a questionnaire on their technology-transfer activities. They comprised a representative mix of public and private institutions, or offices within institutions, that are responsible for making the results of basic and applied research available for commercial use. The majority of the technology transfer centers responding to the survey (77 percent) were established since 1970, although a sizable number (19 percent) were established between 1940 and 1959. Site visits and interviews revealed that few of these centers devoted themselves exclusively to the commercialization of life sciences research findings, although biotechnology was regarded by many to be of "growing" importance in their daily operations.

More than one half of the technology centers (57 percent) were established independently as not-for-profit or as university and government-affiliated institutions, while the remaining centers were incorporated as a private company, or a Gesellschaft mit beschränkter Haftung (GmbH). Only 14 percent are affiliated exclusively with private firms; the remaining 86 percent are affiliated with federal and state governments, research centers and universities, or with a consortium of governmental, research, and/or industrial institutions. All of the nonprofit technology centers and offices, as well as the few research parks responding to the survey were affiliated with and/or situated within another organization. These "parent" organizations included city governments, universities, national research centers, private management corporations, and nonprofit business service organizations, such as the Industie und Handelskammer (equivalent of the American Chamber of Commerce). Site visits revealed that, owing to the cross-appointments of staff and overlapping purposes and services, these affiliations tended to shape the character and quality of services within the technology centers.

As a group, these technology centers and offices are financed primarily from three sources: state governmental funds, income earned from services to clients, or grants from the Federal Ministry of Research and Technology or another federal agency. On the average, they receive approximately 66 percent of their operating funds from one or a combination of these sources, as well as from unspecified "other sources" which contributed an average of almost 20 percent of the total funds. These technology centers are not likely to earn significant other income from renting office or laboratory space to tenants or from gifts from private foundations, so they are forced to rely on other forms of income. Fewer that 25 percent receive financial support from the Ministry of Economics, while only 30 percent rely on overhead cost recovery to finance their operations.

Few of the technology transfer centers offered what might be considered, by U.S. standards, a complete mix of services for technology development and commercialization. Those services offered most frequently were consulting services and scientific services. The technology-transfer centers said they could broker or refer clients to specific regional economic development promotion, in addition to offering economic policy information and advice as well as patent or licensing consulting. Few offered laboratory or office space to tenants; prototype development and testing services were rare.

According to the responses to the questionnaire, three services were most needed by actual or potential clients of technology centers: consulting or advice about funding opportunities, financial assistance, and scientific support services. Patent and licensing was considered necessary also, but to a lesser degree. Services not requested or considered particularly meaningful were business policy information, rental or lease office and laboratory space, and prototype or testing services. The centers were frequently asked to perform services including data bank development, referrals to contacts in the European Community, contract research, marketing and public relations, venture or seed capital, company formation. The technology centers projected less demand for laboratory and office space and many did not see a role for themselves providing regional economic development support.

Technology-transfer centers therefore appear to play a strong role as information providers. However, on review of the other services not provided, these centers do not appear to be involved in meeting the basic business needs of an operating company. They were unlikely, for example, to provide general services such as bookkeeping support and office rooms for clients. As business services, they tended not to provide legal consulting services or public relations support. Access to special scientific equipment and laboratory space was lacking among the technical support services available at German technology centers.

In written responses, the technology centers and offices identified needs that prevent them from better serving the biotechnology industry in their respective regions:

- technical assistance for screening and evaluating new biotechnology products
- better financial mechanisms (investment) for biotechnology firms
- support in advertising and marketing (for biotechnology firms)
- help in information dissemination and contract negotiation on behalf of biotechnology firms
- help for small firms seeking partners nationally and internationally
- regular exchange of skilled people between universities and industry

Respondents repeatedly identified the need for additional personnel skilled in technology management and for additional funding in specific research fields (e.g., biosensor, downstream processing, and food biotechnology) in order to secure the success of their activities.

Entrepreneurship and the Needs of Small Technology-Based Firms

In the United States, responsibility for bringing new technologies to market often rests with the small entrepreneurial company. Interventionist and laissez-faire advocates alike defend the role of small business as vital to U.S. economic vitality. Yet controversy exists over the financial costs and time requirements of such commercialization efforts, which some see as insurmountable barriers to small, technology-based firms. In view of these concerns, the study paid special attention to the needs of Germany's small and medium enterprises (usually referred to as the *Mittelstand*). Site visits and personal interviews revealed that the *Mittelstand* faces many significant challenges, even though it is reaping certain competition-bolstering benefits.

The Absence of **Ansprechspartner** *(Central Point of Assistance).* Small firms appear to have difficulty working with basic research centers and universities principally because (1) there is no administrator within the university to help them identify needed scientific talent, (2) no reliable assistance is available to develop a technology transfer agreement, and (3) faculty consultants often place a lower priority on consulting for small companies. One of the reasons these small firms need good university contacts is that strong scientific input would have a "credentialing effect" that would hasten the acceptance of their technologies in the marketplace, but the affiliation of small firms to universities and other research institutions is problematic.

Forbidding Regulatory Requirements. A great many of these firms are developing products that will come in direct contact with some facet of the German regulatory system. They perceive themselves as ill-equipped to manage the costs and bureaucratic demands of that system. In one instance, a firm requires help in securing recognition for a new industrial standard that resulted from its product research but that would have broad industrial importance. A small firm cannot typically afford the costs of representation at federal regulatory agencies and consequently depends on governmental contracts to develop its product and obtain governmental approval. In yet another case, product development may be slowed for several months owing to laws requiring public hearings before getting research approved. The complexity of biotechnology regulation has discouraged many of Germany's larger firms and caused the location of new research initiatives outside the FRG. What is less obvious, but of equal significance, is that this regulatory system may be discouraging entrepreneurial activity among university scientists and hindering the formation of small biotechnology companies.

The Need for International Connections. Virtually all of the respondents expressed interest in the development of international contacts that would lead to new product-oriented research relationships and open up new markets for their products. They required contacts both in the United States and elsewhere in Europe. Two things prevented these companies from developing adequate international contacts: (1) the high costs of international travel and communication and (2) the lack of a networker and team builder in the foreign country to help them find the right contacts, thus saving them precious time and money. (The need for international contacts was confirmed by the responses received from the administrators of the German technology centers.)

Additional Management Talent. Many of the firms surveyed lacked adequate management talent to ensure the successful growth and survival of their companies. Few of the company managers understood the biotechnology product approval process and fewer still were able to acquire risk financing and to position their firms competitively against the larger German chemical and pharmaceutical firms. The management of small firms is often troublesome (few scientists and corporate professionals choose entrepreneurial careers); the lack of management talent in the emerging German biotechnology industry is particularly acute.

Vulnerability to Acquisition. Most of the biotechnology firms surveyed were either service providers or single product companies, with the result that they were very dependent on contracts offered by larger German chemical and pharmaceutical firms. Others were the virtual captives of a large German firm that had made an early-stage investment in the firm. Many of the large German firms are confident that they can acquire new products simply through contract relations with these dependent, small firms or through outright acquisition of them. A lack of diversity in the German venture capital industry makes these firms even more likely to depend on or sell a large portion of their stock to larger firms. The combination of these factors causes many small German biotechnology firms to be vulnerable to acquisition and, in general, restricted in the options they have for expansion and diversification.

Strengths and Weaknesses

It is easy to find numerous individual examples where some of the activities required for successful technology transfer are established and working smoothly at German technology transfer centers. The cataloging of technical information, a necessary instrument of technology transfer, is an outstanding service of the Aachen Technology Center and Wirtschaftsförderung Berlin. The Kernforschungszentrum in Julich is an exceptional example of an industrial licensing office. Company formation appears to work well in Heidelberg and Aachen because of the many support organizations located there. The marriage of basic and commercial research appears to be harmonious at the Institute for Microbiology in Göttingen. The coordination of a regional economic development strategy focused on biotechnology, with all the many required strategic alliances, is well under way in Braunschweig, facilitated by the Gesellschaft für Biotechnologische Forschung and Biozentrum. These individual examples notwithstanding, there are opportunities for improvement.

The German government has made significant commitments to research and development in biotechnology that are certain to generate research findings of both scientific and commercial merit, while also serving to train research personnel for the industrial jobs of the future. However, this commitment of research funds to the generation of ideas is not necessarily matched by support at administrative levels and by the training of technology managers and entrepreneurs. The burden of technology transfer still rests with the larger German chemical and pharmaceutical firms.

The *Mittelstand*, an equally strong and essential component of the German economy, is not receiving the same support as the German biotechnology research community. As a rule, these small and medium-sized firms need help in negotiating the cumbersome regulatory environment, better working relations with the universities, scientific credentials for their newly developed products, international contacts and technical support, protection from the theft of ideas and know-how, and seed and venture financing for company formation and new product development. Although the burden for helping the *Mittelstand* should not rest exclusively on the German government, it must find new ways to stimulate and enable greater private collaboration. Because small companies afford a necessary economy of scale for certain products, such support should also seek to protect the independence and growth potential of the *Mittelstand*.

The technology transfer offices and centers, while strong on the cataloging of information about new technologies, are not actively promoting business transactions (e.g., joint ventures and new companies) that better allow market forces to commercialize new technologies. Several reasons may explain this:

1. These centers typically receive substantial outside funding and are not required to cover their costs or generate additional revenue.
2. Staffing is often inadequate.

3. Incentives or contractual mechanisms to allow researchers to work in partnership with their parent institutions are rare.
4. The technology centers are often viewed as mere shelters for inadequately managed companies.

Although these observations cannot be easily verified, they reflect commonly held beliefs.

Comparison with U.S. Practices

A recent report of the Organization for Economic Cooperation and Development (OECD), entitled *Biotechnology and the Changing Role of Government* (1988), cites four conditions for the successful establishment of a biotechnology industry:

- excellence of research
- communication and information exchange
- flexibility
- industrial research and development (R&D) investment incentives

These conditions provide a useful framework for comparing the strategy and functioning of the German technology transfer system with that in the United States.

Clearly, at least two conditions for a biotechnology industry—excellence of research and communication or information exchange—are present in both Germany and the United States. Perhaps then, the best points of departure for comparing technology transfer in these two countries are in the remaining two conditions: flexibility and industrial R&D investment incentives. These latter two conditions are manifest in virtually all of the current trends in technology center and science park development in the United States.

In the United States, one finds an expanding array of services offered to small, technology-oriented businesses. Financial products range from seed capital to venture capital, each product addressing the needs of companies at separate stages of development. Services are most likely to be provided through a partnership between government, industry, and the university, with each partner sharing the eventual risks and rewards. Incubators no longer provide simple shelter and office support but seek to offer the most comprehensive range of marketing, business planning, management, or administrative services, as well as scientific and technical resources to ensure the success of small and medium firms.

Formerly passive bystanders to the technology transfer process, institutions are now active managers of technology. University administrations are creating separate offices for the identification of commercially relevant technologies, the development of industrial partnerships as joint ventures, and the aggressive formation of new companies. Often, university-based technology transfer offices are organized as profit centers and expected to generate revenues that will at least cover their own costs of operation. Independent incubators and technology centers are becoming active shareholders in the development of companies and are thereby expanding revenues for their own institutions.

Technology centers are, furthermore, playing a greater leadership role in regional economic development by becoming honest brokers and/or managers of regional economic development strategies. Their combined technical and business expertise, as well as political neutrality, allow them to build strong links between the public and private segments in their regional economies.

Possibilities for Improvement

Three general goals seem essential to the continued development of technology transfer in the Federal Republic of Germany. First, future programs and policy must aim to increase the availability of services to small and medium-sized firms. Future services must strengthen the working relationship between small companies and university or research center programs. These services should also be expanded to meet a broader range of business needs. Second, future programs and policy should furnish increased support for technology-transfer programs within universities and research centers with the aim of identifying and more fully exploiting the commercial potential of biotechnology at an earlier stage in its development. Such programs and policies must work within or in service to those research institutions that are currently the storehouse of technologies of strategic economic importance. Without challenging or significantly disrupting the current structure and operating procedures of those research institutions, programs must more aggressively bring innovation to industry, placing balanced emphasis on working with small and larger enterprises. Third and finally, the FRG needs to provide additional incentives, greater flexibility, and still-untried enabling mechanisms. These will allow researchers, institutional administrators, entrepreneurs within small firms and managers of larger companies to share financial rewards through the commercialization of biotechnology.

Principles that are common to successful technology-transfer programs in other countries (specifically the United States) include:

1. the management of technology-transfer programs with the specific intention of using innovation to generate a return on investment;

2. the development of contractual relations concerning intellectual properties that maintain the incentives for researchers, the parent institution, and the private sector partners up to and beyond the point of market entry;
3. the corresponding sharing of development costs and risks among a wide set of interested parties, including innovators, their parent institutions, investors, business partners, and civic or business leaders who will benefit from higher revenues and collateral economic efforts of a successfully commercialized scientific development.

The fundamental premises on which German research, development, and technology transfer are founded may need to be changed to reflect these principles of successful technology transfer. While these principles may seem to violate traditional boundaries between government, industry, and the university or research establishment, they can be accommodated within those boundaries by the properly skilled individuals.

Several models and approaches may be appropriate for improving the transfer and commercialization of biotechnology in the FRG, but the following deserve particular consideration because of the success they have demonstrated in the United States.

Forming research development corporations. Such corporations are often established through a government charter with the purpose of going beyond a simple licensing of patents and know-how to the actual formation of joint ventures and companies around commercially viable technologies. Such corporations take responsibility for technology auditing and marketing, venture capital financing, and, at times, near-market R&D. They aim to generate revenues that eventually will reward the institutions and inventors responsible for the technology developments. They can be committed to specific technologies (e.g., gene technology, biosensors, or neurobiology) or have a more general focus.

Mandating technology transfer from federal laboratories. Such an approach forces technology developed through tax-supported research into the private sector through mandate or order of the executive branch of government. Improving this kind of technology transfer (i.e., from national laboratories to the private sector) was accomplished largely through the United States by the Stevenson-Wydler Act. Because the initiative was only recently implemented, its success has not yet been fully demonstrated. However, the logic of mandating commercialization of nondefense technologies seems to hold for any developed nation that spends a significant portion of its gross national product on research and development.

Developing regional technology transfer assistance centers. These centers should have three purposes: (1) serving the technology transfer needs of universities and research institutions from promotion of intellectual property to industrial liaison and including new company formation; (2) brokering relations for small firms who require easier access to scientific know-how and product ideas with special emphasis on universities and research institutions; and (3) enhancing the competitive abilities of existing firms and entire economic regions through the widest range of technology-oriented economic development and promotion activities. Such activities are already partially established in Germany's existing technology transfer centers, but they suffer from inadequate staffing and lack of support. The only existing institution that approaches the regional technology-transfer assistance centers proposed here with this sort of needed service is the Steinbeis Stiftung in Stuttgart, Baden-Württemberg.

Establishing industrial liaison offices. Programs in research institutions or regions strong in technologies of strategic importance would be modeled after the University/Industry Cooperative Research centers established by the National Science Foundation (NSF), of which there are now thirty. (In contrast to the NSF model, however, these centers should make special efforts to open their research institutions to working with small companies.)

Training and recruiting management. In order to address the growing needs of future German biotechnology companies, the government must act with the same decisiveness and financial support as it has previously invested in basic and applied biotechnology research. Among other steps, the FRG should establish a fellowship and training program for technology transfer specialists skilled in the commercialization of biotechnology. This program should seek persons with a unique blend of technical and business skills.

Internationalizing biotechnology commercialization activities. International cooperation with the United States is mandatory for several reasons: (1) essential talent and scientific resources are dispersed around the world, (2) regulatory issues present a common barrier to be overcome before products can be fully commercialized, and (3) the markets for biotechnology products are such that they should be entered quickly and simultaneously on a global basis. Three worthy options for collaboration between the United States and the Federal Republic are:

1. Development of joint programs in setting standards for and testing biotechnology products, specifically recombinant DNA technology;
2. Establishment of carefully planned and executed reciprocal agreements with specific regions to promote (a) collaborative research on precompetitive technologies in areas of mutual strategic economic importance, (b) development of mutual understanding or common regulatory standards that would allow more open market competi-

tion, and (c) mutual representation or referrals for companies across national boundaries for the purposes of research and development;
3. Cooperation on the training of technology-transfer specialists and the further development or implementation of the BMFT biotechnology transfer programs and policy.

Collaborating along such lines could prepare the FRG to compete more successfully for research and development projects in the European Community and avoid trade tensions with the United States. Agreements are already in place with the United States or other countries that could serve as models for such collaboration.

Conclusion

Notwithstanding the shortcomings of the German system, it does have some strengths. Biotechnology transfer in the FRG appears determined to take place regardless of any particular policy or program. For example, in spite of the intense public controversy over biotechnology in Germany at the time this research was conducted, efforts to generate technological innovation based on biotechnology proceeded virtually without interruption. Researchers, institutional administrators, and businesspeople alike have remained mindful of the commercial potential of these innovations and sought—often through institutional mandate rather than entrepreneurial drive—to develop that potential.

In comparison with the system of technology transfer in the United States, the German system appears to be a more integrated, seamless process of moving innovation to the marketplace. Although this impression warrants further research, technology transfer in Germany does not appear encumbered by the same structural impediments to technology transfer in the United States such as the splintering of regulatory responsibility for biotechnology among multiple agencies or overlap in regional, state, and federal programs.

The integrated quality of technology transfer in Germany may be best attributed to a *Weltanschauung*, or a shared assumption, among the various individuals involved in the technology-transfer process. This worldview surpassed the parameters or objectives of any particular program. To the extent that this overriding involvement in technology transfer is successful, it depends on ingrained German bureaucratic traditions. It also relies on an enduring commitment to education and fundamental scientific investigation among German policymakers at the local and national levels. Above all, this enduring support for fundamentals has much to teach policymakers who may seek some simple programmatic solution to building economic competitive advantage.

Notes

This research was conducted by the author during the fall of 1988 under the auspices of the German Ministry of Research and Technology. All observations, conclusions, and possible errors drawn from that research are the author's sole responsibility. Nothing stated in this essay is intended to reflect the policy of the BMFT, the German government, or its affiliated agencies and contractors. The author expresses his appreciation to the BMFT for their assistance in this effort.

1. Technology transfer carries many different meanings, but here it refers specifically to movement of know-how, patented or copyrighted inventions, skilled people, and valued goods from a domain of basic, undirected, or precompetitive scientific investigation to one where the results of that investigation suggest and eventually prove to have commercial value in a competitive marketplace. It is a bias of this study to search for technology-transfer activities that bring ideas to the point of production and distribution and where that exchange of produceable goods or services in turn generates other economic returns (e.g., employment opportunities) that result in regional economic development.

11

Negotiation and Compromise in German Environmental Politics: Government, Industry, and the Public

Carol Deck

The Federal Republic of Germany is one of the most densely populated countries in Europe. Perhaps this is why its citizens exhibit such a high level of environmental consciousness. The Green political and environmental movement began in West Germany, where the Green party consistently received more than 5 percent of the vote in elections between 1983 and 1990.[1] Because of its location in the center of Europe, its dense population, and the desire of its citizens for stringent environmental controls, the Federal Republic is one of the most advanced countries in Europe in terms of environmental protection. It is a leader among the European Community (EC) nations in the application of pollution-control technology and in national levels of voluntary recycling.

Germany has achieved these successes through a variety of means, not all of them strictly set out by laws and regulations. Because of its geographical position and the practical weakness of international law, it has relied on negotiation with its European neighbors to control cross-border pollution. Negotiation and compromise also play an important role domestically in the relations between the federal ministry of environment and the state governments, and between governments and industry.

To say that negotiation and informal consultation are widely applied in Germany does not mean that environmental protection is carried out without regulation. In fact, market-based incentives that encourage companies not to pollute, such as the emissions trading policy in the United States, are viewed with suspicion by federal and state governments and are rarely, and then only narrowly, implemented. Instead, government officials first attempt to reach an informal agreement with industry before they take the first steps toward regulation. Frequently, these "voluntary" agreements obviate lengthy regulatory procedures. Compared to the United States, the work of environmental protection in the Federal Republic of Germany is characterized by a higher degree of negotiation and informal cooperation and less by rigid command-and-control rules. At both the federal and state levels of government, officials rely heavily on informal mechanisms and relationships to develop, implement, and enforce policies. This reliance can have significant implications for the public's ability to be aware of and participate in governmental decision making.

Federal-State Cooperation

Under the Basic Law, or constitution, which was ratified by a majority of the states (*Länder*) in 1949, the Federal Republic is a decentralized federalist country. The authority of the individual states is not derived from federal authority. Each state has its own constitution, a democratically elected parliament, an executive government, administrative agencies, and independent courts. The federal government and parliament (Bundestag) have power to create broad legislation. The state governments are responsible for interpreting and implementing the legislation.

The tradition of federalism in Germany is strong. Until 1871 the area which is now Germany was composed of independent principalities and kingdoms. Between 1871 and the end of World War I, the individual German states held a strong legal and political position vis-à-vis the federal government in Berlin. Although after World War II many of the original boundaries of the individual states were redrawn (according to the occupation zones), the newly created states, under the Basic Law of 1949 and in practice, retain many of their nineteenth-century powers of independent action.

The Lack of Federal Government Leverage

Compared to the United States, the German federal government has relatively few formal levers to ensure that the states implement environmental legislation according to federal intent. The federal ministry often must persuade states to fulfill federal plans. It rarely has authority under the Basic Law to enforce federal environmental laws itself.

In the United States, individual states receive a large part of their yearly budget for environmental protection directly from the U.S. Environmental Protection Agency (EPA), which often ties receipt of such funds to specific goals and activities that the state has accomplished or promises to accomplish. The state is not necessarily free to spend the money as it wishes. Depending on the state and the EPA officials involved, there may be negotiations between the state and EPA over how the federal money will be spent. At issue recently was the extent to which EPA can direct a state to perform activities for which it does not receive federal funds but finances on its own.

In the Federal Republic of Germany, such financial strings between the federal and state governments do not exist. Federal aid funds are transferred from federal to state governments in one lump sum, without being tied to particular agencies or programs and without specific instructions how the money should be spent. The states are free to set their own priorities. Wealthier states receive very few federal funds.

The German federal government's specific legal authority over states is also limited. Technically, under Article 37 of the Basic Law, the federal government can force a state to fulfill its obligations under federal law (*Bundeszwang*), but only with the consent of the Bundesrat.[2] In the summer of 1988, Environment Minister Klaus Töpfer threatened to use Article 37 to force the state of North Rhine–Westphalia to issue a permit for the fast-breeder reactor in Kalkar, but he ultimately backed down. According to several environmental law experts, this *Bundeszwangsinstrument* has never been applied to environmental protection issues.[3]

In a landmark decision in May 1990, the Federal Constitutional Court in Karlsruhe decided that the states did have to obey federal orders in certain areas of national importance such as air traffic control, federal freeway construction, and nuclear energy facilities. The Kalkar reactor was again at the center of the controversy. The Social Democratic (SPD) government of North Rhine–Westphalia wanted to require additional environmental and safety tests before issuing a permit for the reactor. The federal environment ministry thought the tests were unnecessary. The court ruled that the state had to obey the federal order.[4] The Karlsruhe court reiterated this position in a 1991 decision involving the repository for low-level radioactive waste being constructed at the Konrad mine near Salzgitter in Lower Saxony. After the Social Democrat–Green coalition had come to power in June 1990, it announced it would require additional environmental safety studies to be performed before work on the site could continue. The court decided, however, that the federal government could order that no additional tests would be performed. This federal supremacy does not extend beyond these limited federal issue areas, however.

In the United States, it is also envisioned that the state will bear primary responsibility for the work of protecting the environment. Yet under most of the U.S. environmental laws, the EPA has the authority to enforce regulations itself or to delegate the authority to an individual state, stepping in if a state is not enforcing them properly. In the drinking-water program, for example, states are granted "primacy" from EPA to implement and enforce federal drinking-water regulations themselves, and EPA receives periodic reports from them and oversees their progress. If a state is found to be misusing this authority, the agency can and, at the very least often threatens to, take away this primacy. However, this power must be used with restraint and tact. In practice, even if EPA wanted to assume more of the day-to-day authority of the states, it rarely has the resources available to perform those tasks itself.

Federal-State Coordinating Groups

Notwithstanding their differences, federal and state environment ministry representatives in Germany meet often. Several working groups organized according to environmental medium provide the framework for these meetings. Officials responsible for controlling air pollution, for example, meet approximately four times each year as the State Committee on Air Pollution (Länderausschuß für Immissionsschutz). Other working groups exist in areas such as waste, water, and nature conservation. The most important group is the Conference of Environment Ministers (Umweltministerkonferenz), made up of all the state and federal environment ministers, which meets every six months.

The lower-level working groups discuss current technical and policy issues affecting several states or affecting a few states and the federal government. Their members coordinate rather than make decisions. Representatives of the federal government play a large role in the working groups, evidenced partly by their permanent place at the head table next to the rotating chair of the group.[5]

It is at the larger and more significant Conference of Environment Ministers that hard negotiations take place and the federal environmental minister must cajole and convince the states to step to the beat of the federal government. The current environment minister in Bonn, Klaus Töpfer, is well suited to this role. Unpopular among many state officials for his persistence in pushing the federal line and slowly increasing the power of the federal ministry vis-à-vis the states, he is nevertheless an effective and competent leader who is respected, if not well liked, by states.

The Role of Political Parties in Federal-State Cooperation

Political parties play a crucial role in relations between federal and state governments, and in most other facets of environmental politics in Germany. The centrist Christian Democratic Union (CDU) has held power in Bonn with its coalition partner, the relatively small Free Democratic party, since 1983. The third member of the coalition is the Christian Social Union (CSU), the CDU's conservative sister party in Bavaria.

Political parties play a much more significant role overall in the Federal Republic than they do in the U.S. Party discipline is rarely broken and votes in the parliament are cast strictly along party lines. And, because of the parliamentary system of government, the chancellor and members of his cabinet are usually chosen from the parliament itself, thus reinforcing the party ties. In the state-federal working groups, and especially during the Conference of Environment Ministers, positions on issues are formed along party lines. In the United States, by contrast, states often join together on issues to form a unified front against the federal government. Whether the state is led by a Democratic or Republican governor makes little difference. In Germany, however, this unified bloc of states countering the federal government rarely forms.[6]

The Power of the States and the Federal Government's International Role

Because the states are responsible for implementing almost all environmental treaties and agreements, the federal government's ability to operate internationally is often constrained. European Community officials have recognized this limitation and attempt to meet with representatives of state governments or state working groups in addition to meeting with federal officials. In international negotiations during the last few years, the federal ministry has frequently included representatives from state governments as members of the German delegations. If state officials later balk at implementing an international agreement, the federal ministry can remind them that they were represented on the delegation.[7]

Despite the relative power of German states, the federal ministry plays a lead role in environmental decisions. Sometimes the amount of federal influence depends on the relative level of expertise of the states in a particular area. In a complicated area such as waste disposal and cleanup technology, for example, states may rely on the federal government for direction. In other areas like drinking water that are clearly of local or regional interest and have been for hundreds of years, the federal government may have much less control.[8]

Through the Conference of Environment Ministers and the state working groups, the federal ministry is able to coordinate with the states to work toward accomplishing environmental goals. Although the federal government has little direct power, it is able to steer the debate through persuasion and through working with its like-party states. In the end, however, it has little power to force a state to follow through.

Government-Industry Relations

Compared to the United States, there is more contact in the Federal Republic between industry and government at the highest levels, and it is more informal. Yet EPA often draws its political appointees directly from industry, while Germans in similar positions have worked their way up the ladder in their ministry or in their political party. As in the United States, industry groups are organized into associations (*Verbände*) that have varying degrees of political influence depending on the industry and its presence in an elected official's district.

The relations between state and industry in the Federal Republic differ depending on whether one is considering a state controlled by the Social Democrats or by the CDU or CSU. As might be expected, industry has relatively more difficulty with SPD states, and less with CDU/CSU states or the federal government. Some of the following observations may not necessarily apply to SPD-controlled governments.

Voluntary Agreements: Negotiating Instead of Regulating

Interaction between government and industry in the Federal Republic occurs behind closed doors. This does not mean that the relations between the two are always friendly or cordial. Although there is a complex system of environmental laws, regulations, and permits in the Federal Republic, the government frequently tries to negotiate with companies or with a particular industry before it attempts to regulate.[9]

In general, many government officials in Germany believe it makes little sense to promulgate regulations if one is not sure that companies will follow them. The belief in achieving compliance through inspections and enforcement procedures is not as strongly held as it is in the United States. Germans may be more constrained than their U.S. counterparts because their powers to inspect industrial facilities are more limited.

The federal government negotiates with industry mostly because of the difficulty involved in achieving the necessary consensus with states in order to pass a new law or regulation.[10] Sometimes in state government a close relationship between industry and political appointees plays a role in a program manager's decision to seek an informal agreement with a company. Ministry staff may be hesitant to promulgate or enforce regulations strictly or to fine a company if they believe that the top political appointees in their ministry will not support their actions.

Often the government's threat of new laws or regulations is enough to coax a voluntary agreement from industry. In 1989 in Bavaria, a new industry-government group was formed to address the problem of abandoned hazardous waste sites in the state. Under the initial accord, industry agreed to contribute DM 3 million to a special fund each year for ten years and the state agreed to contribute the same amount. Contributions from individual companies would depend on the size of the firm.

Companies have a strong incentive to make their voluntary efforts succeed. They are deeply fearful that the German government will pass a law similar to the United States' Comprehensive Environmental Response, Compensation, and Liability Act (CERCLA, commonly called "Superfund"), which they believe would be a disastrous burden to industry.[11] Although all parties to the agreement readily admit that DM 6 million per year will not be enough to clean up the abandoned waste sites in Bavaria,[12] they have agreed to attempt to solve the problem without new laws or regulations. (By contrast, the state of Bavaria and a local community are spending DM 90 million to clean up one particularly notorious site, and the U.S. spends approximately $2.5 billion on Superfund each year.) Industry is happy because they have forestalled increased taxes and regulation in the near future, and government is satisfied because industry will contribute in the short term and because remediation efforts begin immediately. Moreover, few German government officials are convinced that they want a program like Superfund, whose results they view as negligible, given the cost of the program.

Broken Agreements and the Government's Response

When a voluntary agreement is broken, the government must make good on its threat to regulate. A recent example was the introduction of 1.5 liter plastic softdrink bottles into the German market. Several years ago the federal government developed an agreement with softdrink companies banning the sale of such drinks in plastic bottles.[13] The disposable bottles, not easily recycled, rapidly turn into a trash disposal problem. They would be quickly noticed in a country in which a high percentage of softdrink and beer bottles are glass returnables.

The voluntary agreement on the 1.5 liter plastic bottles worked well until the middle of 1988 when Coca-Cola decided to renege on the agreement. Although they were not certain, officials in the federal ministry believed that the German subsidiary was under pressure from its Coca-Cola parent in Atlanta to introduce the plastic bottles and would not have abrogated the agreement on its own.[14] The federal government responded with plans to slap a high deposit (50 pfennig) on the plastic bottles, which would discourage sales of the product. (Deposits on returnable glass bottles are between 5 and 30 pfennig.) In choosing 50 pfennig, the government did not give weight to the effect the additional cost would have on product sales, nor exactly how high the deposit should be to encourage customers to return the bottles to the stores where they were bought.[15]

Costs to industry or to consumers play a smaller role in regulatory decisions in Germany than in the United States. There is no equivalent to Executive Order 12291 issued by President Ronald Reagan and reissued by President George Bush, which requires the EPA to consider cost and benefit impacts as it regulates.[16]

The willingness of German government to cooperate with industry has many roots not only in the proindustry bias sometimes evident in CDU-controlled governments but also in its relative inability to execute environmental policy in the states. The states, for their part, lack confidence in inspection and compliance-monitoring systems and have developed an aversion to the feeling of distrust between state and industry that such systems can create. As for German industry, it is willing to work with government to avoid regulations that would almost probably be stronger and costlier than any voluntary agreement.

Implications of Informal Government-Industry Cooperation: Problems of Public Participation and Accountability

The cooperation between state and industry means that some of the high costs of creating, implementing, enforcing, and litigating regulations are avoided. Assuming that German industry does not renege on an agreement and pollute in secret (on the whole, government officials believe that industry representatives keep their word), the voluntary agreements should protect the environment as well as comparable regulations. That the agreements are usually less stringent than a regulation may imply that the environment is less well protected. However, the likelihood that a regulation or law would ever be put into force must also be considered.

A negative consequence of voluntary agreements is that they are made outside of a formal framework, thereby excluding the participation of those who are neither industry nor government. Because of the informal relationships and agreements, major governmental decisions are made outside of the public arena. In general, scrutiny by the public of governmental decisions, whether informal agreements with industry or more formal legislation and regulation, is not anchored in the German system of government or in the German culture. A meaningful role for citizens is neither written into environmental laws nor observed informally.

Limited Public Participation

Information about how government makes decisions is rarely available to German citizens. There is no German equivalent of the Freedom of Information Act.[17] In addition, although almost all committee hearings in the U.S. House and Senate are open to the public, no hearings are open in the Bundestag.

In both countries, industry groups meet regularly with federal officials to offer their advice and opinions. In Germany, these meetings occur without the public's knowledge. In the United States, federal agencies are bound by the Federal Advisory Committee Act to allow the public to scrutinize the advice received and, in most cases, to attend the meetings.[18] Although it is true that the act is not followed to the letter by all agencies, it and the Freedom of Information Act do afford citizens a window into the decision making of the agencies. Under both acts, citizens can sue an agency to force it to comply with the legislation.

In contrast with the United States, there is no significant private right of action under German law for citizens and groups to force the government to implement environmental laws or to question environmental standards that the government has set. German citizens and groups are not allowed to sue the government to force it to implement environmental laws or to question environmental standards that the government has set. However, as in the United States, German individuals are allowed to comment during the process through which a facility receives permission from the government to operate, and the government must respond to the public comments. When permitting large facilities or facilities that will have an effect on the environment, the government must hold a public hearing. Under the federal air pollution law (Bundes-Immissionsschutzgesetz), for example, state agencies must give the public notice of the permit application, make the applications and supporting materials available for review over a two-month period, invite the public to raise objections to the project, and arrange for a meeting with the persons who have filed objections. Only people who have raised objections to the project are entitled to participate in the meeting. Other citizens or the press need special permission from the agency to attend. State agencies are not required to inform the public if permit modifications are not expected to cause additional or different emissions or risks to the public and the neighborhood.[19]

Compared with the United States, German restrictions on who has standing to file a lawsuit are more stringent. For example, under Germany's federal atomic energy law, to file a suit against a potentially dangerous facility, a citizen must live within a certain radius of a facility *and* be able to prove that he is directly affected by the potential danger. A person living upwind of a leaky nuclear power plant and receiving 20 millirems of radiation as a yearly dose when the government safety standard is 30 millirems is not allowed to bring a suit against the plant. Only his neighbor living downwind of the plant and receiving 45 millirems is allowed to take action.[20] The federal air pollution law imposes similar restrictions on who may bring a court action.[21]

Such stringent requirements have prevented the rise of sophisticated state- and national-level environmental activist groups like the Environmental Defense Fund or the Natural Resources Defense Council.[22] Increasingly in practice, however, groups like Greenpeace try to locate a citizen who fits the specific criteria, and offer to pay all the legal fees and to provide other support.[23] The suit must still be led by that individual, though. In Social Democrat state governments, environmental groups may be allowed to bring such suits themselves (*Verbandsklagen*), provided they have members fitting the necessary criteria. The success of these suits brought by groups has been uneven across the different states, depending on whether the courts in the states are liberal or conservative. Suits by environmental groups cannot be brought against nuclear facilities because atomic power is controlled by federal, not state, law and such suits are not authorized under federal law.

Public Involvement and German Culture

Given the successful informal cooperation between industry and government and between governments at the state and local level, one questions why the public is also not considered by government as an informal player. Tradition is one reason—public participation has not been integral to German culture. Until a few years ago when the environmental movement took hold, there were few demands by people to participate in or be informed of decisions. Another factor preventing citizens from increasing their level of participation is the attitudes of the players already in the game, that is, government and industry representatives.

Whether in the United States or Germany, it is an indisputable fact that citizens have lost trust in government. In Germany more so than in the United States, though, government does not trust its citizens. Over and over, with few exceptions, German government officials speak of the "hysteria" of the population when environmental matters are concerned, and the public's lack of understanding. There is little support in government quarters, from highest official to lowest analyst, for allowing these "uninformed" citizens to take part in environmental policy decisions. When told of EPA's regulatory negotiation program, in which representatives of environmental groups, industry, EPA, unions, and others, sit together at a table and literally negotiate a regulation, the listener, whether Green or CSU member, expressed skepticism that such a program could work in Germany. (The ultimate goal of regulatory negotiation is to avoid costly lawsuits, a problem that does not present itself in the Federal Republic.)

Are government and industry representatives really antipublic, or are they just afraid of losing control over decisions that they have always made themselves? In a democratic society—and Germany is without question democratic—one must assume the latter. Fear of what citizens will do with information in any society can lead to the withholding of that information by those who control it. When there are few systematic checks and levers on the holders of the information, such as the Freedom of Information Act, congressional inquiries, or an inquisitive press, it is indeed possible that the information can be kept successfully from public view.

Informal relationships between government and industry and between state and federal governments in the German system mean that government is held less accountable than in the United States. If the public is not informed and has no authority, it cannot serve as a check on the powers of the government. The legislature does not serve as a check on the government because of the parliamentary system in which the cabinet is drawn from the legislature and because of strict party loyalties. Within the federal government checks are provided by the coalition partners of the Christian Democrats (the Free Democrats and the Christian Social Union). It is difficult for the CDU to push through a measure with which its coalition partners do not agree. In state governments without coalitions, especially where one party has been in office for many years, there is no effective check on the power of the government. It is virtually accountable to no one.

Conclusion

Do informal agreements between government and industry protect the environment better than a strict regulatory and inspection regime? Without detailed technical studies, no one will ever know. Also, in most areas of environmental protection, Germany, like the United States, does rely on strict regulatory measures. The two countries are more alike than different in their approach to environmental standards and technologies. It is only in the ways that each nation goes about attaining its environmental goals that differences can be noticed. These differences center on federalism and the power of subnational governments, and the role of the public in the governing process. They reflect values at the core of each society.

Notes

1. The western Green party in West Germany failed to achieve the necessary percentage in the 1990 elections to remain in the parliament although the eastern German Green party received sufficient votes in that election to enter the Bundestag.

2. Article 37 of the Grundgesetz (Basic Law) provides as follows: "(1) If a Land fails to comply with its obligations of a federal character imposed by this Basic Law or another federal law, the Federal Government may, with the consent of the Bundesrat, take necessary measures to enforce such compliance by the Land by way of federal enforcement. (2) To carry out such federal enforcement, the Federal Government or its commissioner shall have the right to give instructions to all *Länder* and their authorities."

3. Interview with Dr. Peter Horst, special assistant to the state secretary, Bavarian State Ministry for Regional Development and Environment, spring 1989.

4. Finally in March 1991, however, the federal government, for political reasons, gave up its effort to persuade the North Rhine–Westphalia government to allow the reactor to become operational.

5. State Committee on Air Pollution, Aachen, 13–15 February 1989.

6. Interview with Dr. Barbara Schuster, director of federal-state relations and general environmental policy, Federal Ministry for Environment, Nature Conservation, and Reactor Safety, 14 November 1988.

7. Interview with Dr. Friedrich, director-general for water, Hesse State Ministry for Environment, 10 October 1988.

8. Interview with Dr. Koopman, vice-president, German Hydrographic Institute, Hamburg, 14 December 1988.

9. Lawrence Ng, "A Drastic Approach to Controlling Groundwater Pollution," *Yale Law Journal* 98(1989): 773, 789; see generally Craig Reese, *Deregulation and Environmental Quality* (London & Westport, Conn.: Quorum, 1983).

10. The Bundesrat (Council of Constituent States), the upper house of the German Parliament, is composed of representatives of the state (*Land*) governments. The concurrence of the Bundesrat is required for enactment of most laws.

11. Industry Committee for Hazardous Waste Cleanup in Bavaria, 26 January 1989.

12. Ibid.

13. Interview with Dr. Karl-Heinz Lindner, director for solid waste disposal and cleanup technologies, Federal Ministry for Environment, Nature Conservation, and Reactor Safety, 7 October 1988.

14. Interview with Mr. Dietrich Ruchay, director-general for water and waste, Federal Ministry for Environment, Nature Conservation, and Reactor Safety, 7 October 1988.

15. Lindner interview, 7 October 1988.

16. 5 U.S.C. § 601.

17. 5 U.S.C. § 552; Implementation of the Freedom of Information Act is uneven across U.S. agencies. See, for example, Jane Rissler and Margaret Mellon, "Public Access to Biotechnology Applications," *Natural Resources Law Journal* 4 (1990).

18. 5 U.S.C. App. I.

19. Eberhard Bohne, "Politics and Markets in Environmental Protection: Reforming Air Pollution Regulations in the United States of America and in the Federal Republic of Germany," Report to the German Marshall Fund of the United States, 1987, page 44.

20. Horst interview, 28 March 1989.

21. Bohne, "Politics and Markets," p. 45.

22. Interview with Christa Morawa, director of international and bilateral cooperation, Federal Environmental Research Agency, Berlin, 11 November 1988.

23. Horst interview, 28 March 1989.

12

The Future of the German Electronics Industry

Lauren Kelley

International attention has focused recently on the current difficulties of the European electronics industry. National giants such as Phillips and Olivetti have been forced to lay off large numbers of employees, Groupe Bull of France is faltering in spite of huge government subsidies, and Germany's Siemens has switched from a traditional policy of going it alone to forming strategic alliances with competitors such as IBM. Almost everyone agrees that problems exist, but there is little consensus on what the solution might be.

This crisis has a particular significance in Germany where jobs and economic leadership are at stake not only in the electronics industry itself but also in the automotive, machine tool, and other major manufacturing industries. The German government is caught between pressures on one side to preserve jobs and local production in a strategic industry and, on the other side, arguments that free trade policies and open competition are fundamental for a healthy industry. It is becoming more widely accepted that major electronics companies, whether German, British, or American, can succeed only through increased international competitiveness rather than through government policies aimed at protecting or subsidizing them. This paper looks at some of the reasons why so much attention is focused on the health of the electronics sector, the perceived threat posed by foreign electronics investment in the Federal Republic, and the status and potential of the German electronics industry.

Electronics as a Building Block of the Economy

The electronics industry has developed over the past several decades into a sector that most developed countries consider vital to their national economies.[1] The production of electronic goods and services provides direct employment for many highly skilled, relatively well paid persons. At the same time, employment in numerous other industries—from the automotive and aerospace industries to machine tools—also depends on the electronics industry. In many cases, these secondary industries require access to the latest electronics technologies in order to remain competitive in their own sectors. For example, today's automobile is relying more and more on electronics to help it do everything from using fuel efficiently to measuring the weather outside in both Fahrenheit and centigrade. Companies such as Daimler Benz and Volkswagen work closely with electronics suppliers such as Bosch in the design of new cars. Other important German industries (e.g., machine tools, medical equipment, environmental-monitoring industries) rely heavily on the latest electronics technology in order to continuously develop more advanced products that are internationally competitive.

The Economics Ministry in Bonn estimates that the German electronics sector employs just over half a million highly skilled workers.[2] Almost 40 percent of these jobs fall in the telecommunications services sector, almost 20 percent in telecommunications, 23 percent in software and data processing, and only 2.5 percent in the production of microelectronics, the key components on which all other sectors of the electronics industry depend.[3] Of course, this is the direct employment in the electronics sector; the European Community (EC) estimates that 60 to 65 percent of the working population in the EC nations are employed in jobs that are directly or indirectly related to electronics and its applications.[4]

In the introduction to a 1989 concept paper on German government electronics policy, the ministers of Research and Technology and of Economics write that information technology, unlike any other technology, leads to deep structural changes in all aspects of daily life. The paper further contends that information technology stimulates innovation in sectors that are the basis of the Federal Republic's export strength. Its increasing strategic importance for the service sector and the provision of public services such as environmental protection, communications and transportation make information technologies a vital concern of policy makers.[5]

The Status of the German Electronics Industry

In 1989 approximately DM 99.1 billion worth of electronic goods and services were produced in Germany.[6] This can be viewed in relation to a world electronics market of approximately $607 billion, of which approximately $253 billion is the U.S. market, followed by the European market, which was estimated to be about $164 billion.[7]

Looking at the microelectronics portion of German production, roughly DM 1.6 billion worth of integrated circuits were manufactured in the Federal Republic in 1989. This is almost four times German microelectronics production in 1982. Employment in the German microelectronics industry increased slightly from twelve thousand in 1982 to thirteen thousand in 1989. German microelectronics exports increased dramatically from DM 750 million in 1982 to approximately DM 4 billion in 1989. However, German microelectronics imports also increased greatly during this period from DM 1.35 billion in 1982 to DM 4.6 billion in 1989. According to the Economics Ministry, the fact that more microelectronics are exported from Germany than are produced in the country implies that much of the import volume represents components imported into Germany for further manufacturing, then reexported as part of another electronic product.[8] While semiconductors and microelectronic components represent only 1.6 percent of German electronics production and 2.5 percent of employment in the electronics industry, these products constitute the basic technology around which almost all other electronic products are built.

The largest German electronics company by far is Siemens AG. Siemens ranked number two in microelectronics sales in Europe during 1990, after Phillips, and in the German computer market, it was ranked second after IBM in 1989. After acquiring the ailing Nixdorf computer firm, Siemens is now Europe's largest computer company, with sales estimated at $7.8 billion for the year ending September 1991, followed by Olivetti, whose 1990 sales stood at $7.5 billion.[9]

In telecommunications, Siemens dominates the German market for products and services. In contrast, it only occupies fifteenth place in worldwide semiconductor sales, after the leading Japanese and U.S. semiconductor companies. In computers, Siemens ranks thirteenth in world computer sales. Only in telecommunications does Siemens achieve a leading world position: number three in sales after AT&T and Alcatel.

Founded in the mid-nineteenth century, Siemens quickly became one of the first true multinational corporations in the world. Shortly after the establishment of Siemens & Halske Telegraph Construction Company in Berlin in 1847, Werner Siemens sent his brother Carl Siemens to Russia, where he obtained the contract to install extensive telegraph lines throughout western Russia. The Russian contracts maintained the company's growth during financial downturns during the initial years.

The company's next major international project began in 1868 when the London office, run by another brother, William Siemens, obtained the contract to build the world's longest telegraph line. Almost 11,000 kilometers, this telegraph line connected London with Calcutta via Berlin,

Teheran, Bushire, and Karachi. In the mid 1880s Siemens laid the first direct transatlantic cable from Ireland to the United States.[10]

The Siemens Corporation continued to grow through the end of the nineteenth century and into the beginning of the twentieth century by being first with the leading technologies of the day. From telegraphs to electric railroads and subways to the early power stations, the energies of the three Siemens brothers and their company contributed to Europe's early technical developments. In the nineteenth century advances in communications from telegraph to early telephones and improvement in living standards through electricity and electrical lighting resulted in a strong impact on social and political developments. For example, the first long-distance telegraph line in Europe was laid between Frankfurt and Berlin in order to transmit as quickly as possible the decisions of Germany's first parliament, called the National Assembly, at St. Paul's Church in Frankfurt to the Prussian court in Berlin in the aftermath of the 1848 revolution.[11]

Today, the qualitative change in our ability to process information is revolutionizing the way we go about our daily lives. From placing a computer on the desk of an average white-collar worker to improving understanding of the environment through the analysis of a billion times a billion pieces of data, the computer revolution is as important to society today as the telegraph and telephone were at the beginning of the twentieth century. The key players today, however, in the development and use of information technology are American and Japanese companies, a fact confronting German policymakers and industry.

Dependence on Foreign Suppliers for Key Components

In view of the electronics sector's contribution to employment and the competitiveness of user industries, policymakers are concerned about the increasing dependence on foreign suppliers for key technologies. This concern is echoed in studies conducted by the U.S. government, the European Community, and the German government.[12] In particular, the activities of Japanese electronics firms are coming under greater scrutiny as Europeans and Americans question their dominance of key segments of the electronics sector, particularly relating to the strength of domestic, high-technology industries. For example, Japanese dominance of high-speed, large-capacity memory semiconductors is causing great concern in both the United States and Western Europe. Dependence on Japanese semiconductors is seen as a threat to a variety of semiconductor user industries, such as the computer, automotive, and advanced machine tool industries. Japanese dominance is particularly threatening because the same companies that produce semiconductors, such as Toshiba or NEC, are also giant competitors in the down stream industries, such as consumer electronics or computers.

In contrast to the Japanese situation, components suppliers and end-user industries in the United States represent different companies that do not, in general, compete against each other. This led to very different perspectives in the United States regarding Japanese sales of semiconductors at very low prices during the 1980s. U.S. semiconductor companies saw this as "dumping," a strategy of selling at below cost in order to drive competitors out of the market. U.S. computer companies viewed low Japanese prices from a competitive perspective—the lower the price of components, the more competitive U.S. computers could be on world markets. However, this analysis is complicated if the component supplier is also a competitor at the systems level. Because the leading Japanese semiconductor companies are also computer manufacturers, it is considered natural competitive behavior to withhold chips or other advanced components and technology from customers who are also competitors at the systems level.

Competition in Electronics Investment in the EC and Germany

Concern about dependence on "foreign" suppliers is complicated as it becomes more difficult to determine the nationality of a company when the ownership may be in one country, production in various different locations, and target markets in yet another region. The situation is complicated by intertwined strategic alliances among various international companies, the increasingly global nature of production, and trade actions by local governments that aim at making it difficult for nonnational companies to sell in a domestic market. Ten or twenty years ago it was clear which companies were American, which Japanese, and which European. Today, it is not clear whether the nationality of a company should be determined by the nationality of its owners, the country where it employs the most people, or where it adds the most value to its products.

According to the German Economics Ministry, the following electronics companies are manufacturing microelectronics in the Federal Republic: Siemens, Telefunken Electronic, Phillips Components, Hitachi, Mitsubishi, Toshiba, Texas Instruments, and IBM.[13] For the policymaker, it becomes increasingly difficult to evaluate whether these companies should be treated similarly or differently. All contribute to employment and all sell in the local market. It is feared, however, that companies with "foreign" ownership have a different commitment to local employment and the local market than "national" companies. In the United States, this fear has often been dispelled by practices of several foreign manufacturers. A large number of U.S. companies moved offshore, particularly during the recession of the mid 1970s and early 1980s, to find cheaper production costs in the Far East and elsewhere, while foreign investment moved into the United States. For example, in the U.S. television industry, more workers are employed by foreign companies in the United States than by U.S. companies.

During the 1980s an increasing number of non-European-owned electronics companies, particularly Japanese, increased their manufacturing presence in the European Community. Initially, Japanese companies chose the United Kingdom as the premier location for production facilities. In 1989, 73 percent of Japanese investment in Western Europe was established in the United Kingdom. Japanese companies had established 39 electronics and electrical equipment manufacturing operations in the United Kingdom as of 1 January 1989, out of a total of 120 in Western Europe.[14] This location preference reflected various factors, including Japanese familiarity with doing business in English, a less regulated marketplace—particularly under Prime Minister Margaret Thatcher—than other European Community nations, and overall good investment conditions.

Germany is the second most popular location for Japanese electronics production currently, and one that is increasing in importance. As of January 1989, there were twenty-six Japanese electronics facilities in the Federal Republic. Influencing factors in the decision to locate electronics investment in the Federal Republic include a low inflation rate, high productivity, an undervalued stock market, a rather conservative dividend policy in Germany, and high educational standards. For Japanese management, the drawbacks of a German location are the difficult language for Japanese, strong labor unions, and a large number of holidays and vacation time for workers. On balance, however, Germany's well-trained workforce (especially its engineers and technicians), a stable and growing economy, and, for semiconductor companies the pure water and clean facilities necessary for electronic components production have proved to be deciding factors in these investment decisions.[15] One also suspects that proximity to the wealthy German market and German competitors may have had a major influence on Japanese corporate thinking.

EC Policies Regarding Foreign Investment

Why have Japanese and, to some extent, U.S. electronics companies been increasing their investment in the European Community? These moves came about as a result of several EC policies and an overall global approach on the part of international electronics companies. The initial impetus most likely came from trade policy actions by the European

Community and fears that a unified, strengthened community after creation of the internal market of 1992 will take even more aggressive action.

The most important trade actions affecting non-EC electronics companies have taken place under the rubric of antidumping actions. Antidumping actions are initiated when a company sells a product overseas at a price lower than in the home market, resulting in injury to local producers in the overseas market. In order to help local producers avoid being driven out of the market by the foreign "dumping," antidumping tariffs are set in place by the local government to increase the end cost of the product in the local market to the same level as in the home market.

In order to circumvent antidumping duties, companies may in some instances shift production to the foreign market so that the product is regarded as a local product. To counteract concerns that little more than so-called screwdriver factories are being established to get around dumping actions (i.e., factories where imported kits of parts are screwed together with very limited local value added) the European Community now requires at least 40 percent local content before a product is considered to be EC in origin. EC antidumping tariffs ranging from 10 to more than 40 percent on a wide variety of electronic products, including semiconductors, act as a strong inducement for foreign electronics manufacturers to locate within the European Community in order to avoid high tariffs.

Another factor in the decision to move production facilities to Europe is the need to be geographically close to a booming market. Growth is expected to increase even more over the next few years as European companies modernize facilities to compete in the new single European market. More chips, computers, and telecommunications equipment than ever will be needed as the unified European economy becomes the largest economy in the world. As technical standards and requirements for doing business are harmonized among the various EC countries, it becomes more economical for foreign companies to locate within the community. This means that competition for sales, market share and resources will make it even more difficult for Europe's electronics giants to maintain not only their position in the European market as a whole but also in the domestic market in which most of these companies draw their greatest strength.

Enhancing Competitiveness

As trade barriers drop within the EC, German industry is contending with increasing competition not only internationally but also on the home front. For government policymakers, the importance of electronics for employment and contribution to GNP—not to mention exports—gives greater urgency to this challenge. The companies themselves see the precarious condition of major European electronics companies and hope to avoid the same situation. Heavily subsidized Groupe Bull in France is confronting increasing losses, Phillips in the Netherlands and IBM Europe are both laying off large numbers of workers, and ICL in Britain has been bought by Japanese giant, Fujitsu. German industry must learn to dodge the pitfalls and not just survive, but become adept at international competition.

Germany possesses many strengths that may enable it to retain leadership in the electronics sector. Technological innovation requires excellent scientific and technical skills; Germany's well-developed university and research structure plays an important role in supporting technology companies. As with other German industries, the highly skilled and disciplined German workforce contributes to the health of the German electronics industry. In addition, German economic stability and the availability of capital make it possible to carry out the long-range planning and investment required by global electronics markets.

The quality of demand is another aspect of competitiveness that is relatively less well known but appears to play an important role in enhancing competitiveness. This factor is a weakness of the German electronics sector and contributes to German difficulties in leading the information technology revolution.

Quality of demand means that companies are kept competitive because their customers demand the newest and most innovative products from a supplier. For example, it could be argued that one factor in the success of the German automotive industry is the quality of German automotive demand. German car customers demand the latest and the greatest and are willing to pay some of the highest prices for the newest models. This type of demand has driven the German automotive industry to design and sell some of the world's best cars. The German automotive industry competes worldwide, even in Japan where almost no non-Japanese companies are successful.

According to a recent EC paper and proposal for action,[16] European electronics demand is estimated to be two to three years behind that in American and Japanese markets. The study found that European industrial electronics purchasers hesitate to buy until innovative products are successful in external markets:

> The lack of leading-edge users in Europe, in contrast to the United States and Japan, prevents the European information technology and electronics industry from exploiting all the advantages of being first to market in new fields. However, for the development of the information technology and electronics industries, the existence of a dynamic and demanding market plays a decisive role. . . . The advantages of leading-edge demand are not

only technological, but also commercial and financial. Indeed, it is during the period when a product is introduced that prices are high and profit margins sufficient to release the resources needed to finance R&D and prepare subsequent generations of products.[17]

Given these various factors, what can Germany do to increase competitiveness and vitality of its electronics sector? As a starting point, it must be generally understood that the role of the government should be to enhance competitiveness, not to protect domestic industry from competition. Protectionism tends to stifle innovation and risk taking, without which the electronics sector cannot compete either globally or domestically. A good example of the adverse effects of protectionism is the experience of the European automotive industry. France and Italy have strongly protected their car industries from foreign competition by restricting Japanese imports. Germany, on the other hand, has not limited foreign car imports, yet the German car companies dominate the domestic market and are extremely competitive internationally. The French and Italian car companies are asking for greater protection and have far greater difficulties competing outside their local markets.

Government procurements and procurement practices are often an area of hidden protectionism. Domestic companies can be clearly favored over foreign suppliers in the granting of government contracts and the establishment of technical standards for the public market. Transparency of public procurement was a major issue at the GATT (General Agreement on Tariffs and Trade), in U.S.-Japanese trade talks, and in the U.S.-German telecommunications procurement talks during the 1980s. Government procurement is of unusual importance to the electronics sector because governments and the public sector in most industrialized countries are major electronics consumers—from the communications network to military purchases. Orders placed by national governments for the most expensive electronics equipment, such as mainframe computers and telephone exchanges have created captive, protected markets.

More should be done to open up government procurements by establishing international rather than national technical standards for the market place. This would allow companies to compete in markets other than their home market, thereby strengthening their capabilities and opening them up to new demands. Open, international technical standards also encourage the growth of small and medium-sized technology companies instead of protecting the preserves of the large, established companies. Small and medium-sized companies have historically been vital to the health of Germany's economy.

Captive, protected markets have helped national giants such as Siemens, for example, or Bull in France to grow to their current size. With the completion of the European Community's internal market and the opening of public procurement to competition, German companies must break away from captive markets and compete in an open, international marketplace. It is only through enhanced competitiveness that German electronics companies can survive the aggressive competition of the global electronics market.

It is also important to remember that while governments can help to provide a healthy environment in which companies can grow to compete internationally, in the end, the private sector alone will determine whether or not the electronics sector will survive. In this context, the German government has done quite a good job in providing many of the factors required for competitiveness: a highly skilled and stable workforce, a strong economy, and a good educational and research system.

Overall, Germany possesses many of the important factors for a healthy electronics industry. However, the competitiveness in today's evolving electronics sector, where the stakes are larger than ever imagined and the potential losses devastating, requires rare combinations of creativity, flexibility, and quick adaptability. German companies must learn to follow an ever-changing market and be able to adapt both production and management to changing trends. A captive domestic market in the past has ill prepared many German companies for these new challenges. The first steps toward increased competitiveness have been taken through an increased awareness of the problems. On this point, there appears to be a fairly broad consensus throughout German industry and government.

Over the next ten years, it will become apparent whether the German electronics sector has made the necessary adjustments and will succeed in the new international environment. A failure would have significant impact on the German economy as a whole. Nonetheless, success, in view of past German technological contributions and innovations, could have far-reaching consequences to the development and use of electronics all over the world.

Notes

1. The term "electronics" is very imprecise and covers a wide variety of products that change as technologies develop. For the purposes of this discussion, the electronics sector will be considered to be that segment involved in the production of electronic devices for industrial use, as compared to consumer use. This includes the following industries: business equipment, computers, software, electronic components, instruments, semiconductor test equipment and telecommunications. The U.S. Department of Commerce used this definition in its 1990 publication, "The Competitive Status of the U.S. Electronics Sector, from Materials to Systems." The Commission of the European Community and German Econom-

ics Ministry use somewhat similar definitions as well in recent publications on the electronics sector.

2. "Informationstechnik in Deutschland," Nr. 310, Bundesministerium für Wirtschaft, Bonn, pp. 11 and 12.

3. Ibid.

4. "The European Electronics and Information Technology Industry: State of Play, Issues at Stake and Proposals for Action," Commission of the European Communities, 26 March 1991, p. 2.

5. "Zukunftskonzept Informationstechnik," Der Bundesminister für Forschung und Technologie and der Bundesminister für Wirtschaft, Bonn, August 1989.

6. Ibid., p. 16.

7. "Informationstechnik in Deutschland," BMWi, p. 11.

8. Ibid., p. 16.

9. Company reports, as reported in "The Last Hurrah for European High Tech?" *Business Week*, 29 April 1991, p. 14.

10. Sigfrid V. Weiher and Herbert Goetzeler, *The Siemens Company—Its Historical Role in the Progress of Electrical Engineering, 1847–1980* (Berlin and Munich: Siemens Aktiengesellschaft, 1977), pp. 183–184.

11. Ibid., p. 11.

12. For example, see the "Zukunftskonzept Informationstechnik," as well as the aforementioned EC Commission paper and U.S. Department of Commerce study on the status of the U.S. electronics sector.

13. "Informationstechnik in Deutschland," BMWi, p. 18.

14. From an unpublished survey of leading Japanese electronics companies by the Japanese External Trade Organization, completed in August 1989.

15. From an unpublished study by the Japanese Ministry of International Trade and Industry regarding Japanese electronics companies' current or planned investment in the European Community, February 1989.

16. European Electronics and Information Technology Industry, p. 9.

17. Ibid., p. 9.

Appendix One

The EC Internal Market: Internal Integration, External Trade Restrictions?

Martin Bangemann
Federal Minister of Economics, Bonn (1986–1989)
Vice President, European Community (1989–   )

I welcome the opportunity to address this distinguished audience on a topic of interest to both Europeans and non-Europeans.

The year 1992 will indeed be an important one. You in the United States will be celebrating the 500th anniversary of Columbus's discovery of America. We in Europe have set 1992 as the completion date for a historical imperative—the formation of a single, integrated market within the European Community.

In very few years the world economy will have a new partner to welcome, one whose economic might and political creativeness cannot be estimated from our present perspective. One thing is certain, however. Its 320 million inhabitants will make the single European market larger than any other industrialized market, exceeding even that of the United States.

The internal market will fundamentally alter Europe's economic and political weight. It will strengthen Europe and help it meet the future's challenges as a free continent. All this is reason enough for our partners in the global economy to ask: "How will European integration affect third countries?" Will it bring them new opportunities? Or must they fear serious disadvantages?

The EC Commission has attempted to quantify the anticipated impact of the internal market on the European Community. It has concluded that

---

This speech was delivered to the Annual Conference of the Robert Bosch Foundation Alumni Association, 22 October 1988, New York City.

Appendix One

there will be benefits amounting to hundreds of billions of dollars and growth impulses that will boost gross national product by several percentage points. I do not feel called on to try to corroborate these calculations. A billion dollars or a percentage point one way or the other is relatively insignificant in relation to the overall amount. The decisive aspect for me is that Europe's industry is aware of the enormous potential the internal market will create for capable and efficient companies.

Day after day, industry is forced to experience the difficulties and, above all, the high costs generated by barriers at the Community's internal frontiers. Industry feels tied down by the myriad of national regulations.

This explains why Europe's industry emphatically demands the completion of the internal market. Thirty years after the establishment of the EC, industry seeks the possibility of finally producing according to uniform rules and of buying and selling within a large area unrestricted by internal frontiers. In a manner that has made an impression on the governments concerned, Europe's industry is gearing its plans to bring them in line with the completion of the internal market.

The high level of acceptance of the internal market is important for our policy: all of the governments in the EC now know that we cannot turn back, that every step forward is a step toward the internal market. And should the governments lose heart, industry's support will provide the motivation to carry on with negotiations to achieve our goal.

The commission has already submitted to the council two-thirds of all of the proposals necessary for completing the internal market; the council will soon have passed one-third of the total. Very difficult problems, such as the harmonization of indirect taxes, lie ahead. But we are convinced that they can be solved.

European integration is of course first and foremost of importance for the Europeans themselves.

1. The internal market will completely eliminate internal borders. People will be able to move freely; goods, services, and capital will be able to circulate unimpeded.
2. In the internal market, national regulations will be harmonized; they will no longer act as barriers. Rigidities will be overcome, growth forces released, and signs of "Eurosclerosis" removed.
3. Finally, the internal market will help narrow the economic and social disparities in Europe. In handicapped regions and in areas hit hard by structural change, new opportunities will arise. One of the most positive aspects of the internal market is that people in Europe's deprived areas will be given new hope and encouragement.

Not only Europe but also its partners throughout the world will be offered valuable opportunities by European integration. We expect they will make use of them. If you Americans seek to export to Europe in the 1990s, you will find a dynamic and single market there. You will be able to export mass-produced goods of uniform specifications; your merchandise will be able to circulate freely throughout the community. If you want to import from Europe, you will be able to place your orders with the most efficient supplier, no matter where its operations are headquartered in the community. Finally, if you are interested in investing, you will be able to reach the entire community from a single location within its borders, whether you seek to establish a new company or acquire a firm already in existence.

A more capable and efficient Europe will also be able to improve the situation in other parts of the world. The EC will be more able to assist the fifty associated countries in Africa, the Caribbean, and the Pacific, most of which are among the world's poorest nations. The community will be able to extend its cooperation with the Mediterranean states, thus helping to relieve the situation in this tension-filled region. Finally, within the framework of détente, the EC can lend a hand in the effort to restructure Eastern Europe's economy. It can thus support the social transformation now under way in the Soviet Union and elsewhere, the successful outcome of which is our common hope.

So far so good, will be your response to the news I have presented thus far.

But I am sure that you will also be asking: "Will not the community that has completed its internal market begin to look inwards, perhaps for the very reason that its successes are arising from within?" "Will the EC not become 'Fortress Europe,' turning away competitors from abroad that also seek to profit from the internal market's benefits?"

A number of arguments tend to support this fear:

- The member-states that bear the burden of the community should be the ones to reap the harvest of their efforts;
- The structural adjustment measures required for harmonization are easier to implement in the closed internal market;
- Third countries can be granted benefits if they are willing to do the same.

For this reason, the questions arise: How can we prove that Europe will remain open to its partners? Why are the Community member-states so fond and ready to speak of "community preferences"?

We take these questions very seriously and are not inclined to give a quick answer just for the sake of replying. It is, of course, impossible to

Appendix One

peer into the future with any degree of exactitude. No one knows how the global economy will develop, what turbulence lies ahead, how we will react.

But setting aside the unpredictable developments, I can find good arguments for an answer that should eliminate the fears of our partners in the world. I find these arguments in the history of European integration, in the interests of the Community, and in the most important instrument of our global economy, the GATT with the present negotiations in the Uruguay Round. My response, which I pass on to you with confidence, is: There will be no "Fortress Europe" engaged in constant dispute with the rest of the world. Rather, the community of a single internal market will be one that is open to its partners, one that contributes constructively to facilitating international trade in goods and services.

The willingness of the other world trading powers to work with the community as partners will naturally also be a crucial factor. Let us look back for a minute to the history of European integration, to the sixties and the seventies, to the community's first two decades.

The establishment and first enlargement of the EC represented a disturbance in GATT's multilateral system of trade because a customs union such as the European Economic Community violated the most-favored-nation principle that rules the GATT system. The EC formed its new common external tariff from the average tariffs of the six founding member-states. As welcome as the tariff reductions were in high-tariff countries such as France and Italy, our partners were just as upset by the tariff increases in low-tariff countries, above all in Germany.

What has become of the common external tariffs? The Kennedy Round and later, after the expansion of the community, the Tokyo Round sharply lowered the community's external tariffs. The EC today boasts one of the world's lowest customs tariffs. The average community tariff is only 5 to 6 percent, and peak customs duties are hardly to be found. The establishment and expansion of the community did not, therefore, lead to a permanent increase in or hardening of trade barriers; rather, it clearly facilitated the worldwide reduction of such barriers within the GATT system.

It is no coincidence that from the very beginning European integration has been accompanied by successful international trade negotiations. Nor is it a coincidence that we are again negotiating on tariff reductions within the GATT, in the wake of the enlargement of the community to include Spain, Portugal, and Greece.

Do not forget the community's own interests! Exports account for a large share of the community's economy, more than twice as large as that of the United States.

The strong export orientation of the community will remain if the internal market proves a success. It would be a major error if the community's enterprises neglected the large markets throughout the world with their high growth potentials on account of the internal market that is, perhaps, easier to sell to. Europe cannot afford to forget about East and South Asia, Latin America, or East Europe with their large need for merchandise—quite apart from the neighboring EFTA [European Free Trade Association] nations and the non-European industrial states!

And if this is correct, the community can just as little afford to close itself off to imports from these countries. The would-be exporter must also import. No one ignoring this lesson goes unpunished! It would not only be unwise but also quite damaging in the face of the EC's own interest if the community were to erect barriers against imports. Our trading partners would rightfully respond by retaliating against community exports.

I therefore do not envisage an internal market operating at the cost and to the detriment of our partners worldwide. These thoughts determine the policy of the federal government, and we unrelentingly work to ensure an open internal market. I am certain that my friend Willy de Clercq, the community's commissioner for external relations, views the matter just as I do.

After all, and this is my third argument, we have an excellent international instrument to help us achieve an open internal market. GATT's already cited Uruguay Round runs practically parallel to the efforts made on behalf of the internal market. And we are negotiating on some topics concerning the internal market in this very round. Above all, I want to mention services. Thanks to the United States, trade in services is being discussed in the new GATT Round. This issue is highly topical since services are the growth industry, one whose worldwide progress demands an international framework for trade.

The Uruguay Round offers us the possibility of solving the problem of reciprocity now emerging in many discussions on the internal market. If the internal market produces benefits both for us and for competitors from third countries, where then are the reciprocal benefits? Must not the community safeguard itself against the competition, at least as long as the European companies enjoy the same opportunities on third-country markets?

Many in the community are posing this question. And since the United States has made reciprocity one of the guidelines of its trade policy, there is no way around the matter.

This is an area in which the Uruguay Round can and must produce solutions. It must improve the framework for the exchange of merchandise and services so that global reciprocity is created and guaranteed. We

Appendix One 179

emphatically support this and reject the narrow approach of reciprocity that leads us into the deadend of bilateralism and even of unilateral action.

If we can ensure the success of the Uruguay Round, protectionism will have much less of a chance. Although protectionism is not exactly a monster that keeps growing new heads, one more hideous than the next, a functioning GATT will be able to perform quick and efficient decapitations.

My confidence that we will be able to make the internal market an open market also derives from the fact that the EC is bound by a growing number of international ties and commitments. The community is not alone in the world. It has a highly responsible role to play, particularly since integration and the internal market are newcomers on the international stage.

This has also been recognized by those member-states that have not been as strongly integrated in the world economy as Germany. These countries know that the era of comprehensive protection is over, that they must become more open in the interest of their own restructuring and modernization.

Within the circle of twelve member-states, the trade policy discussion in the community is naturally not easy. The economic policy tradition is too different, as is the performance potential of each of the individual member states. The openness of the internal market must be the object of continuous struggle. Amid the dissonant voices of the member-states that range from "world-openness" to "community preferences," there is the voice of the EC Commission members. On the one hand, like us, they underline the previous openness of the EC. Commissioner [Heinz] Narjes did this recently by pointing to the continued validity of Article 110 of the EEC Treaty that commits the common trading policy to liberalization.

On the other hand, the members of the commission also emphasize the necessity of reciprocity, above all in the fields of services and the right of establishment; Article 110 and the [Most-Favored Nation] MFN clauses as respectively found in the Treaty of Rome and in the GATT do not apply to these areas as they do to merchandise.

In a letter to Commissioner de Clercq, who is responsible for foreign relations, I have criticized such pointed references to reciprocity.

Germany will, perhaps, be outvoted in some cases. But we will not give up easily. At any rate, I promise you my government's committed effort for an open Community. In this context, however, we are also in need of the support of our partners abroad. Every protectionist measure outside the EC strengthens the position of those in the community who want to reserve the benefits of the internal market for themselves. It certainly does not help when the EC and United States present each other with long lists of accusations, even though I don't want to overrate this.

Need I tell you that a number of points in Congress's new trade bill seriously concern us? Should the aim really be constantly to refine Washington's trade policy instruments, thus expanding the possibilities, multi- and unilateral, of intervening in international trade? The federal government regrets the intention of the president to sign this piece of legislation that contains elements of clear protectionism.

We share the disappointment expressed on this point by EC Commissioner de Clercq. The act could prove to be a burden for free international trade. It might unleash or worsen trade conflicts and thus impair the work of GATT, in particular the current multilateral trade negotiations in the framework of the Uruguay Round.

The federal government has therefore appealed to the responsible officials in Washington to see to it all the more so that the provisions of the act are applied in accordance with the interest of free world trade and with GATT's rules of open and multilateral trade.

We trust that the America that has courageously advocated free trade in the wake of its terrible experience with the Great Depression will honor its best traditions and principles. This will serve as a model and inspiration for our European integration that is following American integration at a distance of two hundred years.

The German View of the World in the 1990s and Beyond

Rita Süssmuth
Bundestagspräsident

I would like to begin by thanking you for inviting me to this year's conference of the Robert Bosch Foundation Alumni Association. It is an honor and a pleasure to be able to speak to an audience that has contributed so much to the vitality of German-American relations. You, the Foundation alumni, have the benefit of first-hand experience accumulated during your studies in the Federal Republic of Germany. What is done with this experience in your working lives and whether it is used to further the growth of German-American relations will depend on you.

German–American Day

Today we are celebrating German–American Day for the third time, approved by Congress and proclaimed by President Bush yesterday. It reminds us not only of the contributions German immigrants have made to the development of America, but also of the convictions we share with regard to freedom, democracy and human rights. German–American Day is an expression of bridge building across the Atlantic. It bears testimony to the close ties that have developed between Germans and Americans since the end of the worst war ever to take place. They include numerous public and private initiatives such as the Parliamentary Sponsorship Program between the U.S. Congress and the Bundestag, and the Bosch

---

This speech was delivered to the Annual Conference of the Robert Bosch Foundation Alumni Association, 6 October 1989, at Harvard University, Cambridge, Massachusetts.

Foundation's Fellowship Program. Although these two exchange programs feature prominently in the context of German–American relations, they are only symbolic of the many other programs that exist.

German-American Relationship

Just a few months ago, in May of this year, the Federal Republic of Germany celebrated the fortieth anniversary of its founding as a country and the fortieth anniversary of its constitution. In this context we gratefully recalled the American contribution to the reconstruction of our country and of Europe—a contribution associated with names such as Lucius D. Clay, George Marshall, and other outstanding figures of that era. The forty years the Federal Republic of Germany has existed have been forty years of German–American friendship. With its contribution to the reconstruction of European democracies, America promoted the idea of uniting the democracies to form a European Community. As such, the United States was one of the "godparents" of the European unification movement. For these reasons, and due to the close relationship that exists between our two peoples and countries, based on shared values and ideals of fundamental importance for the founding of the Federal Republic of Germany, German–American relations go far beyond the broad range of exchanges we have in government, industry, science and culture. The core factor in our relationship—the "unifying" factor that holds us together—is the values we share—freedom, joint security, and mutual solidarity. For this reason our relationship is more steadfast and resilient than it would be if it were based only on a harmony of interests. We need to preserve this unifying factor for the future. As such, German–American friendship requires constant and very attentive cultivation.

Global Trends and Prospects

I say this quite consciously, in view of the enormous problems with which the world is faced and the current changes with which the governments of our two countries are having to cope. We are not only living in exciting times, we are living in an era in which global political and economic conditions are being defined, the effects of which will carry over far into the next century. Creative tasks lie ahead of us, but also creative responsibilities. This constitutes an immense challenge both for the United States and for the Federal Republic. This is a challenge that will exert an influence on the further development of the German–American relationship, giving it new orientations as well as new impetus.

I would like to mention a number of points in this context:

1. Three major long-term trends will have an influence on global politics in the future. Changes have begun to take place in the East–West spheres of influence. The rigid bloc thinking that originated in the 1940s is beginning to disappear. A world-wide cooperative network is beginning to replace the old power constellations. The current phase of rapid development in Europe is a further trend—one that will continue to increase the importance of what people here in the United States sometimes refer to as the "Old World" as an influential and stabilizing force in a multipolar world. Finally, the political importance of economic and technological potentials will continue to grow, while the influence of military potentials will decline due to the expanding disarmament and arms control process. These three trends are interactive.

2. In addition, there are factors and forces that support the impetus for change:

- the fact that the reform processes in the Soviet Union, Hungary and Poland will not fail to have an effect on the other Warsaw Pact countries,
- the change from confrontation to system-opening cooperation between the West and the East,
- the progress being made in the process of European unification within the European Community—an example of a European peace order that has already been implemented,
- the development of new regional economic centers and new regional associations (examples: ASEAN, the Gulf states, Latin America),
- the technological revolution: in the fields of information technology, biotechnology and genetic engineering, as well as in the area of alternative and renewable forms of energy,
- the expanding reciprocity and networking of interests in a world that is increasingly becoming a "global village" and a survival community for reasons of mutual dependence. The need to restore an ecological balance and international problems relating to the need for environmental protection are but two very visible examples of this. Let me indicate a few more: overpopulation, the threat of climatic disaster, the North-South differential, human rights violations, as well as the worldwide flood of refugees, hunger and poverty in the world.

New Structures

No generation before us was ever faced with as great a burden of responsibility as we bear for the following generations. On the threshold to the next millennium we are faced with the central question as to whether the human race is being drawn into a maelstrom of self-destruction or whether it will use the pressures being generated by rapid change as an opportunity to formulate definitive and decisive policies for the future. This will include new structures, new strategies and a new system of ethics—a system of ethics for a technological civilization, a system of ethics that will take into account the limits of the modern age and questions of human survival. The "pursuit of happiness"—which the American Declaration of Independence of 1776 refers to as an inalienable right, and which to this very day has continued to be an ideal for social welfare and individual development in the countries of the West—would be turned into its opposite if it were not used as a standard for responsible and enlightened "global policy"—particularly by the free and wealthy nations.

Let me expatiate on this subject. First of all with regard to new *structures* and *strategies*, it will not be possible to solve the major problems of the world if the West and the East do not pool their political energies and their economic strength. Gorbachev's reform policies—the economic and social restructuring taking place in the Soviet Union—have brought about new thinking in Eastern Europe and have begun to loosen up rigid postwar structures. Although we must not underestimate the long-term nature of the changes taking place in the architecture of Europe, it still should be noted that in the course of the 1990s we will move a considerable way closer to achieving the objective of a European peace order that will unite all of Europe in freedom. Americans and Europeans are now faced with the task of promoting the process of political and economic restructuring in all of Europe. We will not be given a second opportunity of this kind. Economic cooperation, foreign policy and security policy are major factors in this context. Thus, by definition, the German–American relationship will be of key importance in this. The Conference on Security and Cooperation in Europe (CSCE) agreements reached in Helsinki and at the follow-up meetings, point in the right direction—joint security, confidence building, practical cooperation, respect of human rights and elimination of the separating character of borders in Europe. The NATO summit declaration issued at Brussels in May this year contains a comprehensive concept for this, which—in addition to maintaining our defense—is based essentially on three pillars: disarmament and arms control, East–West cooperation, and joint alliance responsibility in the face of global challenges. I am certain that these will continue to be essential elements for a joint political strategy in the coming years. Elements of a strategy of this kind are contained in the joint German–Soviet declaration issued during General Secretary Gorbachev's visit to the Federal Republic in June. In various passages of the declaration it is indicated that the agreements signed will serve the gradual build-up of all-European cooperation. What we agreed on with the Soviets will remain embedded in the process of detente and cooperation between the West and the East.

European Community

The European Community has a decisive role to play in the world community of the future. In the course of the 1980s the European Community was enlarged to its present status of twelve members. More than that, however, it acquired an additional dimension. In 1986 the Community undertook to intensify political cooperation among the twelve. Now, a single European market is to be established by the end of 1992. With increasing frequency we are noting signs of a wide-spread fear in non-Community countries of a possible growth in the level of international competitiveness among European Community countries. Misgivings are being voiced more and more loudly that this Europe might very well close itself off economically to the rest of the world. Fears of a "fortress Europe" are currently being voiced most loudly here in the United States, in Japan and in Eastern Europe. To those who see in a Western European economic giant a threat to the global economy and a disintegrative factor for the internal community, I would say that potentially they are right. However, it would be in no one's interest for an economic giant of this kind to close itself off to the rest of the world and pursue protectionist policies—it would do the European Community no good, it would do world trade no good, and it would not be of benefit to economic development in the Third World.

More than forty years after the founding of the General Agreement on Tariffs and Trade (GATT) and in the middle of the Uruguay Round, it is obvious to everyone involved in world trade that we will all need to keep our markets open. The raw materials dependency of the European Community countries, our mutual export dependency above and beyond the European Single Market, international division of labor, and the market opportunities deriving from the interpenetration of national economies is virtually forcing us to engage to the greatest possible extent in free and unrestricted trade. Isolating the European Community from the rest of the world would not help make the Community more competitive—quite on the contrary. We learned this from a number of cases in past decades when protectionist policies were pursued in our country and elsewhere in the world. At the same time, we will always demand of our partners in the world that they, too, desist from protectionism, dumping, and other unfair trade practices.

The message that should be projected by the European Single Market in the 1990s can only be: open markets, cooperation based on partnership, division of labor, and a fair balance of interests. We will continue to project this message in the context of world trade, particularly in the economic triangle consisting of Europe, Japan and the United States. Due to its export dependency, the Federal Republic of Germany is a classical free-trade country. It will continue to be committed to this policy in the context of the European Single Market.

A look at the European Community's trade and association policy record thus far shows how serious we are about this objective for the 1990s. In the course of its development since 1957, the European Community has systematically pursued a liberal trade policy towards third countries and is continuing as a region to liberalize trade. The Fourth Lomé Convention is currently being worked on. Under this convention the European Community has developed an exemplary form of cooperation with the Third World. Similar concepts have been developed to promote cooperation with other regions of the world—with the ASEAN countries, with Latin America, with the Mediterranean countries, and with a number of COMECON countries. On this basis, including an intensification of cooperation with the EFTA countries, we will now be able to continue pursuing political issues that are in the interest of Europe as a whole—such as transnational environmental protection measures, development of transport infrastructures in Europe, research and technology. This prospect shows that economic relations are a firm foundation for the shaping of a European peace order that can and must extend far beyond the European Community. The European Community is an economic and political factor in global politics. However, more than that it is, to an increasing extent, becoming a crystallization point for a united Europe. Thus, the European Single Market and the further planning stages for an economic and monetary union not only have an economic dimension, but are building blocks for a European union whose aim will be to move forward politically in all of Europe in the decades that lie ahead.

The more relations between the West and the East are demilitarized, the more clearly Europe's ability to create impetus emerges and the clearer it becomes that Europe does not end on the borders of the European Community countries. We Germans, in particular, have never maintained this. We are aware that everything that serves to bring Eastern and Western Europeans together will also serve to bring our divided nation together. For this reason we have always pleaded in favor of taking Gorbachev at his word and giving him time. This is why we have very consciously turned to our neighbors in Hungary and Poland in recent months as new structures have been emerging and old enemy images have been fading in Central and Eastern Europe.

As President Bush put it in the speech he gave in the city of Mainz this May, "The path of freedom leads to a larger home—a home where West meets East, a democratic home—the commonwealth of free nations." I am grateful for his confidence that the Berlin Wall, probably the most horrible symbol of divided Germany and Europe, will come down some day. The current state of the reform movement in Europe is reflected by

Appendix One 187

the mass exodus taking place from the German Democratic Republic (GDR), mostly involving young people, and the support being provided by Hungary, Poland and Czechoslovakia to these young people in search of freedom. The reform movement in Eastern Europe is both an opportunity and a challenge for us Germans. In this context there can be no doubt as to our own standpoint: we are and we will continue to be firmly integrated in the community of Western democracies, in the Atlantic Alliance and in the European Community. For us there can be no question of neutralist considerations or unilateral initiatives either now or in the future. What we want is a dense network of confidence, cooperation, dialogue and peaceful competition between the various countries and the alliances. The future of the West, the East, and of the international community in general will depend on cooperative structures and joint responsibility.

New Ethics

A joint effort in dealing with the global challenges of our time will require an enlightened change in our thinking. I have already made reference to this fact. Are there elements of a new system of "ethics for a technological civilization," to quote the philosopher Hans Jonas? Where does this system of ethics begin, and who will apply it? We are living in an age in which ideologies are breaking down, in which values are changing, and in which numerous concepts are losing their meaning. The erosion of dogmas is making it impossible to maintain traditional enemy images—the processes currently taking place in Eastern Europe are a tangible example of this. Times of change are also times of reorientation. In the process of change nations and individuals seek islands of security and signposts that indicate to them where things are headed. It is easy to understand, then, that people expect the government to provide a sense of orientation and, as such, give them a sense of confidence in the future. But can politicians simply declare themselves guarantors of the future? I feel they must at least undertake every possible effort to provide for the future, although those in government—like anyone else—have no way of knowing exactly what the future will bring. As Immanuel Kant said some two hundred years ago in his *Condition Politique:* "The necessity to make decisions extends beyond the possibility to acquire knowledge."

What is involved now and with regard to the future is a new quality in the freedom we have gained in the West. To an increasing extent, our freedom is being seen and accepted as a global message. Government responsibility implies responsibility for the future. As such, the freedom protected by government can only be freedom with responsibility. First and foremost freedom involves responsibility of people for people and, for this reason, includes the principle of reciprocity. The first priority of this responsibility is, as Hans Jonas would put it, "the existence of mankind"; the second priority is "the totality of responsibility"—in other words the need not to lose sight of any of the aspects of this responsibility. According to Jonas, "accepting responsibility for the unknown in advance is a condition of active responsibility, what people refer to as courage to accept responsibility."

In an age in which the human race is, to an increasing extent, faced with the alternative of destroying itself or of changing its thinking, habits and lifestyles, the demand for a new system of ethics is becoming an ineluctable postulate. In only twenty years around seven billion people will populate the earth. In about 100 years the world population will be ten billion. We need to prepare for this fact now. But how can we prepare ourselves? Despite all the dangers to peace, to the environment, to the essence and dignity of creation, opportunities are opening up such as never before in the history of mankind to make use of creative and technological potentials to safeguard and shape the future in the form of a peaceful global society. This will require that we stop carelessly and recklessly destroying the foundations of human life in our natural environment. Instead of the ruthless conquest of nature we should concentrate our energies on developing the human factor, on educating the citizens of tomorrow's world.

Responsible freedom also means our preventing mankind from continuing to be divided up into rich and poor nations. It means that we must avoid the accusation that we are incapable of social justice and of gaining general acceptance for political and social rights in the world. A balance of interests between the North and the South, as well as a wide-ranging emancipation of the Third World—these will be the focal social issues in the world at the end of this and the beginning of the next century. It is only by taking a broad approach in reflecting on and understanding our world that we will gain access to a new system of ethics for technological civilization and for all of mankind—understood as a community for survival. The elements of this ethical system are apparent when we finally understand the process of enlightenment and the changes mankind needs to undergo at the end of an age characterized by many useless fictions regarding power, domination, rule by force, war and error-ridden ideologies. I feel we have a duty to undertake a collective effort to improve our awareness in such a manner that we will be brought back out of the dream sphere of short-term feasibility into the realm of realities for which all the nations of the earth bear a common liability. Europeans and Americans will join forces in formulating a common strategy based on ethical standards. More than that, they will play a key role in this context.

Appendix One

Our common responsibility for the future is based on a foundation of mutual confidence, joint interests and common security—these are unifying factors that bolster German–American friendship. This friendship will stand up under the pressures created by the challenges of the 1990s and beyond. In the process of change—in some cases rapid change—taking place in Europe and in East-West relations, the following factors will remain constant in German policy:

- friendship, partnership and close cooperation with the United States of America,
- the Atlantic Alliance as the guarantor of our freedom and security, and
- the European Community as the basis of our European identity.

The political changes currently taking place in the world will—I hope—bring freedom, democracy, affluence and freedom of movement to more people. Borders will lose their separative character and a forward-looking policy of dialogue and cooperation will develop. We must join forces in making use of these trends for the benefit of all the world's nations and peoples. We are bound by the task of safeguarding the survival of mankind and of moving together towards a future that will bring welfare, peace and freedom to everyone.

I would like to conclude by calling to mind something Henry Kissinger said in 1987 when he was awarded the Charlemagne Prize in Aachen for his merits in connection with European unification: "History knows no resting places. That which does not progress will sooner or later be subject to decline." There must be progress in politics. There must also be a change in our conception of mankind in a global society.

Germany in an Era of Change

Carola Kaps
Frankfurter Allgemeine Zeitung

It is a particular pleasure for me to address the alumni of the Fellowship Program of the Bosch Foundation since I value very highly its work in the promotion of German-American relations. I would like to mention two particular activities: the Bosch Foundation's support of the Youth for Understanding Exchange Organization, of which I am an alumnus, and also the founding of the Bosch Management Institute at Carnegie-Mellon University in Pittsburgh this year. This engagement of a German industrial concern is not only unique but also testifies to the breadth of vision of the Bosch Foundation and its sense of responsibility for the preservation and creation of good international relations. In addition, it is proof of its readiness to be a pioneer in this challenge that results from the growing globalization of world markets and economic relations.

My respect for the achievements of the Bosch Foundation has made my difficult responsibility of selecting a topic for my address a little easier. Because of the recent events, there has been practically no other topic for a German correspondent in the United States than the political developments in my country. For an economic correspondent as myself this boils down to, or extends to the aspects of, the economic significance of German unification and its consequences and effects on the rest of the world.

However, for two reasons I have not selected this topic. First, you probably know from your own observation of the events much about German problems, and you have witnessed more directly than I the various birth pangs of a unified Germany. Perhaps it would be better if I were to listen to you on this topic rather than vice versa. Second, and

---

This speech was delivered to the Annual Conference of the Robert Bosch Foundation Alumni Association, 7 October 1990, Washington, D.C.

more important, you heard an address last evening from a prominent speaker about the new Germany. I have no interest in attempting to compete with Fritz Stern in this respect.

Instead, I will speak to you about my deep conviction that friendship between peoples must be tended with care, above all on the level of private contacts, involving the relationships you developed during your nine-month stay in Germany, which I hope you will maintain, deepen, and expand. This also includes good relations between business entities, and the good corporate citizenship of German companies in the United States and of American companies in Germany. It is certainly true and always good to remember that between countries there are no friendships, only common interests. Friendships exist only between people.

These propositions may appear banal and, in light of your recent experiences, not worth being mentioned and discussed. In my more than twenty years as a correspondent, however, this thought has ripened into a deep conviction: official relations between governments, even when they are best of allies, are like a roller coaster ride through the continual hot and cold baths of compatible and conflicting interests.

In published opinion, relations are described according to whether they are faring well or poorly: either they are "warm relations" based on deep agreement and on "special relationships," or, on the other hand, there is deep disagreement, frigid relations, disappointment, and mutual misunderstanding.

Especially in German-American relations over the last twenty years there have been recurring occasions in which the tone of the relations was bitter. One could sense little in the way of friendship, a community of values, and alliance partnership. I remember, for example, that in 1981, during the high point of the debate over NATO rearmament, then Chancellor Helmut Schmidt found himself exposed to a hateful press campaign and subjected to the same doubts about his fidelity to the Atlantic Alliance as Helmut Kohl and his government found themselves in the spring 1989 before the NATO summit in which a decision on rearmament for short-range missiles was to be made.

In both cases—and please remember that only a year and a half separate us from the last incident—the quiet yearning of Germans for the East was criticized, and Bonn was accused of feeling a greater closeness to the USSR as a European power than it felt to the United States. In both cases there were discussions about a pullout of troops, "burden sharing," credits for the East, the weakness of the dollar, and disruptive German trade surpluses.

It is also worth recalling the indignation in American public opinion to reports that Helmut Schmidt lectured Jimmy Carter in a sharp and arrogant fashion.

The reputations of the Germans sank just as deeply after the Libyan affair. And the infamous engagement of German industry in the construction of an indigenous arms industry in Iraq is planting the same seeds of deep disharmony and invidious presumptions that can hardly be considered "friendly criticism" and thereby rendered harmless.

I emphasize all of this because I am convinced that the new, unified Germany, involved in its search for its place and role in *Mitteleuropa* and the international arena, will cause wrinkled brows and prompt many more doubting questions.

You have perhaps read the excellent lead article in the *Economist* this week with the title "Prost Deutschland." This article presents, in eloquent form, the fundamental challenges that the new, unified Germany confronts at a point in time in which its own massive internal problems could require more than ten years to resolve.

Germany has not been granted the luxury to concentrate on itself, however. From Eastern Europe come appeals for financial and technical help. From Western Europe come the demand that Germany accelerate European integration as a guarantee for the permanence of its Western ties. From this side of the Atlantic a stronger German engagement is sought in international affairs, in the sense of President Bush's proclamation of "partner in leadership." Not to mention financial undertakings.

German policy must first learn how to come to terms with the greater weight of the united Germany in the world. Until now Chancellor Kohl and Foreign Minister [Hans-Dietrich] Genscher have attempted to satisfy all demands, and to promise something to everyone and to make all neighbors happy. I quote the *Economist*:

> This is understakable given that Germany is in the middle of Europe and wants to keep both sides happy. It is also unrealistic. Tradeoffs and hard choices cannot be ducked. Can Germany satisfy the east's demand for aid and open borders? Will it stay in NATO if Germany voters turn against the idea? Will Europhilia really make Germany ready to give up sovereignty when it just has got it back, or give up the D-mark when east Germans are experiencing its security for the first time? Where interests conflict, the Germans will put their own interests first.[1]

There will be, I fear, many problems and many occasions for doubts and misunderstandings. Too much is in flux, and too many things must be reordered before a new, stable European order will emerge from the rubble of the postwar order.

I firmly believe that America should have a place in this new, peaceful European order. However, I also believe that there will be friction and

Appendix One 193

occasions for mistrust and animosity between our governments along the way to this new order.

Particularly in our relationship there is always the danger of a primitive anti-Americanism on the German side and equally primitive anti-German feelings on the American side, stoked by certain representatives of the media.

Here I see your obligation, your important role. Because you and other alumni of the numerous bilateral exchange programs have had the chance to study the intellectual and spiritual energies that sustain the culture of the Federal Republic of Germany or, vice versa, the United States, you must work at the grass-roots level in order to ensure that sympathy, shared values, and mutual respect are not overshadowed by political disputes and conflicts of interest.

I can only mention again in this connection the exemplary achievements of Otto Graf Lambsdorff, who plays exactly the kind of role which, in my opinion, should be emulated by others in order for our friendship to be solidified. He has, over many years, expended much time and great personal effort in order to create friendly relations. As a result, he is now able to state his own opinions in every political situation without being accused of an anti-American attitude, neutralism, or other such tendencies.

Klaus Happrecht, also a knowledgeable friend of the United States, said in his quite charming book, *The Foreign Friend*, that one is not able to understand a person or an entire nation without sympathy, indeed without love. Here lies your, or perhaps better said, *our* common challenge and task.

Notes

1. The *Economist*, 29 September 1990, p. 14.

Appendix Two

West German Federal Governments Since 1949

CHANCELLORS

Year	Government	Chancellor
1949	CDU/CSU/FDP/DP*	Konrad Adenauer
1953	CDU/CSU/FDP/BHE/DP*	Adenauer
1957	CDU/CSU	Adenauer
1961	CDU/CSU/FDP	Adenauer
1963	CDU/CSU/FDP	Ludwig Erhard
1965	CDU/CSU/FDP	Erhard
1966	CDU/CSU/SPD	Kurt Georg Kiessinger
1969	SPD/FDP	Willy Brandt
1972	SPD/FDP	Brandt
1974	SPD/FDP	Helmut Schmidt
1976	SPD/FDP	Schmidt
1980	SPD/FDP	Schmidt
1982	CDU/CSU/FDP	Helmut Kohl
1983	CDU/CSU/FDP	Kohl
1987	CDU/CSU/FDP	Kohl
1990	CDU/CSU/FDP	Kohl

PRESIDENTS

Year	Party	President
1949	FDP	Theodor Heuss
1959	CDU	Heinrich Lübke
1969	SPD	Gustav W. Heinemann
1974	FDP	Walter Scheel
1979	CDU	Karl Carstens
1984	CDU	Richard V. Weizsäcker

*Several smaller parties also participated in the 1949 and 1953 coalition governments.

The CDU does not campaign in Bavaria, leaving the field to the CSU, which in turn does not campaign nationally. At the federal level, the two parties form one joint parliamentary block in the Bundestag.

Chronology of the Division and Unification of Germany

December 1943	Teheran Conference
February 1945	Yalta Conference
7–8 May 1945	German unconditional surrender
5 June 1945	Allied Control Council: Berlin divided into 4 sectors Germany divided into 4 zones of occupation
July–August 1945	Potsdam Conference
January 1947	"Bi-Zone" created by merger of American and British zones
1948–49	Berlin blockade
23 May 1949	Federal Republic of Germany founded
6 October 1949	German Democratic Republic founded
17 June 1953	GDR Uprising
23 October 1954	NATO admits FRG to membership
May 1955	Warsaw Pact established, including GDR
13 August 1961	Berlin wall erected
1970	Treaties by FRG with Moscow and Warsaw
1971	Quadripartite Agreement on Berlin
1972 FRG-GDR	Treaty on the Basis of Relations
Summer–Fall 1989	Exodus of GDR citizens via Hungary (also via embassies in Poland and Czechoslovakia)
7 and 9 October 1989	GDR public demonstrations against SED government in Berlin and Leipzig ("Monday demonstration")
9 November 1989	Berlin wall breached
28 November 1989	Chancellor Kohl lays out ten-point program to overcome the division of Germany and Europe

(*continues*)

(continued)

5 May 1990	"Two plus Four" talks begin; foreign ministers of Great Britain, France, U.S., USSR, FRG, and GDR meet in Bonn for first talks on German unity
1 July 1990	Economic, monetary, and social Union of FRG/GDR
31 August 1990	Unification Treaty between FRG and GDR signed in Berlin
12 September 1990	Treaty on the Final Settlement with Respect to Germany ("Two plus Four") signed
19 September 1990	GDR People's Chamber ratifies Unification Treaty
20 September 1990	German Bundestag ratifies Unification Treaty
1–2 October 1990	Document to suspend Four-Power rights is signed
3 October 1990	In accord with Article 23 of the *Basic Law*, GDR accedes to territory and five new states formed
2 December 1990	First Bundestag elections in unified Germany

Articles of the German Basic Law with Respect to Unification

Preamble: The German people have also acted on behalf of those Germans to whom participation was denied. The entire German people are called upon to achieve in free self-determination the unity and freedom of Germany.

Article 23: For the time being this Basic Law shall apply to [all West German states plus Greater Berlin]. In other parts of Germany it shall be put into force on their accession.

Article 146: The Basic Law shall cease to be in force on the day on which a constitution adopted by a free decision of the German people comes into force.

The New German States

1. *Mecklenburg-Western Pomerania (Mecklenburg-Vorpommern)*
   Area: 23.838 sq. km. (6.7% of the FRG)
   Population: 1,963,909 (2.5% of the FRG)
   State capital: Schwerin
   Minister president: Bernd Seite (CDU)

2. *Brandenburg*
   Area: 29.059 sq. km. (8.1% of the FRG)
   Population: 2,641,152 (3.4% of the FRG)
   State capital: Potsdam
   Minister president: Manfred Stolpe (SPD)

3. *Saxony-Anhalt (Sachsen-Anhalt)*
   Area: 20.445 sq. km. (5.7% of the FRG)
   Population: 2,964,971 (3.7% of the FRG)
   State capital: Magdeburg
   Minister president: Werner Münch (CDU)

4. *Saxony (Sachsen)*
   Area: 18.337 sq. km. (5.1% of the FRG)
   Population: 4,900,675 (5.9% of the FRG)
   State capital: Dresden
   Minister president: Kurt Biedenkopf (CDU)

5. *Thuringia (Thuringen)*
   Area: 16.251 sq. km. (4.6% of the FRG)
   Population: 2,683,877 (3.2% of the FRG)
   State capital: Erfurt
   Minister president: Bernhard Vogel (CDU)

About the Book and Editors

The incorporation of the German Democratic Republic into the Federal Republic ignited excitement over the prospect of bringing democratic reform and better living conditions to the East but also gave rise to concern over united Germany's ability to do so while maintaining its own economic vitality. This volume examines many of the issues integral to the tremendous challenges—in foreign and security policy, politics, economics, technologies, and public policy—that Germany confronted even before unification and continues to confront today.

Gale A. Mattox received a Ph.D. from the University of Virginia in 1981. She worked as an analyst with the Congressional Research Service from 1974 to 1976 and has been a Fulbright Scholar, NATO Research Fellow, and International Affairs Fellow, Council on Foreign Relations, at the State Department. As a 1984–1985 Robert Bosch Fellow, she served with the German Defense Ministry and the Office of the Governor, North Rhine–Westphalia. Mattox is coeditor, with C. Kelleher, of *Evolving European Defense Policies* (1987) and, with J. Vaughan, of *Germany Through American Eyes* (Westview, 1989). She is associate professor of political science at the U.S. Naval Academy.

A. Bradley Shingleton received his J.D. in 1982 from Duke University School of Law and was a recipient of a DAAD Fellowship in 1979–1980 at the Phillipps-Universität in Marburg, Germany. As a 1986–1987 Robert Bosch Fellow, he served at the Federal Ministry of Justice and in the Legal Department of Robert Bosch GmbH in Stuttgart. He has published several articles on legal topics in German and in English as well as a chapter on international litigation in *Germany Through American Eyes*. Shingleton is an attorney in Washington, D.C., with McGuire, Woods, Battle and Boothe.

About the Contributors

Dana H. Allin received a Ph.D. in 1990 from the Nitze School of Advanced International Studies (SAIS), The Johns Hopkins University. He has worked as a staff reporter for the *Montgomery County Sentinel* and the *Montgomery Journal* in Maryland and the Market News Service Inc. in London. In 1990 he was a professional lecturer in European Politics and American Foreign Policy at the SAIS Bologna Center, Italy. As a Bosch Fellow, 1990–1991, he was assigned to the *Frankfurter Allgemeine Zeitung*, FDP-Bundestagsfraktion, and the Economics Department of the Deutsche Bank.

Jon M. Appleton received his M.A. in International Relations and his J.D. from the University of Southern California in 1989. He is a member of the California Bar Association. He was awarded a Deutscher Akademischer Austauschdienst (DAAD) Fellowship to the University of Bonn in 1985–1986. As a Bosch Fellow, 1989–1990, he worked in the East Asian division of the Foreign Ministry and in various ministries of the State Government of Baden-Württemberg. He is currently an associate, specializing in general commercial transactions and foreign trade, with Baker & McKenzie, an international law firm headquartered in Los Angeles.

Martin Bangemann was the Minister of Economics of the Federal Republic of Germany from 1984–1988. From 1989 until the present he has served as Vice President of the Commission of the European Community. Bangemann has been a member of the Free Democratic Party since 1963, and was chairman of that party from 1985–1988.

Carol Deck holds an M.A. from Georgetown University. She worked for several years in the policy and planning office of the U.S. Environmental Protection Agency (EPA) and was manager of European Community relations. As a 1988–1989 Bosch Fellow, Deck worked in the Waste and Water Division of the Federal Environment Ministry in Bonn and in the Legal Division of the Bavarian State Environment Ministry. She is currently studying environmental and natural resource law at the University of Colorado.

J. Henrike Garkisch earned a Master's in Public Policy (M.P.P.) in International Trade and Finance from the John F. Kennedy School of Government, Harvard University. She has worked in the Department of Commerce International Trade Administration in Pittsburgh, 1987, and at the Sumitomo Life Insurance Company as a trainee in Tokyo, 1988. As a Bosch Fellow from 1989 to 1990, Garkisch was with the Bundesbank and the Matuschka Berlin GmbH. She is now employed by Deutsche Bank, New York City.

Melinda Hargrave-Kanzow received a Master's in Public Policy from Harvard University in 1989. From 1982 to 1984 she worked as a journalist for Oliphant Washington Service in Washington, D.C. For two years, she studied in Europe at the Institute for Political Studies in Grenoble, France, and at the University of Würzburg, Germany. A Bosch Fellow from 1989 to 1990, she worked at the Bundesbank and at the Dresdner Bank.

Carola Kaps received her training as an economist in the Federal Republic of Germany. She was named the Washington correspondent for the *Frankfurter Allgemeine Zeitung (FAZ)* in 1980. In 1984 she took a four-year assignment with *FAZ* covering West Africa. Kaps resumed her post as Washington correspondent in 1988.

Lauren Kelley received a Master's in International Affairs from Columbia University in 1984. From 1982 to 1984 she was Editor-in-Chief of the *Journal of International Affairs* at Columbia University and from 1984 to 1990 she was a Presidential Management Intern and International Economist at the International Trade Administration of the U.S. Department of Commerce. She is currently manager, Market Development Eastern Europe at Compaq Computer Corporation in Munich, Germany.

John Meakem received his M.A. in Public Policy from the John F. Kennedy School of Government, Harvard University in 1987. He worked in the Office of Massachusetts governor Michael Dukakis from 1984 to 1985, the IBM Governmental Programs Office in Washington (1986), and the Executive Council on Foreign Diplomats in New York from 1987 to 1989. As a Bosch Fellow, 1989–1990, he was posted in the Ministry for Intra-German Relations and the Office of the Mayor of West Berlin. He is now an associate with the Jerome Levy Economics Institute of Bard College, New York.

Richard W. Morris received his Ph.D. from Rice University in 1980 and C.B.A. from the Wharton School in 1985. He is both a manager of technology-based economic development programs and a scholar specializing in comparative industrial policy. He founded the Bioprocessing and Pharmaceutical Research Center at the University City Science Center and served as Vice-President of the Texas Research and Technology Foundation. As a Bosch Fellow in 1988–1989, Morris worked on the international issues of venture capital, technology transfer, and public policy. He is presently a Senior Program Officer at the National Research Council, National Academy of Sciences, where he develops industrial policy for the Republic of Indonesia.

Daniel H. Mudd received a Master of Public Administration at Harvard University in 1986. He served in the United States, Japan, and Lebanon as a Marine Corps

Officer from 1981 to 1984. From 1986 to 1988 he was a senior consultant at Ayers, Whitmore and Company in New York and was a Manager for Strategy and Development with Xerox from 1988 to 1990. As a Bosch Fellow in 1990–1991, he worked in Bonn with the German Defense Ministry on the strategic planning process for the management of military policy following German unification and with the Matuschka Group in Munich.

Barbara Reilly received her J.D. from Georgetown University in 1984 and served as a law clerk to the U.S. District Court in Birmingham, Alabama, 1984–1985, and as an Associate with Davis, Wright and Jones in Seattle, Washington. As a Bosch Fellow, 1987–1988, she was in the Justice Ministry in Bonn and the Federal Cartel Office in Berlin. She is currently an in-house counsel for Krone AG, a telecommunications company with extensive international ties, and is responsible for the company's foreign subsidiaries.

Rita Süssmuth studied romance languages and history in Münster, Tübingen, and Paris. She was a professor at Ruhr University, Bochum, Germany from 1969 to 1971 and in 1971, she became Professor Ordinarius of Educational Science at Dortmund University. She served as Federal Minister of Youth, Family and Health from 1985 to 1986. Since 1986, she has served as Federal Chairwoman of the CDU Women's Association and as Federal Minister for Youth, Family Affairs, Women and Health. She has been a member of the Deutscher Bundestag (German Parliament) since 1987 and is currently its president.

Cole Thompson received his M.A. from the University of California, Berkeley. He served with the U.S. Army in Germany as a Tank Officer. Thompson was a Research Team Manager with Levy & Co., Oakland, in 1989. As a 1989–1990 Bosch Fellow, he was in the Ministry of Intra-German Affairs and with the economics section of the *Stuttgarter Nachrichten*. He is now a consulting associate for Cambridge Associates, an investment consulting firm.

Jonathan B. Tucker holds a Ph.D. from the Massachusetts Institute of Technology with a specialization in defense and arms control studies. In 1989–1990 he was an American Association for the Advancement of Science Fellow in the Office of European Security and Political Affairs, U.S. Department of State. Tucker was a Bosch Fellow from 1987 to 1988, working at the NATO desk in the Foreign Office in Bonn and the military technology division of Dornier GmbH, an aerospace company based in Friedrichshafen. He is currently an analyst with the International Security and Commerce Program at the congressional Office of Technology Assessment (OTA).

Index

Aachen Technology Center, 142
Accountability, 159
Accounting, 105
Acheson, Dean, 11, 34, 36, 45
Adenauer, Konrad, 11, 19, 21, 34, 35, 36, 37, 45, 125
Advertising, 123, 128, 130
Aerospace industries, 17, 19, 30, 31
Aérospatiale firm, 22, 28, 31
Afghanistan, 40
Agriculture, 108
Airbus consortium, 21
Aircraft, 17, 20
    Alpha Jet, 23–25
    costs, 21, 24
    European Fighter Aircraft (EFA), 27, 28
    F-104 *Starfighter*, 20
    Fouga Magister, 20, 23
    Hawk, 25
    Mirage II/III, 20, 23
    Noratlas, 20
    Rafale, 27, 31
    Tornado, 23
    trainers, 20, 23–25
    Transall transport, 21
    See also Helicopters
AL. *See* Berlin, Alternative List
Alcatel, 164
Algeria, 20
Alliance building, 5
ARD. *See* Federal Republic of Germany, Standing Conference of German Public Law Broadcasting Corporations
Arms sales, 25
Asia, 104, 105, 178
Assassination attempts, 78
AT&T, 164

Atlantic Alliance, 187, 189. *See also* North Atlantic Treaty Organization
Automobiles/automotive industry, 30, 163, 169, 170
AV Euromedia, 128

Baden-Württemberg, 61–63
Bahr, Egon, 15(n2)
Baker, James, 75
Balance of power, 5, 6, 30, 35, 36
Balkans, 9, 45
Baltic Republics, 9
Bankruptcies, 116
Barter system, 115
Baur, Winfried, 61
Bavaria, 61, 153, 154–155, 196(n)
    Bavarian Media Agency, 128
BBC. *See* British Broadcasting Company
Belgium, 11
Berlin
    Alternative List (AL), 69, 72, 77–78
    Berlin Economic Promotion, 137
    Berlin wall, 30, 37, 44, 70, 83, 186, 197
    blockade/airlift, 35
    Bundestag representation, 71
    crises, 37
    East Berlin, 72, 74, 77
    elections, 74
    funds for, 70–71
    GDR refugees in, 72
    House of Representatives, 69, 72, 74, 78
    housing, 72
    red-green coalition in West Berlin, 68–69, 72
    senate/cabinet, 69
    unified, 74, 75
Bertelsmann AG, 128, 130

Biotechnology, 135–147
Biotechnology and the Changing Role of Government (OECD report), 143
Bipolar/multipolar systems, 4–5, 8
Bismarck, Otto von, 35, 36
BMFT. *See* Federal Republic of Germany, Federal Ministry of Research and Technology
Bold Sparrow military exercise, 29
Bosch Foundation, 181–182, 190
Brandenburg, 132(n39), 199
Brandt, Willy, 11, 23, 40, 44, 67, 75, 98
Bretton Woods, 42
British Aerospace, 31
British Broadcasting Company (BBC), 125
Bulgaria, 99
Bush, George, 69, 74, 75, 156, 186, 192
 administration, 43
Business Week, 30

Cable/satellite transmission, 123–124, 127, 128, 129, 132(n39), 133(nn 43, 44)
CAP. *See* European Community, Common Agricultural Policy
Capital (magazine), 106
Capital investments, 115
Capitalism, 35
Capital markets, 87, 89–90, 112
Carter, Jimmy, 40, 191
 administration, 39, 43
Catalonia, 63
CDU. *See* Christian Democratic Union
Centralization/decentralization, 53, 62, 63
CERCLA. *See* United States, Comprehensive Environmental Response, Compensation, and Liability Act
Chaban-Delmas, Jacques, 20
Cheney, Richard, 75
Christian Democratic Union (CDU), 59, 69, 70, 72, 73, 76, 127, 152, 156, 159, 196(n)
Christian Social Union (CSU), 76, 153, 159, 196(n)
Coalitions, 31, 68–69, 72, 76, 77–78, 151, 159, 196(n)
Coca-Cola, 155
Cold war, 3, 5, 19, 34–43, 95
 end of, 30, 34
COMECON. *See* Council for Mutual Economic Assistance
Common European House, 9
Communications, 163, 165, 170
Communism, 35, 117
 Communist parties, 42, 98
Compagnie Luxembourgeoise de Télédiffusion, 128
Competition/competitiveness, 107, 130, 135, 162, 166, 168–171, 185
Computers, 164, 165, 166, 168, 170
Conference of Environment Ministers, 152, 153
Conference on Security and Cooperation in Europe (CSCE), 6, 9, 73, 184
Conscription, 43
Consulting services, 137, 139
Consumer goods/consumers, 99, 104, 106–107
 Eastern consumers, 114–115
 See also Demand
Conventional forces/defense, 14, 26, 27
Copyrights, 137
Council for Mutual Economic Assistance (COMECON), 6, 95, 96, 106, 107, 114, 115, 117, 186
Cranes (machinery), 100–101
Credit, 117
CSCE. *See* Conference on Security and Cooperation in Europe
CSU. *See* Christian Social Union
Currency reform, 42
Currency union. *See* Federal Republic of Germany, monetary union
Czechoslovakia, 99, 101, 105, 107, 187

Daimler Benz, 163
DASA. *See* Deutsche Aerospace
Dassault firm, 24, 27
de Clerq, Willy, 178, 180
Defense industry, 14
de Gaulle, Charles, 19, 20, 21, 22
Delors, Jacques, 10
de Maiziére, Lothar, 76
Demand, 114–115, 169–170
Democracy, 62, 159, 181
 social democracy, 75
Denmark, 11

Der Spiegel, 26, 75, 78
Détente, 40–41, 96, 98
Deterrence, 13, 14, 16(n12), 28, 29, 39, 40
Deutsche Aerospace (DASA), 30–31
Deutsche mark (DM)/East German mark, 12, 40, 43, 83, 90, 91, 92, 104, 107. *See also* Federal Republic of Germany, monetary union
Deutscher Sportbund (DSB), 129
Deutsche Welle, 125
Deutschlandfunk, 125
Dienstbier, Jiri, 15
Diepgen, Eberhard, 69
Dietze, Gottfried, 53
DM. *See* Deutsche mark/East German mark
Dollars, 11, 12, 36, 42, 104, 191
Dornier firm, 24
Dresden, 79(n16), 89
Drinking water, 151, 153
DSB. *See* Deutscher Sportbund
Dumas, Roland, 15(n6)
Dumping. *See under* Trade

Eastern Europe, 8, 45, 103, 107, 118. *See also* Federal Republic of Germany, and *Osthandel*; Germany, pre-1949, and *Osthandel*; Warsaw Pact; *under* European Community; *individual countries*
EC. *See* European Community
Economist, 8, 192
ECS. *See* European Communication Satellite
Education. *See under* European Community; Federal Republic of Germany; United States
EEC. *See* European Economic Community
EFA. *See* Aircraft, European Fighter Aircraft
EFTA. *See* European Free Trade Association
Egypt, 19
Elections. *See under* Federal Republic of Germany; German Democratic Republic
Electronics industry, 162–171
 employment in, 163
 world market, 163–164, 169, 171
EMS. *See* European Monetary System
Energy, 63. *See also* Nuclear power plants
Engineers, 105, 167
Entrepreneurs, 137, 140–141
Environmental issues, 57, 63, 69, 73, 86, 117, 149–159, 163, 165, 183, 186
 and federal/state governments, 151, 152–153
 and government-industry relations, 154–159
 lawsuits concerning, 157–158
 negotiation and compromise concerning, 149–159
 public involvement in, 157, 158–159
 regulations, 115–116, 151, 154, 155–156, 159
EPA. *See* United States, Environmental Protection Agency
ERASMUS Program, 58
Ethics, 184, 187–188
Ethnic conflicts, 45
Eurocopter company, 31
European armaments agency, 32
European Atomic Energy Community, 65(n19)
European Bank for Reconstruction and Development, 107
European Coal and Steel Community, 65(n19)
European Communication Satellite (ECS), 128
European Community (EC), 6–8, 30, 31, 36, 89, 149, 182, 183
 Common Agricultural Policy (CAP), 108
 common foreign/defense policy, 7, 8, 32
 Commission, 52, 56, 57, 58, 60, 171(n), 174, 179
 and community preferences, 176, 179
 Council of Ministers, 16(n6)
 and Eastern Europe, 7, 14, 107, 176, 178, 185
 and education, 57–58
 electronics industry issues, 163, 165, 167
 fears concerning, 176–177, 185

foreign policies, 57
German delegations, 61
integration, 51–64
internal market, 7, 52, 168, 171, 174–180, 185–186. *See also* European Community, trade
investments in, 167–171, 176
and German *Länder*, 51, 52, 55–58, 59, 60, 61, 65(nn 19, 35), 153
regional administrations, 51–52, 61–63
regulations/directives, 59, 116
trade, 7, 56, 58, 91, 167–168, 176–180, 185–187. *See also* European Community, internal market
voting, 57
European Council, 32, 57
European Economic Community (EEC), 65(n19), 177, 179
European Free Trade Association (EFTA), 178, 186
European integration, 51–64, 177, 183
European Monetary System (EMS), 90–91
European Parliament, 7
European Single Market, 185–186. *See also* European Community, internal market
Europe of the Regions, 63. *See also* European Community, regional administrations
Exchange rates, 42, 91, 92, 104. *See also* Deutsche mark/East German mark; Dollars

FAR. *See* France, Rapid Action Force
FDP. *See* Free Democratic party
Fecter, Peter, 37
Federalism, 7, 51, 52, 53, 62, 64(nn 1, 2), 150, 159
Federal Republic of Germany (FRG), 8, 11, 51, 185–186
  aeronautics firms, 19
  aerospace industry, 30–31
  arms exporting, 25–26
  Basic Law, 53–54, 57, 125, 131(n4), 132(n24), 150, 151, 160(n2)
  borrowing, 86–87, 90, 118
  broadcasting in, 123–130. *See also* Media
  Bund/Bundestaat, 51, 53, 55, 59, 60, 61, 73, 168(n2)
  Bundesbank, 46, 83, 84, 87, 91, 92, 112
  Bundesrat, 54–55, 59–60, 65(n34), 68, 73, 151, 160(n10)
  Bundestag, 22, 27, 28, 29, 30, 71, 150, 157, 160(n1), 181. *See also* Federal Republic of Germany, Bundesrat
  Bundeswehr, 19, 23, 74
  Central Research Centers, 137
  chancellors, 196
  chronology of division/unification, 197–198. *See also* Federal Republic of Germany, unification of; Germany, pre-1949, division of
  constitutional issues, 52–54, 57, 73, 132(n31). *See also* Federal Republic of Germany, Basic Law; Federal Republic of Germany, Federal Constitutional Court
  cultural policy, 54, 55
  debt/deficits, 90, 118
  Defense Ministry, 20, 24
  Deutsche Bundespost, 127, 128
  Economics Ministry, 112, 138, 163, 164, 166, 171–172(n)
  economy, 12, 20, 30, 42, 83, 85, 92, 95, 106, 170, 171
  education, 55, 62, 63, 167, 171
  elections, 55, 69(table), 71, 73, 84, 149, 160(n1). *See also individual parties*
  environment ministries, 149, 151, 152, 153
  and European Community, 36, 51–64, 189
  fears concerning, 11, 26, 45–46, 47
  Federal Cartel Office, 129, 130
  Federal Constitutional Court, 57, 123, 124, 125, 126, 130, 131(n4), 151
  federal government. *See* Federal Republic of Germany, Bund/Bundestaat
  federal governments, 196
  Federal High Court, 124, 129, 130
  Federal Ministry of Research and Technology (BMFT), 136, 147

Index 211

five new states, 88–89, 91, 106, 127, 131(n18), 132(n39)
formation of, 52
future role, 46
and German Democratic Republic, 72, 97, 118
government spending, 85, 87, 118
and Gulf war, 30, 32, 46
imports, 86, 91, 94, 164, 170
industrial policy, 135
investment in, 90, 106, 118, 166–167
Länder, 51–64, 65(n19), 123, 124, 125–126, 126–127, 132(nn 20, 24), 133(n65), 150, 160(n2). *See also* Federal Republic of Germany, five new states; *individual states*
law-making issues, 51, 55, 56, 59
Luftwaffe, 20, 24
Mittelstand in, 140–141, 142, 170
monetary union, 83–92, 111, 114
municipalities, 53, 69(table)
and North Atlantic Treaty Organization, 22, 36, 189
nuclear capability, 14, 29
and *Osthandel*, 94, 95–98, 101–108
political parties. *See individual parties*
presidents, 196
private sector, 136, 171
rearming of, 19
Regional Committee, 71, 74
regional governments, 74
second television channel (ZDF), 125, 126, 129, 131(n1), 132(n31)
social policy, 54
space research, 28
Standing Conference of German Public Law Broadcasting Corporations (ARD), 125, 126, 129, 131(n1)
State Committee on Air Pollution, 152
states. *See* Federal Republic of Germany, *Länder*
taxation, 12, 86, 87, 92, 112, 117, 118, 119
trade, 91, 94, 136. *See also* Federal Republic of Germany, and *Osthandel*
Treuhandanstalt, 113, 114, 117–118

unification, 12, 30, 36, 40, 44, 68, 70, 72–74, 75, 76, 78(n3), 79(n16), 85, 90, 92, 114, 118, 197–198. *See also* Federal Republic of Germany, monetary union
See also German Democratic Republic; German-French relations; German-Soviet relations; German-U.S. relations; Germany, pre-1949
Five-Year Plans, 95
Flexible response, 39
Food aid, 15(n2)
Foreign Friend, The (Happrecht), 193
Fortress Europe, 176, 177, 185
Forward defense, 38
Foss, Jörg, 94
Four Motors of Europe, The, 62–63
France, 8, 10, 14, 44, 47, 63, 66(n38), 170, 177
economy, 30
elites, 30
Europeanists vs. Gaullists, 27
and German-U.S. relations, 22
isolationism, 22–23, 25, 26
National Company for the Design and Construction of Aircraft Engines (SNECMA), 27
and NATO, 22, 23, 27
nuclear capability, 20, 22, 25, 28–29, 30
Rapid Action Force (FAR), 27
regional governments, 65(n20)
and United States, 20
See also German-French relations
Fraunhofer Gesellschaft, 137
Free Democratic party (FDP), 69, 74, 152–153, 159
Freedom, 53, 181, 182
of expression, 126, 131(n4)
of movement, 58, 175
FRG. *See* Federal Republic of Germany
Fujitsu, 169

Garnham, David, 16(n12)
GATT. *See* General Agreement on Tariffs and Trade
GDR. *See* German Democratic Republic
General Agreement on Tariffs and Trade (GATT), 170

212   Index

Kennedy/Tokyo Rounds, 177
Uruguay Round, 177, 178, 179, 180, 185
Genscher, Hans-Dietrich, 192
German Democratic Republic (GDR) (1949–1990), 37, 97
  aid to, 72, 112, 113, 118
  demand for products of, 114–115
  economy, 85, 86, 112, 114, 115
  elections, 68, 70, 71–72, 75–77, 76(table), 79(n16), 84. *See also individual parties*
  exodus from, 12, 44, 92, 112, 115, 187, 197. *See also* Refugees
  exports, 114
  fears concerning, 20
  firms, 87–89, 111–119
  and Green party, 77
  gross national product (GNP), 86, 116
  secret police, 76
  See also Federal Republic of Germany; Germany, pre-1949; German-French relations; German-Soviet relations; German-U.S. relations
German-French relations, 36
  arms collaboration, 17–32
  autonomy vs. alliance in, 18
  defense arrangements, 23, 26–27, 29, 30
  Elysée treaty (1963), 21–22
  Franco-German Defense and Security Council, 29
  and Germany's increased power, 30–31
  joint exercises, 29
  and pilot training, 23–24
  political objectives in, 18, 25, 29, 31
German-Soviet relations, 4, 47, 95, 184, 191
  German aid, 12, 15(n2), 45, 46
  Rapallo treaty (1922), 41, 45, 47
  and Soviet troops' relocation, 45, 46
  trade, 95, 97, 106. *See also* Federal Republic of Germany, and *Osthandel*; Germany, pre-1949, and *Osthandel*
German-U.S. relations, 20, 22, 34–47, 184, 189, 190, 191, 193
  anti-Americanism, 39, 193

Association of German Industry, 97
biotechnological collaboration, 146–147
burden sharing, 41–43, 191
Center for Foreign Trade Information, 97, 104
economic relations, 41–43. *See also* German-U.S. relations, trade issues
future of, 47
German-American Day, 181–182
and military strategy, 38–39
and monetary policy, 43
Mutual Defense Assistance Agreement (1955), 19
and pilot training, 24
stability in, 38
tensions in, 37, 38, 40–41
trade issues, 43, 94, 170, 191
and U.S. nuclear commitment, 28
and U.S. troops in Germany, 36
weapons purchases, 21
Germany, pre-1949
  division of, 97, 197
  economy, 42
  ethnic Germans, 94
  National Assembly, 165
  and *Osthandel*, 94
  Propaganda Ministry, 125
  Reichspost, 124
  Reichsrundfunkgesellschaft (RRG), 124–125
Giscard d'Estaing, Valéry, 26, 32
Global politics, 182–183, 186, 189
GNP. *See* German Democratic Republic, gross national product
Gorbachev, Mikhail, 4, 39, 44, 73, 95, 98, 184, 186
Great Britain, 8, 10, 14, 17, 23, 27, 44, 167
Great Depression, 43, 180
Greece, 177
Green party, 26, 69, 77, 149, 151, 160(n1). *See also* Berlin, Alternative List
Greenpeace, 158
Groupe Bull, 162, 169
Grundgesetz. *See* Federal Republic of Germany, Basic Law
G-7 countries, 91

Gulf war, 8, 12, 31, 91. *See also under* Federal Republic of Germany

Habicht, Thomas, 67
Happrecht, Klaus, 193
Hard currency, 99, 100, 103, 115
  auctions, 104
Haussman, Helmut, 116
Havel, Vaclav, 9
Hazardous waste, 153, 155
Heinemann AG, 100, 101
Helicopters
  Apache, 29
  Gazelle, 28
  Tiger, 17, 27–30
Helios satellite, 28
Hernu, Charles, 18
Hitachi, 166
Hochbaum, Ingo, 58
Homatek, 100, 102, 103
Housing. *See under* Berlin
Human rights, 181, 183
Hungary, 44, 99, 100, 105, 107, 183, 186, 187

IBM corporation, 162, 164, 166, 169
ICL company, 169
Industry, 116, 135, 149, 154–156, 162, 175. *See also* Automobiles/automotive industry; Electronics industry; Production/productivity
INF. *See* Missiles, Intermediate-Range Nuclear Forces
Inflation, 43, 83, 84, 85–86, 87, 90, 91, 112, 113, 117, 167
Information/information offices, 61, 62, 97, 124, 137, 139, 142, 143, 163, 165, 169
  Freedom of Information Act. *See under* United States
Infrastructure, 115, 118, 186
Innovation, 63, 147, 163, 169
Institute for Microbiology (Göttingen), 142
Intellectual properties, 137, 145, 146
Interest rates, 12, 43, 46, 83, 85, 86, 87, 88, 89, 90, 91
International monetary system, 36
Iraq, 192. *See also* Gulf war
Ireland, 8
Ismay, Lord Hastings, 10, 11, 15

Italy, 11, 23, 27, 28, 42, 63, 94, 170, 177

January Uprising (combine), 100–101
Japan, 42, 43, 89, 105, 135, 170, 185
  electronics industry, 165–166, 167
Joint ventures, 31, 99–101, 102, 103, 104, 105, 106, 144, 145
Jonas, Hans, 187, 188

Kaliningrad, 94
Kalkar nuclear reactor, 151, 160(n4)
Kant, Immanuel, 187
Kennan, George F., 14, 36, 45
Kennedy, John F., 37
  administration, 37, 39
Kennedy, Paul, 41–42
Kernforschungszentrum (Julich), 142
Kirsch, Leo and Thomas, 128
Kissinger, Henry, 3, 40, 47, 189
Kohl, Helmut, 11, 28, 29, 31, 40, 44, 45, 72, 74, 76, 106, 107, 118, 191, 192
  administration, 50
  and agricultural trade, 108
  in GDR, 79(n16)
  and Momper, 68, 69, 70, 75
  and monetary union, 84, 85, 112
  Moscow trip (1988), 97
Korean War, 19
Krupp company, 98

Labor costs, 88, 105–106, 107. *See also* Wages
Labor markets, 88, 89, 104
Labor unions, 88, 167
La Fontaine, Oskar, 78
Lambsdorff, Otto Graf, 193
Lang, Reiner, 102
Language, 58, 59, 63, 167
Latin America, 178, 186
Laufer, Heinz, 53
Lawsuits, 157–158
LeBahn, Axel, 103–104
Leipzig, 79(n16), 89, 197
Lenvest, 101
Licensing, 137, 139, 142
Liebherr company, 100–101
Life science, 135, 138. *See also* Biotechnology
LINGUA Program, 58
Lobbying, 60, 61

Lombardy, 63
Lomé Convention, Fourth, 186
Lorell, Mark A., 18

MacArthur, Douglas, 36
Machinery/machine tools, 99, 100, 165
McNamara, Robert, 39
Managers/management, 141, 146, 167, 171
Market economies, 113
Marks. *See* Deutsche mark/East German mark
Marshall Plan, 42
Maull, Hans W., 106
Maystadt, Philippe, 86
MBB. *See* Messerschmitt-Bölkow-Blohm
Mearsheimer, John, 5
Mecklenburg–Western Pomerania, 199
Media, 76, 79(n16), 123–130
 users' fees, 123, 131(n1)
Messerschmitt-Bölkow-Blohm (MBB), 14, 17, 28, 31
Mexico, 105
MFN. *See* Most-Favored Nation status
Microelectronics, 164. *See also* Electronics industry
Middle East, 25
Militarism, 26
Missiles, 17, 20, 31
 cruise, 39
 Euromissiles, 39, 41
 Hot, 22
 Intermediate-Range Nuclear Forces (INF), 26
 Milan, 22
 Pershing IIs, 39
 Roland, 22
 Short-Range Nuclear Forces (SNF), 69, 191
 V-2, 19
Mitsubishi, 166
Mitterrand, François, 26, 29, 30, 31
Modrow, Hans, 71–72
Momper, Walter, 67–78
 plans of, 72–74
 Washington trip, 74–75
Moral authority, 9
Morgan, Roger, 11–12
Moscow, 94

Most-Favored Nation (MFN) status, 179
Mueller, Dietmar, 117

Narjes, Heinz, 179
Nationalism, 23, 36, 63
NATO. *See* North Atlantic Treaty Organization
Natural gas pipeline, 41, 98
Nazis, 53
NEC company, 166
Netherlands, 47
New Brandenburg. *See* Brandenburg
Newly industrialized nations, 135
New World Order, 5–6, 15, 45
New York Times, 116
Night combat, 27, 29
Nixdorf firm, 164
Nixon administration, 42
North Atlantic Treaty Organization (NATO), 3–4, 9–15, 19, 36, 38, 40, 187, 189
 alternatives to, 6–9
 integrative structures in, 14
 London Declaration (1990), 13
 multinational fighting units in, 13–14
 nuclear sharing, 20, 29
 prescription for, 13–15
 rearmament, 191
 strategy, 39
 theory behind, 10–13
 See also under individual countries
North Rhine–Westphalia, 126, 132(n37), 151, 160(n4)
Norway, 11
NSF. *See* United States, National Science Foundation
Nuclear power plants, 158. *See also* Kalkar nuclear reactor
Nuclear weapons, 8, 10, 14, 20, 26, 29
 dependence on, 39
 nuclear club, 14
 nuclear war, 37, 38
 See also Missiles

Oder-Neisse line, 30, 74, 75
OECD. *See* Organization for Economic Cooperation and Development
Olivetti, 162, 164

Operation Desert Storm, 30. *See also* Gulf war
Opinion polls, 12, 79(n16)
Ordshonikidze company, 100
Organization for Economic Cooperation and Development (OECD), 143
Ossenbühl, Fritz, 52, 53, 56
Osthandel. *See under* Federal Republic of Germany; Germany, pre-1949
Ostpolitik, 11, 23, 40–41, 44, 47, 75, 98
Overpopulation, 183
Ownership issues, 113, 114, 117, 119, 137, 166

Pacifism, 26, 38
Paris Agreements (1954), 19
Parliamentary Sponsorship Program, 181
Party of Democratic Socialism (PDS), 77
Patents, 137, 139
Pax Americana, 11
Pax Britannica, 36
PDS. *See* Party of Democratic Socialism
Pensions, 84, 85
People's Republic of China, 14
Perestroika, 95
Personal contacts, 96, 98, 102, 191
Petra Program, 58
Phillips company, 162, 164, 166, 169
Planned economies, 95–96, 105, 111
Plastic bottles, 155–156
Pluralism, 126–127, 132(n37)
Pohl, Gerhard, 116
Pöhl, Karl Otto, 91
Poland, 30, 44, 94, 98, 99, 107, 108, 183, 186, 187
Pollution, 149, 152, 157. *See also* Environmental issues
Pompidou, Georges, 23
Portugal, 177
Press, 79(n16), 84, 130, 157
Prices, 113, 115, 166, 170. *See also* Inflation
Privatization, 113, 114, 117, 118
Procurement practices, 170
Production/productivity, 86, 87, 88, 89, 113, 116, 166, 167, 171
Proletarian Victory (combine), 101
Property rights, 90, 114

Pro 7 (broadcaster), 128
Protectionism, 135, 170, 179, 180, 185
Public opinion, 124. *See also* Opinion polls

Radio, 124, 125, 132(n20). *See also* Media
Rall, Günther, 24
R&D. *See* Research/research and development
Rapallo treaty. *See under* German-Soviet relations
Raw materials, 115, 185
Reagan, Ronald, 39, 68, 156
administrations, 28, 41, 42, 43
Recessions, 87, 90, 91, 167
Reciprocity problem. *See under* Trade
Recombinant DNA research, 136, 146
Refugees, 72, 84, 108, 183. *See also* German Democratic Republic, exodus from
Regionalism, 62, 65(n20). *See also* European Community, regional administrations
Regulations, 59, 135, 136, 140–141, 142, 146, 175. *See also under* Environmental issues
Republican party (Federal Republic of Germany), 69
Research/research and development (R&D), 17, 31, 32, 63, 135, 136, 137, 138, 140, 142, 143, 144, 145, 146, 169, 170, 171, 186
Responsibility, 187–188
Reuter, Ernst, 67
Reuth, Ralf Georg, 75
Revanchism, 6
Reykjavik summit, 39
Rheinbund of 1806, 52
Rhône Alpes, 63, 66(n38)
Romania, 107
Rome, Treaty of, 6, 56–57, 65(nn 19, 28), 179
RRG. *See* Germany, pre-1949, Reichsrundfunkgesellschaft
RTL plus (television station), 128, 129, 133(n65)
Rubles, 104, 115
Russian Republic, 10

Salamander company, 101, 103, 104

Satellites, reconnaissance, 28
Satellite transmission. *See* Cable/
　satellite transmission
SAT 1 (television station), 128, 129
Savings, 84, 85, 103, 104
Saxony/Saxony-Anhalt, 199
Schiess AG, 102
Schmidt, Helmut, 26, 39, 40, 191
Schöneberg, Rathaus, 77
Schröder, Gerhard, 24
Schumacher, Kurt, 35, 45
Schwarz-Schilling, Christian, 127
Screwdriver factories, 168
SDI. *See* Strategic Defense Initiative
SEA. *See* Single European Act
SED. *See* Socialist Unity (Communist)
　party
Self-determination, 62
Semiconductors, 164, 165–166, 167
Separation of powers, 53
Services, 178, 179
Shevardnadze, Eduard, 4, 45
Shortages, 115
Siberia, 41, 98
Siemans AG, 162, 164–165, 166, 170
Siemans brothers, 164
Single European Act (SEA), 6, 56–57
Skoda comany, 105
SNECMA. *See* France, National
　Company for the Design and
　Construction of Aircraft Engines
SNF. *See* Missiles, Short-Range
　Nuclear Forces
Social democracy, 75
Social Democratic party (SPD), 26, 29,
　69, 70, 72, 73, 75–76, 77–78, 84,
　151, 158
Socialism/Socialists, 35, 78, 99, 103
Socialist Unity (Communist) party
　(SED), 72, 76, 197
Sovereignty issues, 51, 55, 60, 64(n6).
　See also Federalism
Soviet Union, 3, 8, 9, 115
　crises in, 45, 63
　Foreign Trade Bank, 104
　freight in, 103
　and Germany in NATO, 44–45
　and joint ventures, 99, 100–101, 102,
　105
　KGB, 10
　Kola Peninsula, 99
　military, 10, 11
　trade regulations, 98–99
　See also German-Soviet relations
Spain, 11, 27, 28, 63, 177
SPD. *See* Social Democratic party
Sporting events, 129
Springer AG, 128, 130
Stability, 47
Statehood, 54
Steel, 115
Steinbeis Stiftung (Stuttgart), 146
Stock markets, 85, 167
Strategic Defense Initiative (SDI), 28
Strauss, Franz-Josef, 19, 21
Strikes, 77
Subsidiarity principle, 52, 62
Subsidies, 97, 107, 108, 112, 113, 162,
　169
Suez crisis (1956), 19

Tageszeitung, 77
Tanks, 20, 26, 28
　Leclerc, 31
Tariffs. *See under* Trade
Taxation, 175. *See also under* Federal
　Republic of Germany; United
　States
Technology, 63, 115, 183, 186
　cleanup, 153
　information, 163, 165, 169
　technological civilization, 187, 188
　technology incubators, 137, 143, 144
　technology transfer/transfer centers,
　135, 136–139, 141–147, 148(n)
　See also Biotechnology
Telecommunications, 163, 164, 168
Tele 5 (broadcaster), 128
Telefunken Electronic company, 166
Telegraph lines, 164–165
Television, 123, 128, 167. *See also*
　Media
Texas Instruments, 166
Thatcher, Margaret, 167
Third World, 25, 45, 185, 186, 188
Thuringia, 199
Thyssen company, 98
Töpfer, Klaus, 151, 152
Toshiba, 166
Trade, 7, 36, 42, 46, 83, 91, 94, 98–99,
　108, 136
　dumping, 166, 168

free trade, 162, 180, 185
reciprocity problem, 178–179
tariffs, 168, 177
trade fairs, 96
See also Federal Republic of Germany, and *Osthandel;* Germany, pre-1949, and *Osthandel;* under European Community
Trademarks, 137
Transatlantic cable, 165
Transportation, 63, 163, 186
Treuhandanstalt. See under Federal Republic of Germany
Tshikiryov, Nikolai, 102
Turkey, 11, 12
Two plus Four talks, 73, 198

Unemployment, 12, 43, 84, 86, 92, 117
United States, 14, 20, 89, 105, 177, 185
 Commerce Department, 171(n)
 Comprehensive Environmental Response, Compensation, and Liability Act (CERCLA), 155
 Congress, 43, 180, 181
 defense spending, 43
 economy, 41–42, 46, 140
 education, 43, 46
 electronics industry, 164, 166
 environmental issues in, 149, 155, 157. See also United States, Environmental Protection Agency
 Environmental Protection Agency (EPA), 150–151, 151–152, 154, 156, 158–159
 and European Community, 179–180, 182
 Federal Advisory Committee, 157
 Freedom of Information Act, 157, 159, 160(n17)
 hegemony in Europe, 19
 isolationism, 36, 46
 military buildup, 42
 military presence in Europe, 8, 10, 11, 35, 47
 National Science Foundation (NSF), 146
 and North Atlantic Treaty Organization, 47
 nuclear umbrella, 26, 28
 policymakers, interventionist vs. laissez-faire, 135, 140
 Republicans, 36
 states vs. federal government, 153
 Stevenson-Wydler Act, 145
 taxation, 42, 43
 technology transfer system in, 143–144, 144–145, 147
 television, 123, 167
 trade issues, 42, 43, 178, 179–180
 See also German-U.S. relations
Universities, 137, 140, 142, 143–144, 146, 169

Vertical integration (manufacturing), 103
Vetoes, 54
Vietnam War, 42
Vocational training, 58
Vogel, Hans-Jochen, 76
Volkswagen company, 105, 163
von Heynitz, Achim, 106
von Weizsäcker, Richard, 67

Wacker, Gerhard, 102, 104
Wages, 83, 84, 86, 88, 89, 90, 92, 107, 113
Waigel, Theo, 72, 116
Wallace, William, 21
Walters, Vernon, 44
Warfare, coalition, 31
Warsaw Pact, 6, 183, 197
Waste disposal. See Hazardous waste
Water, 167. See also Drinking water
Weimar Republic, 124–125
Western European Union (WEU), 6, 8–9, 16(n6)
Westphalia, Treaty of, 52
WEU. See Western European Union
Wirtschaftsförderung Berlin, 142
Wirtschaftswoche, 94–95
Workers, 58, 103, 115, 167, 169, 171
Work ethic, 103
World economy, 41, 89–91, 107, 111, 179, 182, 185. See also Electronics industry, world market
World War II, 41–42
Wörner, Manfred, 10

Young, Thomas-Durell, 31
Yugoslavia, 6, 63, 99

ZDF. See Federal Republic of Germany, second television channel